NEVER STOP
PUSHING

NEVER STOP
PUSHING

Rulon Gardner
with Bob Schaller

CARROLL & GRAF PUBLISHERS
NEW YORK

NEVER STOP PUSHING
My Life from a Wyoming Farm to the Olympic Medals Stand

Carroll & Graf Publishers
An Imprint of Avalon Publishing Group Inc.
245 West 17th Street
11th Floor
New York, NY 10011

AVALON
publishing group incorporated

Copyright © 2005 by Rulon Gardner

First Carroll & Graf edition 2005

Library of Congress Cataloging-in-Publication Data is available.

ISBN: 0-7867-1593-6

9 8 7 6 5 4 3 2 1

Interior design by Maria Elias

Printed in the United States of America
Distributed by Publishers Group West

To the men and women of the United States
Armed Forces. God bless you and
God bless America.

Contents

One
NEVER STOP PUSHING   *1*

Two
DUMBO FROM THE FARM   *6*

Three
RURAL ROOTS   *24*

Four
THE GARDNER CLAN   *33*

Five
NEVER STOP PUSHING II   *41*

Six
BARN BURNS, HOPE SURVIVES   *56*

Seven
THE BOY WHO MADE EVERY DAY COUNT   *61*

Eight
LEAVING THE VALLEY *83*

Nine
ON MY OWN TWO FEET IN THE HEARTLAND *91*

Ten
TO BE A TEACHER *107*

Eleven
CHASING MY WRESTLING AND COLLEGE DREAMS *116*

Twelve
HEROES *134*

Thirteen
THE ROUTE TO 2000 *139*

Fourteen
JOURNEY TO GOLD *158*

Fifteen
THE MIRACLE ON THE MAT *167*

Sixteen
WHO AM I NOW? *191*

Seventeen
VALIDATION: DEFENDING THE GOLD AT THE 2001
WORLD CHAMPIONSHIPS *203*

Eighteen
MIRACLE IN THE MOUNTAINS *218*

Nineteen
ANOTHER RUN AT THE OLYMPICS *274*

Twenty
ATHENS, 2004 *303*

Twenty-One
NEVER STOP PUSHING, PERIOD *318*

INDEX *327*

One

NEVER STOP PUSHING

THIS IS IT.

The end of an important chapter of my life, almost three decades that have, in large part, shaped me as a person.

As I lace up my wrestling shoes for the final time, to wrestle for the bronze medal at the 2004 Olympic Games in Athens, Greece, I run my hands along the shoes, feeling the soft leather.

I will be taking them off for the last time in less than fifteen minutes. And just two years ago, I thought I'd never be putting wrestling shoes on my feet again. Suffering from severe frostbite after a night stranded in the Wyoming wilderness, soaking wet from five plunges into the Salt River and temperatures reaching 25 below zero, I had nearly lost the front third of both of my feet.

Yet here I am. Back on the world stage. Back where I had become "the farm boy from Wyoming who had defeated the greatest wrestler of all time," by beating undefeated Russian Alexander Karelin for the gold medal at the 2000 Olympics in Sydney, Australia.

During the rehab for frostbite, just seeing my wrestling shoes in my truck or around the house had been painful; I'd wonder every day when I'd be able to put them on again. I think back now to the fall of 2002, months after my ordeal in the Wyoming wilderness when I could first put on the shoes again. The pain was so intense, my feet were so swollen, that I had to move up from my usual size 13 to size 14.

I ruined that pair, and several more, because my feet bled through the leather. Eventually, though, I was able to wear my wrestling shoes without too much pain. My feet still hurt during a tough practice, but I knew I was making progress. Soon, I didn't have to put on my straight face and pretend that my feet didn't feel like needles were poking them. If you can't put on the shoes, you're not a wrestler, I told myself during rehab sessions. Wrestling was my single biggest motivation to get through rehabilitation, my inspiration and number one reason to endure the surgeries, the physical therapy, and the wound-care treatments when the techs sandpapered the dead skin off my feet in order to stimulate growth in the red, raw tissue underneath. In fact, the first time I was without any pain putting on my wrestling shoes was more than a year after the accident in Wyoming, right before U.S. Nationals in the spring of 2003.

Earlier today in Athens, I lost my semifinal match to a wrestler I had beaten two years earlier. I won't get the chance to repeat as Olympic gold medalist. People think I must be devastated. The truth is, I'm not. I wanted the gold medal, no doubt about that. But I am thrilled to just be able to wrestle again.

Now I am putting my feet into my shoes for the last time as a wrestler. Not all of the feeling has come back—and I am told it never will; in fact, another surgery awaits me a few months after the Olympics—but nearly thirty years of wearing wrestling shoes makes me smile. So many memories have come on the mat. So many lessons have been learned through this sport, lessons I apply to "real life." All of those experiences started with my wrestling shoes. Carrying my shoes in a gym bag. Wearing them, tied together, around my neck. Putting them on before practice. I can remember every pair of wrestling shoes I ever wore, including the first pair: Ed Bruce, my coach when I started out as an elementary school-age wrestler, let me wear a high-schooler's pair of wrestling shoes because my feet were so big. Coach Bruce gave me high-school hand-me-downs, since my family couldn't afford to buy new wrestling shoes every time I outgrew my current pair. Over the years, as I did get new shoes, it was always an exciting thing for me, because I'm still just a kid at heart.

"This will be the last time you put these on," I think to myself. It is an amazing, meaningful moment.

All I want from this match is all I want every single time I wrestle: my best effort. If I win, great; but if I lose, I can hold my head high, as long as I give it my best effort. In spite of what I have been through—nearly dying in the wilderness, suffering from severe frostbite, rehabilitating my feet into walking again, getting hit by a car while riding my motorcycle, and dislocating my wrist badly enough to require surgically implanted pins—I have a surprising peace about me. I am once again on the world stage, a far cry from the eastern Idaho hospital I was admitted to a short two years ago, but I feel right at home.

The truth is, while I'm elated to be in Athens, I don't really care about the cameras and reporters at this point; just getting back home on the Olympic mat has been a victory. I even wondered, as I came back, if I was being greedy: after fulfilling my dream in 2000 with Olympic gold, and gold again at the 2001 World Championships, was I asking for too much? But then I remembered the original goal I had set in 1996, of making two Olympic teams; I am realizing that goal only now in Athens. Wrestling is the one thing that has healed my feet—and my spirit: no matter what happens, wrestling completes my recovery.

I was a long shot to make it back to the Olympics before the accident, because I had to beat fellow American Dremiel Byers, the 2002 World Champion, just to make the U.S. Olympic Team.

So the bronze medal match, to me, is every bit as meaningful as the 2000 gold medal match in Sydney, where I beat the previously undefeated Russian legend, Alexander Karelin.

And when the final buzzer sounds, telling me I've won the bronze medal in Athens, I know I have done my best. I haven't won the gold medal, but in this match I have done my absolute best. And this time, my absolute best results in my second Olympic medal in four years.

This will be the last time my shoes come off as a

wrestler. A tidal wave of emotion washes over me as I unlace them. It is a great privilege to be able to wrestle in the Olympics in Athens in 2004, and in Sydney at the 2000 Olympic Games; but then it's a great privilege to wrestle in every match, whether on the world stage or in a tiny rural high-school gym in western Wyoming.

I leave my shoes in the middle of the mat, keeping alive a tradition that marks the end of a wrestler's career. The crowd, which has had passionate fans cheering both for and against the Americans throughout the two-day wrestling competition, finally unites, erupting in applause, sharing in the emotion of the moment.

With the exception of the sixteen members of my family and my coaches, many of these fans have heard bits and pieces of my story, but none of them has been there every step of the way. But I can see that people are overwhelmed, knowing what they know, seeing my shoes lying there in the center of the mat.

I walk off the mat, fighting off the heavy sobs that are overtaking me. Wrestling has gotten me back to this point, and now it's time to say good-bye.

Two

Dumbo from the Farm

FEBRUARY 15, 2002, 7:00 A.M.

I could hear the sound of an airplane over the canyon in which I was trapped. I must've looked like the last piece of cereal in a bowl of milk as the snow swallowed me up—me standing there in a fleece top—not even a winter coat—and that fleece was frozen solid with ice.

"Hey, look, it's an airplane," I said, to keep myself company.

I could never imagine a greater sense of isolation than I felt that night. It wasn't loneliness—I often enjoy being alone. Growing up doing farm chores, often alone in the cold, were some of the times I enjoyed the most. I was used to the subzero temperatures and the sound of my own thoughts, and didn't mind it. No, this was a feeling of complete and utter isolation, being stranded in the world.

No one could hear me talking to myself. No one had

heard me in seventeen hours. No one had seen me in seventeen hours. Once, in school, I had to define "help-less." I knew what it meant, but I couldn't find the words to tell the teacher. Kids in the class laughed. I could show them what helpless was, if only they could see me now.

The airplane continued straight ahead. I stood and used every ounce of energy to hold my hands above my head, certain the pilot had seen me, relieved that I had survived a night in the wilderness of western Wyoming. Even though it sounds like an unforgiving place, you have to remember that in the summer, this was my outdoor back-yard. The white blanket of snow and canyon walls in this particular place were unfamiliar, but I couldn't have been more than six or eight miles from home. And although I knew the general area well, and knew where the Salt River began and where it came out in the town south of us, I had no idea that it turned briefly away from Star Valley, and following the river east along a narrow, almost impos-sible-to-travel path is how I had ended up not only lost, but unfindable to my friends and searchers in this unfor-giving patch of wilderness.

But waving at that airplane used my last ounce of energy. I had to sit down to regain some strength. I felt I was like a flickering candle, but there wasn't much light left in me. The sun was my most welcome visitor that morning: I would find out later that the previous night's subzero temperatures had dropped my body temperature to the 80-degree range, which is fatal whether you are a doctor, teacher, lawyer, or an Olympic wrestler—anyone. Moving was as necessary as it was difficult. My mind *was alive still—I can tell you right now that I had thought of nothing but getting rescued—but there was no question, my body was shutting down.*

The plane continued to circle for the next two hours, disappearing only twice—I assumed, to go notify the search crew of where I was, and to tell them to hurry. The pilot even threw a coat to the ground from the window of the plane. Even though I could've used the warmth, my body simply couldn't move anymore to retrieve it. Because of undulations in the terrain and snowbanks, I couldn't see where the coat had landed, and the difficulty of climbing through drifts was too much for my depleted body. So the coat, just out of my vision and reach, sat uselessly on the snow, a feeling I was all too familiar with after the long night alone in the cold.

After spotting the plane, I expected to see snowmobiles coming over the ridge. Kind of, one noise should lead to another—that sort of thinking, I guess. I was in the Bridger-Teton National Forest, named after pioneer legend Jim Bridger, who, ironically, was known for never getting lost. Where was Jim Bridger when I needed him? If there is ever a Rulon Gardner National Forest, it will have signs every ten feet. And matches. Lots of matches.

"Don't give up now," I told myself. "Whatever you do, don't give up now."

"Don't give up, Rulon," the teacher told me. "You can do this."

When I started kindergarten at Afton Elementary in Star Valley, I was frustrated with how inadequate I felt, right from the first day. Almost immediately I was diagnosed with a learning disability and targeted for special education—at the time, a fairly new program in our school district.

I wasn't at the same level as kids my age. The other students always seemed smarter, faster. Everyone was a better reader than I was. I couldn't spell simple words, couldn't keep up in most of the learning exercises. I had a hard time absorbing and applying what the teachers were telling us.

A teacher, or sometimes a classmate, often had to come over and help me with the assigned tasks. The other kids sensed that I wasn't able to keep up. Some wanted to help me; others would ignore me, making me feel invisible. Some would laugh at me.

The struggle went on day after day. I had been so excited to start school, because I was the youngest in the family, but I missed my siblings, especially my brother Reynold, who was just one year older. I didn't like being home alone. Until the first day of school. Then I was ready to be back home—although I did enjoy, for the most part, the social aspect of school, being around other kids my age.

I had to learn how to deal with the struggle of being the "slow" one. I had to avoid beating myself up every day over it.

"You're okay," I'd constantly tell myself.

At the end of my kindergarten year, the teachers and school administrators called my parents in for a meeting.

"We want to keep Rulon another year in kindergarten," they were told. "Because that will help get his learning skills up with the other students."

I was already the biggest kid in kindergarten. Or first

grade, for that matter. If I were held back, we were looking at *Guinness Book of World Records* kind of big. But Mom and Dad were experienced with the school system. I had eight brothers and sisters, and though none had my learning problems, my folks considered the road the school was suggesting to be a dead-end street. Whatever it would've done to help me, being held back would've also killed any self-esteem I had. It was bad enough being made fun of by kids my age; who knows what it would've done to me to have *younger* kids poking fun at me and pointing and whispering at the "big slow kid."

"That would put him further behind," my mother said. "He needs to keep pushing. We can't have him being held back."

The teachers did tell my parents that my social skills were good. I was a chatterbox, but I would listen, too, to just about anyone. I guess I enjoyed having someone other than my family to talk to. Our farm was on the outskirts of Afton and we made only necessary trips into town, so talking with other kids or teachers was the highlight of my school days. It was only academically that I was slower than everybody else. I don't know how else to explain it except to say it just took me longer to do things, sometimes a lot longer, especially if I, or the teacher, got frustrated.

But my parents stuck by their belief that any step not forward set me back even more, so I moved on to first grade, where I was identified as a special needs student and placed in a special education program. I also received peer tutoring when I was in the regular class. Though I received extra help, I would never come close to catching up with everyone else my age, and actually fell further behind. Reading was especially difficult for me. I just couldn't read like the other kids. Once I could get through individual words, it took even longer for me to understand a complete sentence. Only with the dedication of teachers and the love of my family would I start to close the gap.

First grade was different than kindergarten, because it was all day, not just a morning or afternoon. Despite the challenging schoolwork, I enjoyed first grade because I'd get a carton of chocolate milk halfway through the day. You wouldn't believe what a prize that chocolate milk was to me—to this day, it still brings a smile to my face.

As first grade turned into second, we moved from reading to ourselves to reading in front of the class. I could feel my nerves starting to act up when we were told to "form a circle." I didn't want to read in front of everyone else. Every sentence was a struggle, and building a flow or rhythm was simply not possible.

I was a terrible reader, and I knew it. I knew it because of the finger-pointing or whispers from classmates—or, worst of all, the giggles and laughs. Some of the kids would make fun of me, imitating my slow struggle to get from word to word, sentence to sentence. I was often called "Dumbo" and sometimes "Stupid." Those words hurt a lot. And I wasn't good at defending myself. I knew the other kids didn't understand my learning problems—even I didn't understand why I was slower than them. But it wasn't like I wasn't trying my hardest. I simply couldn't learn at their pace. Kids would see that as a weakness and build themselves up by putting me down. Some of them did it to be mean or to make themselves feel better, but other kids did it just to join in—and once a few kids got laughing, everybody wanted in on it, to be a part of the laughing, regardless of who was hurt by it. It didn't stop at mocking my reading problems either; I was called "Fatso" because of my size—I was over 120 pounds by fourth grade. Those memories are now, decades later, still fresh in my mind, and though I have a better context for them now, it's still hurtful.

The teachers cared, though, and worked hard to help me improve. They also tried to help me deal with the ridicule I faced daily. Sometimes while being laughed at or whispered about, I felt I was drowning; it was a choking, sinking feeling. Eventually, I'd learn how to ignore such ridicule and take some steps on my own to improve, but I was just a kid then and hadn't made that big, independent leap in my mind.

I went to sixth grade in Osmond—named after relatives of the famous family that produced, among others, Donny and Marie—a nearby community that had opened up an elementary school. Our home fell within Osmond's boundaries, so I was to attend this new school. I have good memories of Osmond. I was still in special educa-tion and needed a lot of help. Mrs. Louter, my teacher, was a lot of fun, but she was firm. She believed in me as a person. She said, "You have potential, but you have to work harder." I believed her and began to work harder in the Osmond special ed program than I had in the other program. I started to gain confidence, a feeling I'd have to learn to keep in check when it threatened to mix with anger. For example, a friend of mine, a good kid and special ed student like me, came into class one day and saw me struggling, getting frustrated with myself. He teased me about it, we had a few words, and suddenly I got up; I was thinking about grabbing him. Though I had been mocked all through elementary school, I had never fought back. I remember the anger I felt in my heart that day, and the weird sensation of wanting to hurt this kid, a friend of mine. I had to step back and think about why I would want to hurt him, why I would want to be violent. That was a growing experience for me. I decided that fighting wasn't a way of expressing my feelings. I knew I could only fight when I was backed into a corner.

Life after the school day presented a different kind of challenge, and this one, unlike school, was social. Kids would get ready for the final bell, talking about what they were going to do that day. As exciting as it was to hear about everything they had planned—some things they would do, other things, of course, they wouldn't; but being kids, the afternoon was limitless in our minds—I knew I wouldn't be a part of it. Not that day. Not ever. We—my siblings and I—couldn't go play with town kids at their houses, because we had to get home to do farmwork.

There was one loophole: we were allowed to have other kids over, with the understanding that they'd help us with our chores. At first, the few grade-school friends I had were excited to come over so they could see the inside of a barn, see the cows—even milk the cows. Farm chores, like carrying irrigation pipe and getting it fitted so water could get to the crops, sounded like new, fun adventures to them. This was my chance to show off, and I did. I explained farm life to the kids in great detail. Of course, it never dawned on me to mention that they'd be walking through cow pies, testing the limits of their strength, and holding their noses against strong smells— that was just part of the territory to me. So that first excitement wore off quickly: within the first half hour, they would realize what they had gotten themselves into. It would start with a look, and I could almost see the wheels in their minds turning as they plotted their exit. A look at a watch or asking my parents for the time would signal the end of our day.

"My mother says I have to be home now," I'd hear. Or, "Oh, I have a report due that I forgot about—gotta go now."

Only one of my friends, Rick Johnson, would come out and work with me during junior-high years. I really appreciated his friendship. He never complained about the hard work, the long hours, or the smells. It takes a special breed of person to understand farmwork, much less do it. Rick not only understood it, but also exhilarated in the feeling that comes from working hard for hours at a time. There is a proud mind-set that comes from working with the earth— even as a kid, you tap into it—realizing that you are providing food for yourself and others. Rick felt it. He either enjoyed the mission or was such a good person that he didn't mind spending some time with me in our world; probably both were true in his case, and it meant a lot to me.

But most of the time it was just the family. We'd go out after school and work, not getting in until late evening, sometimes as late as 10:00 P.M. If something broke down, or the tractor got stuck, we'd work until midnight. Every farm family knows that when something breaks down, you either become the world's greatest mechanics or you prepare to spend thousands of dollars to get the machine fixed. Given the typical farmer's finances, most become great mechanics, because fixing machines is a constant effort. Between the high cost of repairing them and the cost of losing crops when they were down, farm machines were one of our biggest worries.

Farm life started early and ended late, sometimes spilling over midnight into early the next morning, meaning a short night of sleep. I don't know any farmers who had sleep disorders. Sleep was sustenance, and you either got it when you could or you collapsed the next day. You worked when you had to, you ate when you had time and if there was food close to you, and you slept when the moon wasn't too high in the sky.

I remember one week when the earliest we returned to the house was 11:30 P.M. Something was always going wrong: the tractor would have a problem when we were feeding the cows, or the vehicles would freeze up, or there'd be a problem with fuel. But these challenges helped shaped my attitude. I learned that no matter how many challenges you solved, you would always face more. So that's what I expected out of life, that it would never get measurably easier, but that hard work and education (whether it was in school or on the land), would get you through—and on to the next challenge.

I can't stress enough what a challenge the weather is in western Wyoming. The area's climate is unforgiving to all life—human, animal, and plant—and at 6,134 feet above sea level, the air is extremely thin.

No matter how bad the weather is one day, there's an even chance it will get worse the next day. And if the weather isn't worse, the effects of the weather from one day will be felt the next day. Snow can melt and wash out roads or crops; rain can freeze and create a dangerous sheet of ice for the animals and ourselves.

Western Wyoming summers had some beautiful days, and even though the work was hard, the views of the mountains and the wide, sweeping valley couldn't be beat. Even in the summertime, however, the nights were very cold. Often it would get down into the 40s in the evening, sometimes dipping into the 30s. But the cold of Star Valley, outside of summer especially—well, that is a memory all of its own. It was always cold. And since we went by the clock and the calendar as to what needed to be done, not the temperature, we did some of our most arduous tasks in the cold.

Summertime was our busiest season; there was no time off. We'd get up at 6:30 A.M.; my dad would get the cows in, and we'd start milking. When that was done, we'd start moving the irrigation pipe. All of the crops needed to be irrigated, because the Afton soil and climate weren't too reliable.

Even though we were a dairy farm, we raised alfalfa, barley, and oats to supplement the farm income, the alfalfa serving as feed for our cows. We had what is called a "gravity flow" irrigation system. The water flowed downhill—the bottom of the line was lower than the top—though there was water pressure where the water was initially dispensed from. We connected our pipes to a valve that provided irrigation water for our farm, and then connected the pipes to water all of our crops. Each aluminum pipe was about forty feet long and weighed about thirty pounds—though it varied, as the older pipes were heavier than the newer ones. I'd go back and forth thirty-two or thirty-three times—the number of pipes I had to carry in order to start irrigating the next section of our farm that needed water. Of course, it was only sixteen or seventeen trips if someone was helping, but usually you changed the pipe for one field alone after you reached a certain age, normally about nine years old. You'd hook the pipe together and then straighten the line out, which was harder to do if you had started the water without the line being straight, because with water in the pipes, they were heavier.

When I was a kid, we changed four lines of pipe for our 160 acres, with thirty-three pipes constituting one line, each line going to a stationary sprinkler. So one line would water about 40 acres, in other words.

It took about an hour to change the pipes. Depending on how many siblings still lived at home, changing pipe could take up a significant part of the day. Changing pipe was just as draining mentally as it was physically, because it was so monotonous—getting the pipe, moving it, pulling or pushing to straighten it. Usually one sibling was assigned to change the water for a particular field alone, because in addition to our own fields, we'd often rent other adjacent pastures to grow more alfalfa and other crops. During the busy season, several fields of pipe had to be changed twice each per day over the 700 to 800 acres, so each person would handle one line of pipe on his or her own, although if there weren't a lot of people on the farm that year, you could spend several hours each day going from field to field changing pipe. It wasn't high-intensity cardiovascular work, but walking miles each day and constantly lifting and carrying pipe built a fitness level that I'd carry with me for the rest of my life.

To complicate our farming even more, the soil in Afton doesn't hold water well, because the terrain is so rocky. That was why we had to constantly move our irrigation pipes. But there was a delicate balance between watering that nourished crops and watering that drowned crops. Of course, you also had to figure in the amount of raiq0n or snow, and hope like heck you didn't get hail before harvest.

Wash away a little too much of the topsoil, and the crop would be gone, not to mention that the soil would need a long time to rebuild for the next growing season. Miss moving the pipe, time it wrong, or get too much rain, and the quality of the crop would suffer. Meaning, of course, less money for what we'd sell, or more money spent on feed crops to make up for what we were unable to grow.

Since the work was monotonous, the older siblings would use their imaginations to escape. They'd finish part of the work, take a short break, and talk about running away from home to find an easier life. This was news to me—since I was the youngest, I thought this was how everyone lived. The older kids would plan for us to pack sugar and potato chips and hike up into the mountains to live like hermits. There'd be a lot of talk; but before we settled on a destination or plan of action, we'd get the call to get back to work, and we'd save our dreams for later.

Even on Sunday, after church, we had to go move pipe.

By mid-summer, the hay got so high and thick that we were exhausted just getting to the pipe, and we'd still have to move and set it. I remember how good I felt when we finished. The feeling of accomplishment really built me up. There was nothing like "gettin' done changin' pipe," watching the water flow out onto the field to nourish the crops, knowing that it would help make the farm thrive. I'll never find words to explain how successful I felt knowing that all the hard work we did, we did right.

And we did right by our four-legged friends, too, because in many ways the farm animals were part of our family. We took care of them, and they provided for us, literally, either as food or as revenue when sold. We milked our cows twice a day and fed them once a day.

Being the youngest Gardner kid, I didn't have a lot of say in things. We'd be out working on the farm, and I'd have an idea. Of course, I thought it was the best suggestion ever made. But my brothers and sisters would say, "You don't know what you're talking about." There was a pecking order, and I was at the bottom. One of my best ideas, shot down practically before I said it, had to do with "picking up strings."

Some farmwork chores were more enjoyable than others. One of the least enjoyable was "picking up strings." When the hay was dumped for the cows to eat, the string holding the bales was cut and left in the field. When that season was over and it was time to plant, we had to go out and pick up thousands and thousands of pieces of string. The alternative was to let it sit there, plow it over, and have it in the ground. The string didn't help the crops, and it could damage the equipment or hurt an animal, so it had to be gathered up. Feeding thirty bales of hay per day for four months left a lot of string. I always thought it would have been better to pick up the strings as soon as they were cut. Of course, it was cold when we cut the strings, so I know it wasn't too appealing to add another task with the temperature dropping by the minute. Maybe my idea wasn't so great after all. Though it would've only taken twenty to thirty minutes to pick up each batch of strings after dumping a load of hay, that would've added hours a week, and in the winter, adding even an hour of work a week—even if it prevented having to do the work in the spring—wasn't welcome. The idea wasn't to add work to our already-full schedule, so I didn't pursue implementing it to my weary family.

While we were in school during the day, my father tried to do what farmwork he could alone. I think he didn't start some of the work, because he wanted to give us hands-on learning about the importance of hard work. My father ruled with an iron first. I never back-talked my father, because my parents, and our church, taught us to always respect your mother and father. And I knew their decision would be the right one, just as it would be the final one, no matter what.

Because my brother Reynold is only a year older than me, I worked with him more than with anyone else. Reynold was always my best friend. He says that two of the toughest days in his life were related to me. When I was stranded overnight in the wilderness in February 2002, he got the word in Oregon, where he teaches animal science at Oregon State while getting his doctorate. He said he dropped to his knees sobbing, "worried that I was going to lose my best friend." He says the other toughest day was his first day of kindergarten, as he watched me crying at the screen door pleading for him not to leave me. "I didn't want to leave my best friend," he says of that day.

There were times when I was jealous of Reynold, because it seemed, being a year older, he got to do things I didn't, or at least got to do them (logically, of course) before I was allowed to do them. I never drew as close to other people as I did to Reynold, for a variety of reasons, including my special education needs and my size— Reynold was also big, as big as me or bigger; my whole family is physically big—but he didn't have the learning problems and was more secure with who he was than I was. So Reynold was always there and always my best friend. But like most brothers similar in age, we were rivals in anything we did, from work to play.

It was that rivalry that instilled in me a competitive fire that burned nonstop. From the minute we climbed out of bed each morning until we crawled, exhausted, back into bed each night, Reynold was constantly a measuring stick for me, as I was for him, from athletics to simple, everyday life.

We'd set up competitions to divide our chores. To the victor went the easier tasks. It was a no-brainer agreement for me, because, as the youngest, I always got the work no one else wanted to do anyway. I accepted that, because that was the structure on our farm, a structure put in place by our parents. While I believe we kids could think for ourselves, I believe with even more conviction that we needed, and benefited from, rules set by parents. If our parents told us to go do some work, we closed our mouths and did the work. It was doing those chores or taking that direction that allowed us to think for ourselves, to learn what hard work is and how it impacts a family.

But my sense of discipline didn't always carry over into school. By eighth grade, I was acting up fairly regularly in class, getting in trouble almost every day. Looking back now, I am sure that I had attention deficit disorder (ADD), because I could not focus on anything for more than a few seconds or, at the most, a few minutes. After that, my mind would wander, and I'd have trouble coming back to what I was doing. I'd have to start all over again instead of picking up where I left off. The special ed program provided some assistance, and later, wrestling helped me even more. But there was no better treatment for ADD than parental discipline. Caring and firm parents helped me learn to control myself and to pay attention to authority figures.

One day, after I had been kicked out of class for probably the third day in a row, I was sitting out in the hallway, and who should come down the hall but my father.

"What're you doing out here?" my father asked.

"Oh, you know, just hanging out," I answered.

My teacher came out of the room.

"No, Rulon has actually been getting kicked out every day lately," the teacher said.

My father looked at me.

"This will be the last day he gets kicked out," my father told the teacher, but I got the message too.

When we got home, my father offered to help me learn to behave in class. Very simply, he told me, I could either shape up or see how I liked the feel of his belt on my backside.

I shaped up and my disorder disappeared. After that day, I didn't get kicked out of class again. When I felt myself starting to slip away and lose focus, I thought about the consequences awaiting me if I acted up and got thrown out of class again. I didn't need any pill; my father's antidote—his stare, and his belt—worked.

I was cured, started making progress again in school, and was no longer a disciplinary case

Three

RURAL ROOTS

YES, THE FARM was the center of our lives. Our hard-earned money came from it, and as kids we got our exercise from it; the farm is where I learned to compete. All of us kids would have to do certain chores. Obviously, the older kids got the jobs with more responsibility. As we grew stronger, each of us drew more physically challenging assignments, ones that required strength and stamina. Actually, that describes every aspect of farm life, from milking a cow (which also requires agility, dexterity, and a lot of common sense) to baling hay, moving pipe, carrying calves across the frozen pastures, and all the dozens of other tasks.

People hear my story and say things like, "Oh, it was too cold for you to be out there," or "That work is too hard for kids." On the farm, we were taught that hard work helped you acheive your goals. We understood that any meaningful accomplishment would happen only with hard work. Anything that came easy wouldn't mean as much.

My parents taught me that nearly everything on the farm was measurable. Because goals had to be met, there was no way to wriggle out of the work, no way to cut corners. I knew that if I cut off a milker early and said, "That cow is done," it meant I was shorting my family's milk check—a big percentage of our income.

The cows would try to kick me, but I had to keep milking. We usually had forty or fifty cows, so it was quite a chore for us younger kids, but I wanted to get the job done and do it right. I had to do my part to help the family succeed. Ironically, dealing with the feisty, kicking milk cows wasn't half the battle that dealing with their calves could be. There were times when we'd have to carry the calves into the barn because they couldn't get there on their own, or they wouldn't respond to being led to the barn. When it was warm, you could pick up a 100- to 120-pound calf on your shoulders—a fireman's carry—and haul it the quarter mile or half mile to the barn. When it was winter, the field icy and slippery or mucky, and there was only a short distance to carry it, we'd just pick up the calf and carry it in front. It was much harder to carry 100 pounds in front than on my shoulders, but if it was a short distance and that was the fastest way to get the job done, that's what we did. It wasn't a question of whether I wanted to do it, but *how* I would do it. Calving season—when the calves are born—falls in wintertime. The calves, being so new to the world, get the shivers right away. With those harsh temperatures, there's only so much a cow can do for its calves. So first we'd try pushing the calves to the barn, trying to get them to follow their mothers. When that didn't work, it was time to carry them. The calves needed to survive, they were vital cogs in the farming operation, so we had to do whatever it took to care for them.

There were some nights it would be 20 or 30 degrees below zero and the cows still had to be fed. Actually, though, some of my fondest memories are of working outside during those bitter cold nights. It would be well below zero—absolutely freezing—but the work made me feel alive, even exhilarated. I knew there were few kids around the area doing this kind of important work at that time of night. I was doing something with my life, doing something to help my family, and that gave me a lot of self-esteem.

In the summer the work was no less demanding. In addition to setting the pipes, milking, and feeding, we would have to stack ten thousand bales of harvested hay, which was used to feed the cows throughout the winter. Feeding cows is expensive, and if we had to get hay from Utah or Idaho, it was more expensive. So we grew our own hay, cut it, raked it, baled it, and stacked it. Those were fun times, but the days spent haying were long, and the work could be backbreaking. At least the soggy, muddy ground was easier to deal with than the icy, slippery ground of winter.

So no matter the season or time, there was always a ton of work to be done. I'd think, "What kind of life is this for a kid?" Now I look back and smile. I don't think that lifestyle was something I had any right to complain about. Though at times it seemed I was living a hard life, today I view it as a great experience.

In addition to the satisfaction of knowing that these grueling chores were helping the family business, sometimes we received a small allowance. I liked getting an allowance, because I could buy candy or the other things kids like. But there were times when the milk check would go out as fast as it came in, and our allowances were put on hold.

We didn't have a lot of money for work clothes either, and almost never had money for nice clothes. Almost all my clothes were hand-me-downs. Although I had some great hand-me-downs because I had my pick of the clothes from so many older brothers, some of the items had passed through several brothers before they got to me, leaving them pretty worn. If they were still wearable, I'd have to wear them. Some clothes were okay, but a hand-me-down still feels like a hand-me-down, no matter what. For a couple of years, it seemed like all I wore was a military coat bought at an army surplus store and an old pair of sweatpants. I remember wearing leather gloves that weren't the warmest gloves in the world; but again, we had to make the best of what we had.

I don't want it to sound like my parents didn't provide for us, because they did. In fact my mother would take us school shopping each year for several pairs of pants and new shoes. That annual trip was a strain on the family finances. I often heard spirited discussions between my mother and my father; my father didn't see the need to spend money on clothes each school year, especially since we were active kids and wore the clothes out rather quickly.

And I don't want it to sound like we never enjoyed ourselves on the farm. The natural beauty around us was magical: on clear nights I'd turn around and see the sun going down over the hills west of Afton. The sky would be more beautiful than any magazine picture or movie scene. I'd pause to enjoy what I thought was the perfect night. Then I'd realize that the sun going down meant it would get nothing but colder, and I had more hours of work left. My gloves were often wet and my hands freezing. Sometimes I'd get off the tractor and put my hands near the exhaust to warm them up and dry them out. It probably wasn't safe, but I needed my hands to warm up and I needed my gloves to dry, and that worked.

When we went school shopping each summer in August, we'd leave for a weekend and go to the Lagoon, an amusement park in Salt Lake City. It was a chance to enjoy ourselves for those three days, Friday through Sunday, and then it was back to work.

But we made our own playground on our farm. There was a two-lane state highway running right past the farm. During the summer, it wasn't unusual for someone passing by on the highway to spot us kids out in the cow trough, which is about twice the size of a refrigerator. We'd be stripped down to our underwear, playing in the thing as if it were a pool—well, a really dirty pool, with moss, cow slobber, and other really nasty stuff. But it was our pool and, because we almost never left the farm, the only pool we had access to. When you work as hard we did, day in and day out, you learn to make recreation and fun wherever, whenever you can.

I started wrestling as a grade-schooler. As I wrote earlier, because of my size, the coach let me wear shoes that had belonged to high-school wrestlers. I wish I could share stories of how wrestling gave me all kinds of self-esteem and pride, but the truth is, I was usually the worst wrestler on the team in Star Valley. I remember in first grade, when I started wrestling in competitions—or even in practice—I always lost. In pee-wee wrestling (elementary-school age), I had to wrestle older kids because I was so big, and since wrestling goes by weight class, there was no one close to my age except my brother Reynold, who was close to my weight. Going against second, third, and even fourth and fifth graders occasionally, I always lost— they understood the technique better and had several more years of wrestling under their belts than I did. At that point, Reynold was already much better at wrestling than me.

I stayed with it because wrestling, or any extracurricular activity, got me out of farmwork and allowed me to socialize, to be around other kids my age. I kept losing regularly through pee-wee wrestling. I couldn't grasp the techniques that were so important for success. I had the strength and stamina even though I was chubby; but going up against a kid who better understood wrestling moves, I was easy prey, though I never gave up.

Staying with it, though, I hoped to make a lot of progress in junior high. During my seventh-grade year of school, our Star Valley club team went to a big tournament over in Soda Springs, Idaho, a drive of almost two hours from Star Valley. We took thirty-five or forty wrestlers to the tournament. Our club wrestled something like 122 matches at this big event. We finished with 120 wins. I lost both of my matches. We returned 120–2 from the tournament, with all the other guys winning all of their matches. Except me—chubby, slow Rulon. On the way home, I was very depressed. "I can't even win a match, I'm a horrible wrestler," I said to myself. Part of me was trying to be positive. "That's okay, keep working, never stop pushing, don't lose focus," I chided myself to avoid getting choked up and increase my embarrassment. The faint dream of getting better kept me going. I can't even say that there was a light at the end of the tunnel, because in that regard it was just pure darkness—no wins at the tournament and none in sight. At the same time, I liked being around my friends, enjoyed learning and the physical part of wrestling, and the fact that it gave me a break from the farmwork.

Finally, in eighth grade I started to improve and won some matches. I even won a few junior-high tournaments. People at tournaments must have been quite surprised to see the kid who always lost now standing proudly on the podium. I wasn't surprised, though, at my success. For me, it was a reflection of everything else I had to learn in life—it was a slow road. The progress came not by leaps and bounds, but in tiny steps. I worked harder and harder and started learning from my mistakes, especially as I better grasped the technique involved and how important that technique is in becoming a better wrestler. By the start of high school, only Reynold, who was already a good wrestler and getting better, stood in my way of making the varsity team.

I also started playing football. As a big kid, I was hard to move. Though technique again kept me from earning a starting spot on the offensive line, I was a good fit for the defensive line and could fight off blockers and fill a good part of the field with my size and strength. Really, though, it was the hard work I enjoyed the most, especially as I realized that the hard work was what was always making me better. In addition to playing high-school football—in which Star Valley was a perennial state champion or runner-up—I wrestled and took up the throwing events in track and field. Using body leverage and figuring out how my body's strength could help me excel, I learned to throw the discus and put the shot in the field events. Again, learning the proper technique—never easy in reading or math, and for years a struggle in wrestling—helped me make gains to where I was among the best in the region and, eventually, the state.

Getting into sports provided another short break from farmwork. By the time we were teenagers, my brother Reynold and I would finish with wrestling practice at Star Valley High School and still have a full evening of hard farmwork waiting for us. But that extra hour or two at school was not all play: we were still working hard— wrestling practice was draining. So we'd start our farm chores already worn out, making the evening and night seem longer. Reynold had a favorite saying: "If it doesn't kill you, it makes you stronger." He used to say that to me all the time, not just on the farm, but during wrestling practice and even while we worked on our homework. I hated that comment, but, looking back, Reynold was right. Those experiences made me stronger, both men- tally and physically. They made me a better person and developed my character. With what I had working against me, in terms of the learning disability and not fitting in at times with the other kids, the tough work on the farm gave me a tangible indication that I was capable of doing meaningful work and doing it well. I'm proud of all that work now, because even though I was a child, I still had to do my best. Several times a week—sometimes several times a day—I would say to myself, "Come on, you can get this done!" and I *would* get it done.

Though we didn't realize it for some time, we kids did have a lot of impact on the farm's success; its success depended on how hard and how smart we worked. We learned that we had to be honest in our assessment of our workday. The results were so easy to figure out: there was no way to blame other people if you did the job wrong. I think that's a great lesson for kids as they prepare for life.

Later, when I was much older, I'd finish a training session at wrestling practice, and guys would look at me and think I was a thousand miles away. What I'd be thinking about was: I've taken that farmwork ethic and brought it to my wrestling training. No matter how tired I get, there will be a point when I get done training that day, and I will be better for it. I learned that from life on the farm. Hard work is tiring, but it pays off. I know that hard work is the only thing that can get you to the top.

Four

THE GARDNER CLAN

FEBRUARY 14, 2002, 6:00 P.M.

As I circled and backtracked, cutting a path on my snow-mobile and then on foot, getting lost in the national forest along the Salt River, I made a trail with my sled, and then with my feet, that in aerial photos looks a little bit like a heart, a wide, sweeping heart left open at the top on one side. I guess that was fitting, because it was February 14, 2002 — Valentine's Day. The evening sun gave me its final weak rays. Still, when the temperature is at or below zero, even weaker rays are welcome; any measure of warmth is a gift when you don't know how much longer you are going to be outside. I would lose the sun long before my friends and family in Afton would, because I was deep in a ravine and the sun would slip beneath the mountains long before it disappeared behind Star Valley's western horizon. As a kid, I always felt a bit of sadness when the sun went down, because it meant I'd have to fight the cold. On this night in this valley, cold was about to have a whole new meaning for me. I said it a hundred times that night and I've said it a thousand times since: I should've known better. I shouldn't have taken off down the ravine alone, without a heavy coat, without a survival kit. I know the valley well, but this area I hadn't explored before, especially not in winter, when snow, ice, and freezing temperatures turn Mother Nature's beauty into an ugly nightmare for an ill-prepared explorer like myself. In hindsight, had I stopped where I went in, or at any of the key points along the way where I pushed through natural barriers—cliffs, ravines—I would've been found. Searchers found my path that night, but never could catch up to me.

Until then, I had accomplished just about everything I had set out to do: getting a college degree despite a learning disability and winning a gold medal in 2000, although no one gave me a chance. (That term, "No one gave us a chance," is clichéd and overused in sports. In my case, though, you literally could not find a member of the media or anyone within the sport who would have picked me to win the gold, or any medal, in 2000; and based on what I had, or hadn't, accomplished to that point, I can understand the prevailing doubt.)

The only thing I hadn't done was become a successful husband and father. I realized that being single was fun, but having someone to share life with might be a whole lot better. And there is nothing I like better than working with kids. I love setting a good example for kids, helping them to overcome whatever they face and telling them to always believe in themselves. I relate especially well to the kids who feel out of place; maybe they are a little heavy, maybe they don't read as well as the others—maybe they simply feel alone sometimes. As I stood in snow up to my waist that night, I began to realize what my life was missing. I was also concerned for my family; I hoped they weren't worrying too much about me.

Because in my life, it all comes back to family.

Our parents, Reed and Virginia, have been the best role models we ever could have desired. I count myself lucky for many things, but having such great parents was the most fortunate blessing, along with our faith—the two are intertwined. Mom and Dad set the tone for everything that has gone right in my life, including my ability to overcome obstacles and to face challenges head-on. My father was married and widowed before he met my mother. The oldest child is my sister Geraldine. She was born to my father's first wife, Gay. However, after giving birth, Gay was ill for about a year and passed away from anaphylactic shock.

My father was fortunate to meet my mother, Virginia, in the year after Gay's death. Some friends introduced my father to her and the two of them hit it off right away. My mother was from the arid heat of Arizona, so Star Valley's unforgiving cold was quite a change from what she grew up with.

When the last Gardner kid, yours truly, entered high school, my mother, who already had a bachelor's degree in home education, went back to college. As a result, as a teenager I ended up spending a lot more time with my father. We had to have some sort of income to supplement what we were making—or were not making—on the farm, because bills were a constant battle, money a constant war. My father did odd jobs in and around Star Valley to earn extra money: fixing pipes, spraying weeds, whatever it took to make the farm, and us, financially successful. In the summer, I used to go with him all over the region spraying weeds. He had worked with pesticides on the farm, so he had a good knowledge of which ones to use and how to apply the chemicals in a safe, healthy manner. My father was also a distributor for a product, Protein Molasses Supplement, and he traveled around, often with me in tow, as another way to supplement our own farm income. Since our family had a good name and my father was known as a hard worker and a good, honest farmer, he built a lot of friendships and business contacts.

My mother's decision to go back into nursing while I was in high school was a big sacrifice on her part, and I now know that it instilled in me a great respect for the importance of education. She had a lot of courage to pursue a nursing degree as she neared her fiftieth birthday, a courage that rubbed off on us kids. To have all of us children graduate from college is the best proof I can offer of my parents' strong commitment to our schooling. Despite the long hours, Mom never complained. Several times a week, she drove over a mountain pass into Idaho for classes. To pay for her degree and associated expenses, and to help make ends meet, she worked the night shift at a convenience store. Between school and work, we saw her only on weekends. Because of her incredible resolve and commitment, she became a registered nurse when I was finishing high school. Since there were no nursing openings at the hospital in Star Valley, she took a position with the Evanston hospital, a ninety-minute drive on two-lane state highway.

Whether it was my mother going back to school or my father developing new business ventures, my parents always demonstrated to us the value of education and continued learning. My mother's nursing degree and my father's master's degree in animal science were inspiring to us. One of my sisters is a neurosurgeon. Another sister is a nurse, one brother an owner of several businesses as well as an assistant principal, another teaching college while getting his doctorate. And I have, a bachelor's degree with a teaching specialty. So all of us kids went on to graduate from college.

My oldest sibling, Geraldine, was a high achiever in school. She went to the University of Wyoming for three years and then to San Jose State for pre-med studies before going on to medical school and becoming a very successful cardiologist. She's married and has a son, Wyatt.

The second oldest is Rollin, a graduate of the University of Wyoming, where he majored in animal science. He came back and took over running the family farm. He and his wife, Tami, have four kids—Jessica, Tyler, Justin, and Sadie. Rollin did his Mormon mission in Little Rock, Arkansas.

The third oldest child, and second oldest daughter, is Evon, another University of Wyoming graduate, who lives in Iowa, though she came back home and spent the 2004 summer in Star Valley. Evon has a business degree and works in the banking industry.

My brother Ronald, whose courageous story I will tell shortly, passed away at age fourteen.

Russell is the next branch on the family tree. We joke that he's the family's 911 dispatcher, because he is a jack-of-all-trades and can fix just about anything that goes wrong with a car, or repair one that's been in an accident—and in our family that was a full-time job in itself. Russell graduated from Utah State, got a master's degree in education, and is assistant principal at Star Valley Middle School. He also owns Gardner's Country Village in Afton, which includes a grocery store, motel, and Rulon's Burger Barn. He also has an auto body shop. Russell and his wife, Trisha, have three kids—twins Brock and Kelsea, and Trayson. Russell has been an especially close brother, friend, and confidant at times to me over the years. He also completely remodeled my parents' house. We joke about how that gesture squares Russell's account with the family, since he was the one of us who was able to escape some farmwork to pursue his outside interests, mostly related to fixing up cars, at a young age. Russell did his Mormon mission in Kobe, Japan.

My sister Diane is the one who I remember, along with Reynold, the most from doing farmwork together. Diane, four years ahead of me in school, is a hard, tireless worker who does not shy away from any challenge. She inherited, as we all did to some degree, the strong work ethic and message our parents instilled in us. She is a University of Wyoming graduate with an elementary-education degree and teaches elementary school in Evanston. Diane did her mission in Manila, Philippines.

Marcella, the youngest of the girls, is another sister to whom I remain very close. She's an amazing, compassionate person who has a good head for business. She managed a lot of my career after the 2000 Olympics and was a selfless helper toward what I was trying to build for my future. I remain indebted to Marcella for her kindness and time. She's married to Dale, and they live in Laramie, Wyoming, with their kids Randy, Blake, Kyra, and Tanner. Marcella is a dialysis nurse. She did her mission in Boston, Massachusetts.

Reynold is eighth of the nine Gardner kids. Just a year ahead of me in school, he was my best friend and constant competitor. When Reynold recounted his stories for this project, his memories didn't always intersect with mine. He claims I dished out just as much as I took and that I was a "Mama's boy" to a large degree. That's okay, I tell him with a laugh, he was Dad's favorite so we're about even in every regard at this point. He's also an amazing wrestler, twice winning the Pacific 10 Conference at Oregon State and National Junior College Athletic Association Championship in 1992, two years after I did. He graduated from Oregon State and is now a professor working on his doctorate in animal sciences. He and his wife, Jennifer, have two kids, Chandler and Evan. Reynold did his mission in Rapid City, South Dakota.

We were a family, an agricultural company, and we comprised competing sports teams in our family games and activities, from kickball (with a ball of tape) in the house (which lost more light structures than I can count) to all kinds of organized sports and "kid games" outside. I can't state strongly enough how much this group of special people helped build me into the person I am today. I learned not only teamwork, but also the importance of enjoying time alone. Every member of my family has several characteristics that rubbed off on me so deeply that it shaped my character. During those times when I was working on my own on the farm, I knew I was doing it for all of them, too, and by example they shaped the work ethic that helped me gain self-esteem and security about who I was and my place in this world.

Five

NEVER STOP PUSHING II

FEBRUARY 15, 2002, 8:30 A.M.

More than two hours after spotting the airplane, I still was waiting. Waiting. Waiting. Eventually the rush of adrenaline that had surged through my body when I first saw the plane dried up. When you get to that point, hope is almost lost.

Later, I found out that the thing that had given me more fame than I ever thought possible, the Olympics, was now working against my chances of survival. Almost every helicopter in the region had been contracted to Salt Lake City for the 2002 Olympic Winter Games, making it nearly impossible for my family and rescuers to find a helicopter to use to search for me. I had heard about the big "no fly zone" around the Olympics, but I didn't think twice about it when I ventured out for a ride. In western Wyoming, when there is snow on the ground, it's snowmobile time.

The sun was rising higher in the sky, but it was still freezing. Only the top layer of snow was melting. As I squatted down, the snow crunched, the only forgiving sign in an area that isn't known for letting careless sportsmen out alive. I sat and hoped that someone was on the way. Come on, I thought, doesn't anyone know I'm out here?

I didn't think about the gold medal I had won at the 2000 Olympic Games in Sydney, the thirteen-time world champion Russian wrestler I'd upset, the "Miracle on the Mat"—none of it meant anything anymore.

It's weird, because in Olympic/International wrestling each match consists of two three-minute rounds. After working as hard as you can for only 180 seconds, your body feels like the round lasted a week. Toward the end of the second period in a match, fatigue works on your mind. Here I was, and while I couldn't do the math in my head, I knew I had been outdoors for the equivalent of easily a hundred rounds—maybe even a thousand. And my opponent—Mother Nature—was undefeated no matter who her opponent was, at least in this area of the country.

All I could think about was living, taking one breath at a time at this high, familiar altitude. It had been a long, cold night on February 14, 2002; I wasn't going to let myself believe it would be my last. As I prayed for help, I realized that hope was all I had left—that and the will that had carried me through the previous night without a winter coat, soaked from neck to toe after falling into the Salt River not just once or twice, but five times. Five times! Can you believe that? I kept going, thinking I'd find my way out. Had I never fallen in the river trying to cross it on my snowmobile—I eventually decided to set off on foot after the fifth and final plunge into the river on the sled—I would not have been dealing with frostbite and hypothermia to this degree, both of which hit me within an hour after I realized I was lost. Then again, that's par for the course for me; my life has been one of extremes, losing it all, winning it all, never an in-between—from schoolwork to the farm, and our cows, my life, my sudden stumble into fame, or anything else. What works for us country folks, though, is perseverance. We think if you don't give up, there's really no way you can lose.

My great-great-grandfather was Archibald Gardner, a key figure in the building of the Mormon Temple in Salt Lake City. Archibald was committed to the Church, but his biggest contribution to the economy, and to the communities he served, was the building of sawmills and flour mills, a trade in which he excelled.

Archibald was from Edinburgh, Scotland. He and a brother, and possibly a nephew, came across the ocean and landed in Quebec, Canada. Once there, he learned about the land and started to learn about mills. In Quebec he met Elder Workman, the man who converted Archibald to the Mormon faith. Around 1830, he crossed into the United States and met up with the large group of Mormons who, seeking to avoid persecution, were heading west. It was about this time that the first Mormon Temple in Kirtland, Ohio, was destroyed and Mormons were being massacred. The founder and leader of the Mormon Church, Joseph Smith, was killed in Missouri in further attacks on Mormons.

Archibald spent the hard winter of 1846–47 at Winter Quarters in Nebraska, where the group was preparing to carve out the Mormon Trail across the West to Utah. The group followed the Mississippi River north, until it met the Platte River in Nebraska, at which point they switched directions and followed the Platte west.

The elements and starvation took a toll on the Mormon pioneers. While other settlers heading west followed the Oregon Trail, the Mormons stayed on the southern side of the Platte River for two reasons: to avoid conflict, and because they knew that on this less-traveled side of the river there would be more vegetation for the livestock and more consistent access to water.

When the group arrived in Utah, they settled on the southern outskirts of Salt Lake City. Archibald, who eventually became a bishop in the Church, is said to be the first builder of sawmills and flour mills in Utah, Idaho, and Wyoming. The new leader of the Church, who had taken over after Joseph Smith was killed, was Brigham Young. He liked working with the man he called "Archie." Archibald was one of the leaders and engineers in the building of the famed Salt Lake Temple, though it took forty years to complete the structure. Eight-ton blocks of marble were hauled by oxen from sixty miles away, out of the Cottonwood Canyon, which was south of Salt Lake City, to build the temple.

Archibald had one wife when he arrived in Salt Lake City, Margaret Livingston. He had to marry ten more before my family tree would connect to him. Archibald's eleventh and final wife, Mary Larsen, is my great-great-grandmother. When the U.S. Congress passed the Edmunds-Tucker law, outlawing polygamy, the Church came out with a mani-festo forbidding future "plural marriages." Since the gov-ernment had agents in Utah trying to track down men with multiple wives, the Church sent many to neighboring states, where the marriages were preserved, more children were born, and the families became part of new communi-ties. A good number of the original Mormon pioneers who relocated to my home region of Star Valley came at the urging of the Latter Day Saints Church, of which my family and I are proud members.

An often-misunderstood faith to the general public, the Latter Day Saints is based on service to God, family and community, and hard work. When the media focuses on some guy living with six or seven wives in a remote out-post and labels him a "Mormon Fundamentalist," the truth is that this person is not a Mormon. He either has never been a part of the Church or has been excommuni-cated because he chose to marry more than one woman. There's no longer anything "Mormon" about polygamy. The Church has outlawed it for more than a hundred years, so anyone practicing polygamy can't get away with doing it under the guise of Mormonism. It's unfair that our Church is sometimes publicly linked to an unlawful practice it specifically forbids. At the same time, it is part of my personal history, and if Archibald Gardner hadn't had eleven wives and forty-eight children, I wouldn't be here—that's not an endorsement of polygamy, just a fact of my history and how I got here.

While the Church's manifesto against polygamy played a big part in splitting up families, sending mothers and their children to neighboring states, it was not the only reason many families moved to Wyoming. In fact, after acquiring statehood in 1890, Wyoming's government wanted to see residents gain a foothold in southwestern Wyoming, homesteading the area and making a living as farmers and ranchers to develop the state's economy and add to the population base.

Star Valley was then, as it is now, a spectacular setting. According to figures in the weekly *Star Valley Independent*, later reproduced in the *Independent*-published "Reflections of the 20th Century in Star Valley, Wyoming," the valley sits more than six thousand feet above sea level. It runs approximately fifty miles from north to south, and is anywhere from five to ten miles wide. The valley is boxed in by four mountain ranges: Salt River, Caribou, Wyoming, and Gros Ventre.

There are actually two separate valleys that together comprise Star Valley. A set of "narrows" separate the upper and lower valleys. Also bordering the valleys are the adjacent Bridger-Teton, Caribou, and Targhee National Forests. So it really is a natural wonderland, with mountains and huge forests in every direction as far as the eye can see.

After the Salt Lake Valley was settled in 1847, Church leaders looked to colonize the rest of the "Great Basin" with families of the Latter Day Saints faith. The families were organized and carefully selected, with the directive to start new communities in the various regional mountains and valleys in order to further establish the Church in the region.

Mary Larsen's family was one of those blessed and told by the Church to head to western Wyoming. At the time, it was thought that the land had good soil and would be a perfect area for an agricultural community. Homestead laws at that time encouraged settlers to take huge acreages of land and turn them into something they could live off, building local economies. With all the timber and water in Star Valley, it seemed like a perfect habitat for this lifestyle. However, the soil isn't very deep, and the growing seasons are limited. It's also possible that no one anticipated how cold and long the winters would be in the area, mainly because no one had lived there long enough to learn that information and pass it along to Church leaders.

Afton became the regional hub and largest town in Star Valley, though nearly a dozen communities in all comprised it: Smoot, Osmond, Fairview, Auburn, Thayne, Bedford, Turnerville, Freedom, Etna, Grover, Alpine, and Afton.

The economy in the region was known then, as it is now, as a hay–grain–cow economy. Milk cows were a staple, and though they had a short "working" life and were not always profitable within the valley market, their butter and cheese could be shipped to outside markets. Creameries sprang up in several communities.

Butch Cassidy—who was known locally by his given name of Robert Leroy Parker—also lived briefly in Star Valley. Because the valley was basically shut down seven months a year—almost no travel in or out because of the weather and bad roads—Cassidy spent a winter there in the early 1890s, according to the book *A History of Star Valley*, after he and three outlaw friends robbed a Telluride, Colorado, bank of $10,500. The outlaws lived a quiet life in the valley, gaining a "Robin Hood" status, bringing in the money they stole and spending generously in Star Valley, even on occasion helping out those in need. Eventually the law, chasing Cassidy for stealing horses, traced his post office box and caught up to him in his Star Valley cabin. He was arrested, grazed in the head by a bullet (reportedly during a close-range shootout), and put in the Star Valley jail. He was transferred to Evanston, served two months, and was released. Cassidy was later arrested and served two years in Laramie before receiving a pardon (for reasons unknown) by Governor William Richards. After that release, Cassidy and some outlaws supposedly robbed a bank in Montpelier, Idaho—to pay a fellow outlaw's legal fees in Ogden, Utah—and left the area for good. And while folklore traces the last years of Butch Cassidy's life to South America, Cassidy reportedly corresponded with friends in the Star Valley from the West Coast, meaning he possibly returned to the United States after his trip to South America.

Archibald Gardner knew that the fledgling Star Valley community needed mills to both fuel its economy and feed its families. So at the direction of the Church, he set out in 1889, at age seventy-five, to build the first sawmill and flour mill in Star Valley, since the closest mills were fifty miles away over rough roads.

Star Valley settlers were excited to have their own mills, and a group of men quickly assembled for work. According to Gardner family diaries, Archibald reached into his pocket and pulled out a five-dollar gold piece and said, "This is all the cash I have to begin with. But if you people will help me, I will pay you back every cent and the mill will be ready to turn flour out for you by Christmas." The sawmill opened by the promised date, and Archibald's son-in-law, Brigham Gardner, took charge of both the sawmill and flour mill. Archibald returned to Salt Lake City, where the Church instructed him to take his youngest family, with wife Mary Larsen, back to Afton.

Mary Larsen was born in Denmark in 1850. She was my great-great-grandmother and had given birth to all eight of her kids before she moved to Wyoming in the fall of 1890. The family loaded everything they owned into a wagon, leaving just enough room for the kids, including two-year-old Frank Gardner, the last of Archibald's forty-eight children. All but Frank walked most of the way to Star Valley. When they got to Afton, there still wasn't a lot there, just the early settlers and the new mills. The family settled in the mouth of Swift Creek Canyon as homesteaders. Archibald already had a two-room log house built for Mary and the children; they shared this house with son-in-law Brigham Gardner's family.

The Afton flour mill often ran twenty-four hours a day. Temple Bench, in the Star Valley foothills on the edge of the community, had a thirty-foot waterfall that they could use to flume water into the flour mill and sawmills. The flour mill used grain to produce flour and bran. Archibald and the other settlers realized the hardship those in Star Valley faced. So if someone needed flour and didn't have money, they still got all the flour they needed to feed their family. There are dozens of stories of penniless men who were too proud to ask for flour but for whom Archibald left sacks of flour at their houses anyway. They knew he had been there only after seeing his huge footprints (he was said to wear size 14 shoes) in the snow. At the same time, if someone showed up with a lot of cash and wanted to buy a lot more than he needed, Archibald would sell him only what he needed so as to have enough for those in need.

In 1901, during a visit from Salt Lake City to Star Valley—he had a vigorous travel schedule for regular visits to all of his wives and kids scattered throughout the region—to see his youngest family, Archibald knew his life was winding down. The town had a special meeting to honor him for his hard work and generosity. He told the group to "stick together, work together, and this will be your home. Be blessed. Be happy."

There is a special eight-foot-high granite monument to Archibald in Afton, but he is buried in the Salt Lake Cemetery among the other early Mormon leaders.

Clarence Gardner, my great-grandfather, was born in 1875 in the little house adjacent to Archibald's big flour mill located on the Jordan River near Salt Lake City, some fifteen years before the family moved to Afton. Clarence was another amazing Gardner family member. He and his brother Frank, while exploring and searching for timber strands in 1908, discovered Swift Creek's Intermittent Spring (known also as the Periodic Spring). They were in the area because they operated the water-powered flour mill and sawmill at the mouth of the canyon.

Soon after that discovery Clarence just sixteen years old, started keeping the family's books for the mills. He found a three-hundred-dollar note that needed to be paid in "gold coin to buy machinery for the new gristmill [flour mill]," and balked when his father told him to temporarily disregard the note to fill flour sacks for the needy.

"Father, how can we pay our debts if you keep giving away our profit?" Archibald's answer would stay with his son the rest of his life: "Because you have given of your blessing to the poor, you always shall have wheat in your bins." Clarence cited that moment as something that deepened his resolve to go into public service.

A born leader, at the age of eighteen Clarence became a second counselor to Bishop Waite in Star Valley Bishopric and soon after was ordained a high priest.

My great-grandmother is the former Alice Burton. Alice's mother was among those who moved their children from Ogden, Utah, to Star Valley to escape the U.S. marshals who were tracking down polygamists.

"The marshals became more and more unbearable, spying on us as if we were criminals," Alice wrote in her diary. "They would peek in windows, walk in without knocking and search the house for father. He had to travel most of the time and keep hiding. I lived in constant fear of him being put in prison. I knew he was a good man and we love him—he loved us all deeply. My mother too had to hide sometimes."

In 1866, Alice Burton's father met with a Church official who told him about the almost-untouched, pristine country in the state of Wyoming, and promised "no U.S. marshals would follow him there." The roads to get there, however, were "treacherous, winding through mountain passes and along streams," Alice recalled in her diary.

"The roads were so 'sideling' [sloped] that sometimes the whole family had to ride the brakes to keep the wagon from rolling over. It was very frightening. When we came to steep hills we had to get out and walk, and sometimes push on the wagon or put two teams on one wagon to get up the hills. It was hard work for the horses, and us too."

The family did not pack enough supplies for the trip. They had no idea how treacherous and slow the journey would be.

"Our last camp was made in Crow Creek Canyon," Alice wrote. "The food we had previously prepared was all gone. Other supplies were packed so tightly that mother could get only a little flour out. She mixed it with water and fried it without grease over the bonfire. We were so hungry that it tasted good. Father had gone to bed, too tired to eat, but when he smelled those cakes, he said, 'My stars, that smells good.' So he got up and ate, too."

But by early the next afternoon, their new home was in sight.

"The next day brought us in view of beautiful Star Valley," Alice wrote. "It was soul inspiring! The little valley surrounded by high mountains looked like a green field of waving grass with a small river edged with willows and trees down the center. There were no houses to mar the view. Two or three dirt-roof cabins at Fairview and about a half dozen on the Afton town-site represented all the settlers here then."

Star Valley would be a safe place to live, they decided. After Alice Burton's father staked a claim and prepared to file on it, he returned to Ogden, Utah.

After Clarence Gardner married Alice Burton in late 1897 at the Salt Lake Temple, he did his Mormon mission back East, where among the first letters he received was one announcing the birth and death of his first son, Albert Burton Gardner. My grandfather, Elworth, was born to

Clarence and Alice in 1906; he showed no signs of life for fifteen minutes, but after vigilant work by the doctor and lots of prayer by his parents, he sprang to life.

Alice was a passionate mother, homemaker, and schoolteacher. She taught second and third grades. The diaries and family discussions explaining the history of my family show the courage and sacrifice so many of my relatives made to start scratching out a home and eventually carving out a life, and community, in Star Valley.

Clarence and Alice had three biological sons and one daughter, Marian. All three boys (including my grandfather Elworth, who passed on before he was even forty) died young—the first died at two days old, and Alton died at age fourteen when he was thrown by a horse.

In a family diary, Clarence marked the loss of Alton: "The passing away of our dear son Alton, June 27, 1918, brings vividly to mind the date, when exactly 20 years ago, to the hour, 4:30 A.M., we lost our oldest son at birth, while I was on my mission in the tops of the Allegany Mountains, in West Virginia."

Elworth's life also would be too short. He had a condition where veins in his leg would swell. This was believed to cause a stroke when he was a young man that affected his entire left side (Elworth would die in 1944). In their grief and at the Church's urging and though well past what most would consider childbearing years, Clarence and Alice adopted a son, six-week-old Kenneth, born in Casper, and raised him as well. Kenneth became like a brother to my own father, who after Elworth's death and Kenneth's adoption was raised by Clarence and Alice, too.

Kenneth is still a respected member of the community in Star Valley, where he runs a business.

In 1905, Clarence became the second mayor of Afton, and in 1906 he entered the Wyoming state legislature, where he would serve twenty-two years, eighteen of them as a senator. He served as president of the senate, Speaker of the House, and twice as acting governor of Wyoming. He was reelected to the State Senate in 1914.

In 1918, Clarence bought what would come to be the farmland we have in our family to this day. He and his family plowed the land and put in crops of wheat, oats, and barley. Clarence, who at times had jobs farming, dairying, milling, shingling, planning, and retailing, continued to serve the community. He also was deeply involved in the Church, and upon the death of the Church's stake (which oversees several wards—and wards are comprised of several branches) president Osmond, to whom Clarence served as a counselor, took over the role in 1913 and served in that position for twenty-seven years.

In the late 1930s and early 1940s, Star Valley's economy was hit hard by unemployment. The Depression found its way into Star Valley, where bread lines formed. The Star Valley State Bank had been getting help from banks in nearby Kemmerer and those farther away in Cheyenne and Salt Lake City. When that help stopped, Clarence journeyed to Salt Lake City and spoke with Latter Day Saints Church president Herbert J. Grant. Before the meeting, president Grant called Clarence at the Temple Square Hotel. He asked how Clarence had slept the night before, to which Clarence replied, "not well," because of worries related to the bank.

"Neither did I sleep very much, as I also was worried about your bank," President Grant told my great-grandfather. "I thought what a calamity it would be to the people of Star Valley if your bank should fail. Where can you meet me?"

They set up a 9:00 A.M. meeting at President Grant's office, where he made out a check for $6,500 to keep the bank afloat. In accepting the check gratefully, Clarence gave his word that the entire amount would be paid back, with interest. The bank survived, and once again Clarence Gardner had helped his beloved Star Valley make it through another crisis.

Of course, on a personal level I am also very grateful to Great-grandfather Clarence for taking in my father and raising him as he would his own son after my grandfather Elworth passed away as a relatively young man. My father, Reed, was often mistaken for being Clarence's son, and people were surprised to find out he was actually a grandson. This brings me to more modern times, when my story starts to take shape, and there's no doubt that I followed in the footsteps that my great-grandfather took as I found my place in Star Valley, and in life.

Six

BARN BURNS, HOPE SURVIVES

FEBRUARY 15, 2002, 1:30 A.M.

*Long before the airplane, there had been noises. Between
1:30 and 2:00 A.M., I heard snowmobiles, and then voices,
several sounding familiar, though louder than I was used to.*

"Hallucinating." I said to myself. "Be tough."

*Hours earlier, I had focused on the sounds of nature
and how they changed as I moved around, even slightly.
On one side of the tree that I was using as a lean-to, the
trickling water sounded like a tiny stream. On the other
side, nearer the water, it sounded like a raging river. But
the engine noises kept coming, and then stopped. And
then the engines again. And voices. Getting closer.*

"Snowmobiles!" I realized.

*My head was starting to clear. Maybe it was the rush
of adrenaline from realizing it really was snowmobiles
carrying my potential rescuers, and not a hallucination.*

"I'd better get over there and let them see me," I thought.

Then I heard Danny Schwab's snowmobile. Danny had been out snowmobiling with me just twelve hours earlier. His engine had a very distinctive sound because of how his piping was set up. When he opened the throttle, it sounded more like a motorcycle than a snowmobile.

My legs were numb, and the waist-high snow would impede any long strides I hoped to take. I knew it would take at least a half hour to get back to the riverbed, because it had taken a good fifteen minutes to get from the water to where I was now, and that was before my legs were frozen stiff. Besides, if I worked my way out and the searchers were gone, I knew I would have to hike all the way back to my little protected area against the trees, where I was shielded from the wind. The voices got closer.

I tried to yell, but nothing happened. So I whistled. I always had been a good whistler, so I used every ounce of energy I could find to whistle like I never had before.

The searchers were only two hundred yards away. I kept opening my mouth to yell, but no sound would come out. So I whistled and whistled. I heard two distinct engines. One would go hard, and the other would stop. And on and on.

Eventually, the engines came to life and were roaring.

And then the noise started to fade. There go the snow-mobiles. There go my friends.

They were headed the other way, away from me. Was that the faded sound of all hope leaving me? As I slipped in and out of consciousness, I wasn't sure.

The heat from the fire was incredible. It was the only moment during that long winter of 1978 when we actually wanted any rain or snow we could get. A wet snow, sleet, would be perfect, but it was too cold for sleet. Even too cold for snow, for that matter. I'll never forget the bitter cold from that winter; it's on the books as one of the coldest in the history of Wyoming. I remember milking in open air one night and the milker kept freezing up; I found out why later—the windchill had reached seventy-seven degrees below zero that night.

Flames from our barn were reaching skyward. As the thicker wood caught fire and dried, it popped, sounding like small firecrackers. For a farm family, there is nothing beautiful about a fire, unless it's in the living-room fireplace or burning weeds under our watchful eyes. Otherwise, it's only bad news.

On the family farm the barn is the hub of activity: a storage facility for supplies and equipment, a home for livestock, and an office. So this was really bad news.

That year had already been a rough one on our farm. In October of 1978, my father had been diagnosed with a bleeding ulcer. A few weeks later, it got so bad that he was hospitalized. They gave him a special diet—no celery, tomatoes, or carbonated soft drinks—and told him to take it easy. That was a tough prescription, because Thanksgiving was coming up, and while giving thanks was important, it was the big feast we all really enjoyed, and Dad especially. He had to take it easy that Thanksgiving, his favorite meal of the year.

A few days after Thanksgiving, one of the kids was out milking and turned on a space heater that we often used to stay warm on the cold nights. There was a bit of smoke from the space heater and it smelled funny, but that had happened before. Apparently, as the night wore on, the heater, which was left on or somehow shorted out, caught fire. A neighbor saw the fire from three miles away, drove to our house, and pounded on our door.

"Your barn is burning!" he yelled.

Once the fire caught the hay, it burned even more out of control; there wasn't anything we, or the volunteer fire department, could do about it. The firefighters tried to save the front area, where Dad had put in a milking parlor. But it was no use; the fire was too hot and had spread too fast.

Everything was working against fighting the fire. The straw and wood fed the flames; the freezing temperatures froze the water hoses. The barn could not be saved.

My father stood in the dark, his face illuminated by the shooting flames.

"What are we going to do now?" he asked, shaking his head. "Just what are we going to do?"

So there we were. There'd be no milk check coming, because all the equipment—except for the bulk tank (which stored milk)—was destroyed. This was an older barn, one of those big, open structures you see on post-cards, so we didn't keep the animals in there. So, thankfully, no animals died in the fire.

But hope was a hard commodity that night. Only bills would keep coming, plus a new one if we wanted to rebuild the barn. But we lived in a great community, and our neighbors joined together to pull us through this awful time. Six miles away was a neighbor's inactive barn. We used it to milk our cows until we could raise a makeshift barn, and in time we rebuilt the barn.

That summer—I was eight years old—when we had to bale hay, neighbors brought seven bale wagons to help us haul the hay from the field; there were twenty-five men from the community helping to elevate it. A neighbor isn't just someone who lives next door; he's someone who lives the life you do, who understands when you need a helping hand, 'cause, heck, he's needed one before and he knows he'll probably need one in the future, too. You help in a community because you can. Having all of that help was phenomenal.

My father was no stranger to the devastation of fire. Due to World War II, the family flour mill, established by Archibald Gardner during the early days of Star Valley, had shut down—it had closed down decades earlier as other, newer mills were built and technology evolved—so my father was able to store his barley in the vacant mill. One spring, on the high school's prom night, some kids were seen goofing around the mill. All of a sudden, flames were shooting toward the sky; the mill burned down, taking all of my father's barley. But this second fire hit closer to home, because the barn was such a big part of our daily lives and family business.

As what was left of our barn gave in to the fire that cold winter night in '78, our family held on to each other. We knew we were lucky; we had each other, our faith, and our neighbors.

Seven

THE BOY WHO MADE
EVERY DAY COUNT

FEBRUARY 15, 2002, 4:30 A.M.

I was torn: I could either deal with the complete exhaustion that was consuming me, or I could concentrate on blocking out the bitter cold. Coping with one of them was possible, but fighting on two fronts seemed impossible.

To stay awake, I stood up and leaned against a branch. It may have been frozen solid or it may have been just a strong branch, because it bowed only slightly.

"Bleak," I thought to myself. "The situation can get only worse if . . ."

If I die. Death was close—I'm as sure of that now as I was then. As soon as the branch took my weight, I faded into a deep sleep, or perhaps it was a hallucination. But I have no doubt that what I saw next was real.

The cold went away, and I opened my eyes to an area of bright white. Everything, from the ground to the back-

ground to the sky, was white. As I moved closer, I could see three outlines—three beings, I guessed, and they appeared to be conferring about something.

Right away I saw Jesus standing up. We didn't make eye contact, but I am 100 percent sure that I was looking at Jesus Christ. Up on a higher area was God, and though I didn't look directly at Him, I knew who He was.

Lying down on his side was another being.

My brother Ronald.

I was shocked to see his face. Over the years, I had imagined how he would have looked had he lived, what a great wrestler he would have become in high school, and what a great lawyer and father he would have been. He died in 1979 and would have been thirty-five years old in 2002.

I looked into his eyes and face, and he appeared to be only a young adult, perhaps eighteen or nineteen. I didn't know if I should speak, or wait for Ronald to say something. Though it was good to see him, everything else felt wrong. I didn't understand what was happening, though I sensed that the three of them knew exactly what was going on. Why I felt or knew any of this, or why I experienced any of this, is unknown to me.

As I looked at Jesus and back toward Ronald, I felt my whole body start to shake again. I woke up standing, surrounded by darkness, shivering from the bitter cold.

Yet I felt alert for the first time in at least two hours, and my entire body felt a surge from my head to my feet. I had no idea what to make of what I'd just experienced: a dream, a hallucination, or something that no one else in this life can explain.

What I do know is that for whatever reason, my body picked up a rush of energy.

And I had never needed it more in my life.

I'm told that my brother Ronald, seven years my senior, would have been the best wrestler of all of us if his life hadn't been tragically cut short.

He lost only one match his entire career, to a kid one year older. In what no one then realized was the last wrestling match of his life, eighth-grade Ronald beat the ninth-grade kid who had dealt him that one defeat. The boy he beat would go on to become a three-year Wyoming state champion in high school.

Ronald was the small one in our family, the only one to ever be described as wiry. He was ninety-five pounds as an eighth-grader, but had the fight of a bull and the heart of a lion. If there has ever been a tougher kid anywhere, I never met him.

The older brothers learned quickly that testing Ronald wasn't a good idea. He'd punch and kick any of them who thought they could take him.

"One of these days, Rollin is going to deck you, Ronald, so don't you come running to me," my father told Ronald one day when he was going after the oldest boy in our family. Ronald never had to.

I thought Ronald was a daredevil. As I'd sit watching with awe, he'd jump down the stairs in one incredible bound. I wanted to be like Ronald when I got older, because he had no fear.

One time, some older boys were picking on Ronald and he didn't like it. So he took one of the boys' keys and threw them out into a nearby field. The older boys chased him down and de-pantsed him. Well, Ronald didn't like that too much, so he found an iron bar and chased the boys into the old barn, swinging at the ringleader. Fortunately, Ronald missed, but he left a huge dent in the metal pipe that he did strike. Those boys never messed with Ronald again.

The kid had no fear.

Yet he had a huge heart. In school, Ronald was known as the kid most likely to befriend the kids who were being picked on or left out of the cliques—kids who felt alone for various reasons. He didn't like to see kids alone or, worse, lonely kids. His teachers say he always reached out to the kids who were pushed aside. Ronald was always well liked by the popular kids, too, so I guess you could say he was especially likable. And everyone in the family liked working shifts on the farm with Ronald, because no one worked harder than he did.

He was active and very bright—"sharp" was a word used often to describe his intelligence. In fact, he wanted to be a lawyer, just like my mother's father had been. There's no doubt he would have been an outstanding lawyer had he lived. He talked all the time about his plans, telling my brother Rollin, who planned to (and since has) become a farmer, taking over Dad's farm: "I'll be a lawyer so I can support your farming habit."

Ronald always lived each minute of life three times, so in a sense, he lived to a pretty good age. One night, in the year that he would fall ill, he was taking a friend home on his motorcycle. He left at 8:30 P.M., and an hour later we hadn't heard from him. We called up the friend's house and were told Ronald had left "a long time" ago.

My mother and sister Diane went looking for him. On the way to Ronald's friend's house, there was a gravel pile that the kids used to run their motorcycles over, with a sort of a ramp on each side. On the way home from dropping off his friend, Ronald had gone up the side, not realizing the back side of the mound had been dug out and moved away. He had fallen probably twelve feet, been knocked out cold, and sprained his ankle. The gas cap on the cycle had been loose, so he had been lying there, unconscious, for a good forty minutes, inhaling the gas fumes. We got him up to the car and took him to the hospital. Like everything else that happened before he fell seriously ill, Ronald quickly recovered.

On April 9, 1979, Ronald had a bad bloody nose, the worst in a series of smaller bloody noses. My parents packed his nose and, minutes later, had to pack it again. There were little bruises on his legs, too, and no one knew what they were from.

My parents took Ronald to Star Valley Hospital that evening where he was quickly referred to the hospital at the University of Utah in Salt Lake City. We had never heard the two words the doctor uttered when he came into the room. We could tell the severity of the diagnosis from the look on the doctor's face. This was bad, and everyone knew it right away.

"Aplastic anemia," he said.

Aplastic anemia involves inadequate blood-cell formation from the bone marrow, and it comes on in a hurry. White blood cells have a short life, something like a few hours. So when the bone marrow shuts down, the body's process of shutting down is accelerated.

The disease would take his life only four and a half months later, but it wouldn't prevent Ronald from living until that last day came. While we were in Salt Lake, Ronald was allowed to leave the hospital for a day to go with us to visit friends in the city. My mother came outside looking for Ronald, and there he was, jumping off the roof. Had he broken a bone, he could have bled to death. But his approach to life always had been to live each day to the fullest. And that was just another day, another chance to have a lot of fun and smile.

After a week in Salt Lake, he was flown to Seattle for further treatment. A fungus developed in his leg in June, and the leg had to be amputated just above the knee.

When the doctors came in to tell my brother that he was going to lose his leg, you could see by the look in my parents' eyes that their hearts were sinking. Not Ronald's, though.

"Dad, it's okay," Ronald said. "I still can wrestle with one leg."

He had the will not only to live but to keep on living a real life. A lot of people don't realize how much they have until they are at the point of losing it. Not Ronald. He was counting what he still had as blessings, and not worrying about anything else. He had a passion for life like no one else I've ever met. His will carried him to the very end. He had very bad gangrene, and his skin was falling off. Yet his face would light up when we'd come to see him. He wanted to hear how everything was going—as if he were still on the farm or at school. And the truth is, he was still with us. And is to this day.

Two bone-marrow transplants—from Rollin and

Marcella—helped him put up a fight, but the disease wasn't going to slow down. Since the marrow didn't take, there was nothing else that could be done. We had heard that 60 percent of marrow transplant recipients survived and could return to a normal life. We never saw that happen. All of the transplant patients we saw while we were there were dying, day by day, transplant or no transplant.

Toward the end, Ronald had to be in a protective bubble in his Seattle hospital room. Everything, and everyone, had to be sterilized to enter the room.

"In my mind, there was something always there, holding Ronald's growth back," my father says. "I just can't help but believe that he was born with something that led to this. He had all the fight you could ask for. I just don't know if his body was born with the means to live a long life."

Some of my friends and relatives were laid-back, conservative in spirit. Ronald was a free spirit, always wanting to have fun and learn what life was about. Though I was only eight when he died, the way he lived left an indelible mark upon me; that is, I chose at a very young age to live my life the way Ronald lived his, and I can see his influence in the way I've pursued my ambitions. When my father wanted me to go to the University of Wyoming, as had all his children, I fought back, seeing a better opportunity at another school, one that I believed would better help me realize my dreams and goals. I found the courage to set out on my own because of the will Ronald showed every day of his short life.

Ronald Walter Gardner died from complications relating to aplastic anemia on August 28, 1979.

But just as surely as my heart beats every day, his memory is alive in me, just as it carried me through a cold winter night on Valentine's Day, 2002.

While Ronald went after and conquered danger as a kid, I fell into it all the time, or it found me. After I was born, the doctor who delivered me said something strange to my father: "Your son's accident-prone." Perhaps I was a squirmer coming out. My father must've shaken his head, and maybe laughed. But that doctor was on to something.

Over the years, I have acquired what I would consider—and hope—to be more than my share of scars, scrapes, broken bones, and my specialty, it seems: freak accidents.

The list, arranged chronologically, is impressive, or scary, by any standard.

On my upper arms I have what look almost like tattoos. They are actually scars made by the hot sticks one of my brothers poked me with. We often built outdoor fires, sometimes to burn trash, sometimes just to stay warm, and this time one of my brothers decided to give me a good branding when I was about four years old.

One winter when I was six, I was chopping kindling with my brother Russell. Hacking away at kindling is dangerous, because the wood ricochets when you hit it. But on this occasion I wasn't paying close enough attention after chopping a piece, and on the next stroke I hit myself on the left thumb. I have hit that thumb more than once over the years and still have a few scars to prove it. Once I even embedded the hatchet in my hand; one of my brothers pulled it out.

Another time, when I was seven, I had found some

change and decided to spend it on a candy bar at the golf course shop across the road from our house. As I crossed over the fence to get there, the barbed wire caught me and cut a two-inch gap in my leg. Back to the hospital for stitches.

Another "typical" accident occurred when I was just eight years old. Ronald was in the hospital, and my parents were with him. That meant the kids left back on the farm had to make do and pick up the slack. My sisters Diane and Marcella took charge. We had taken the pickup to go turn off the irrigation water—remember that in addition to our own land, we also sometimes rented nearby parcels for other crops. Farm kids drive when they are able to. In the "old" days, farm licenses were granted, for farm use only, for kids as young as fourteen, but the reality was that if a kid needed to drive to get farmwork done and could see over the steering wheel, they'd drive. I was in the truck bed, and we were going about thirty miles an hour. We had gone out to a main road, and Marcella, being the twelve-year-old younger sister, wanted to take a turn driving. Diane, thirteen, let her, but Marcella was so little in that big truck that she could see the road only through the steering wheel. It was only about a half-mile drive, but Marcella apparently was letting the truck drift toward the other lane. When Diane reached over and yanked the steering wheel to straighten out the truck and keep it on the road—we had drifted all the way into the other lane at that point—she whipped the truck back so abruptly that I flipped right out of the pickup bed. It was summer, and I wasn't wearing a shirt. I landed on my back and skidded down the road. "Hey," Marcella recalls telling Diane, "Rulon's not back there anymore."

They stopped, came back and got me, and took me to the hospital, and I had to go through a series of cleanings, the most memorable of which was the first one, with a sponge soaked in iodine used to remove the gravel and clean the area. Boy, did that sting! Because we were short-handed at home, I didn't miss any farmwork. However, because of the healing scrapes, my shirt stuck to my back every night and I had to have help peeling it off. I remember going to church that next week in pain. There was so much swelling and pus that I had to go back to the hospital to have more gravel picked out and have the wound cleaned with iodine again. Amazingly, there was no concussion or head trauma from that accident.

Later that year, when I was third grade, my insecurities were becoming more apparent to me. I started trying a little too hard to prove my worth. For show-and-tell that year, I brought a killing arrow and a practice arrow—used for bow hunting—that had been given to my brother and me by a family friend. I thought this would really impress the kids, showing them something I had that they didn't, since they seemed to always point out what I didn't have. At the end of the class, I went to put the arrows away in a closet. I dropped the practice arrow, and when I bent down to pick it up, I stabbed myself with the killing arrow. The sharp point went into my stomach right beneath my last rib. I was taken to the hospital with the arrow hanging out of me; it was quite a gruesome scene. The hospital was right next door to the elementary school (was this town laid out with forethought, or what?). The doctor there said that because of the angle I was at when the arrow went in, I was "pretty close to doing some major damage to internal organs." He removed the arrow and stitched me closed; I have about an inch-and-a-half-long scar that is still clearly visible.

There were other incidents that I'm sure most kids go through, mostly bicycle accidents. I loved to ride my bike, but it seemed like I had an inordinate amount of difficulty staying on it. When I was nine years old, Reynold and I were racing home once—not unusual, as we competed in everything—and just when I was ready to catch him, he cut me off, my front tire hit his back tire, sending my bike out of control and me to the ground. Again, it was just scrapes, but farmwork was always a little more challenging with raw flesh, even covered with gloves. Of course, when I talk to my brothers and sisters now about those incidents, they usually forget the role they played, claiming I was to blame for everything that happened. I guess we all have our own memories.

Another time, at age eleven, my sister Diane and I were riding bikes at night; she had a ten-speed and I had a neat BMX. She wanted to ride my bike, so I got on her ten-speed, a real treat for me. The cable that connected to the gearshift interfered with my pedaling. So I reached down to move it and ran into the back of a parked pickup truck. I was thrown from the bike into the back of the truck and suffered a concussion.

From bikes to the bale wagon. The bale wagon, used to pick up hay bales after they were cut and bound in the field, didn't always function right, so a lot of times we had to assist some of the machinery manually. The bales would stack on a "table," and once the table was full, it would rise up and stack the bales onto the others already in the wagon. I was thirteen when I made the mistake of standing on a hay bale—as it was picked up—to trigger the mechanism that drew the bales up on the wagon. My extra weight was needed to push the bale down and trigger the machinery. Then I'd jump up and let it rise up again. Once when I jumped up, my foot went into a hay bale and I got stuck. Well, the mechanism didn't know that, so it just lifted. Since I was prone underneath the table as it started to rise, the chain used to lift the table went across my face, gained traction, and kept going. It was a hydraulic system, so it could do serious damage. Diane was driving and didn't see that I was trapped, but noticed the loading process, from my end of it, had stopped. She climbed out and came back and saw me. Her concern wasn't for me.

"What are you doing!" she yelled. "This is so stupid!"

I could've been seriously hurt, but what irritated Diane was that my predicament was wasting valuable work time and I had slowed our schedule during a very important period. Hay is money on a farm like ours, a resource that we can produce ourselves and not have to buy from out of state. So I didn't get a lot of sympathy, but because she thought I was messing around and not respecting the work, Diane was mad as heck.

As I got older, I didn't get much wiser when it came to accidents. Heading into my sophomore year in high school, I was getting excited about the upcoming football season. Unfortunately, that July while feeding cows, I cut my knee on a piece of concrete. Being farm kids, we did our own diagnoses, and when my brother Rollin stuck a Q-tip a full inch down into my knee, we deemed the wound serious enough to seek professional medical attention. What I remember most about that accident is that when we got to the hospital, everyone on the staff recognized me and someone said, "Hey, Rulon's here again." And I got stitches again.

It was an untimely injury, because the football coach had told me earlier in the spring that if I did well in the big preseason scrimmage in August, I might make the varsity team. The next day in our bedroom, Reynold and I were having our usual disagreement about work. He demanded that I do a certain task, and I said I no way. I hit him and he hit me back, and then he kicked me in the stitches, which completely ripped out, leaving raw, torn tissue. The doctor said there was nothing he could do: "I can't restitch it, because the tissue is so torn out. It'll just have to heal on its own." I still played in the preseason scrimmage, but I was on antibiotics because the tissue was damaged and infected.

I don't want to make it sound like Reynold pushed me around all the time . . . well, maybe he did, but I pushed back. I could play as rough as he did. He says I shoved him into a metal door once during one of our disagreements and ruptured his eardrum—though I don't remember that. Another time, he claims I was wearing heavy boots and, during a disagreement, kicked him in the throat—again, I don't recall that. Yet another time, he claims I threw a stick at him—one I had pulled from a fire we had built—and hit him in the eye. He still has a scar from that accident, a little black dot on his eye. I don't remember that, either. But I have a scar in my eye, too, from a piece of metal that I think came from him—of course, he recalls it differently!

Here's one more accident for the record books: in my junior year of high school, I wasn't interested in watching the Super Bowl, so I went outside to pull hay bales, a necessary chore in winter for feeding cows. It was hard work pulling the bales down, because they were frozen. I kicked at a piece of reinforced metal called "angle wire," trapping my leg and cutting my right shin. I didn't worry about it, assuming the gash would heal on its own. Instead, it got infected and my leg swelled up. So back to the hospital a week or so later, this time for stitches and antibiotics. It took forever to heal. I didn't want to worry about it, because that weekend we were going to drive down to watch the University of Utah play Wyoming in a basketball game, a heated rivalry year-round, but my leg was too swollen to travel. I ended up being admitted to the hospital because the swelling got worse. The doctor said my leg had gotten so bad that if it didn't heal properly, I might, in a worst-case scenario, have to get it amputated. That caught my attention.

I had started beating Reynold in wrestling practice his senior year—this was my junior year—and wanted to face him at the wrestle-offs, where the varsity team for the regional and state championships would be determined. My coach came by the hospital that Saturday or Sunday, because the wrestle-offs were that Monday. "It's Reynold's senior year, and you need to get all healed up," my coach said. I felt like I had just lost my first chance to go to state. Again, Reynold has a different recollection of this—I'm sure he would say he would've beaten me if I'd been healthy—he would go on to win the state championship in the following two weeks—but that's how I remember it.

Another incident born out of my rivalry with Reynold occurred when I was at college in Lincoln, Nebraska. I had a part-time job at a local motorcycle factory. Reynold, who was living with me at the time, also worked there. We competed like crazy at that job, trying to see who could do the various jobs faster. One day when I was working on the line, I put my arm down on a hot surface used to bond parts together and singed the inside of my forearm. It was so bad, I suffered from blood poisoning.

My hospital "rap sheet" is indeed long. But like my brothers told me: if it doesn't kill you, it makes you stronger.

As I progressed through my freshman and sophomore years at Star Valley High School, I was becoming not only a much better wrestler, but also a good player on the football team and improving in track and field in the shot put and discus. Again, it was a steep learning curve in all three sports, but across the board once the so-called "light" went on in my head and I picked up the technique, my physical strength and stamina helped me push to a whole new level of success in all three sports.

When I was a junior in high school, I started to believe I would have a chance to earn a college scholarship in athletics. But I wasn't sure if I'd try to play football, wrestle, or compete in track and field. I was never a varsity wrestler until my senior year. It's ironic, looking back, because most of my college teammates were multi–state high-school champions, and in the Olympics everyone had stories of winning every match they had ever wrestled from a young age. That just wasn't my path. My route was much more circuitous, and because it took me longer to learn—in the classroom, and in sports—I was quite a late bloomer. Having Reynold a year ahead of me—and in the heavyweight class—kept me on the junior varsity, and I still wonder to this day if I could've been a state contender as a junior.

During that year, I was getting to the point where, at times, I could beat Reynold in practice. But when it came time to wrestle-offs to determine who would be varsity for the meet that weekend, Reynold always won. He had a way of getting into my head and making me doubt myself.

In retrospect, these wrestle-offs were very positive learning experiences for me, because I had to develop more mental toughness and focus. I had to learn to not let Reynold, or anyone else, make me doubt myself. That's where it dawned on me that wrestling—and all sports, and even everything else in life—is only partially physical, that a big part of success is mental. I had to condition myself mentally, as well as physically, if I ever hoped to compete to the best of my abilities.

As a senior in high school I went 23–1, losing to a really good wrestler from Idaho. Losing to that kid made me angry with myself, because I had beaten him during my junior year. The kid was being coached by a Star Valley native, a guy who had seen me wrestle before. So he coached his wrestler, as he should, on how to beat me. Because I had beaten him before, I was very cocky going into the match; I was already focusing on upcoming matches. I was overzealous, too, and didn't stick to my game plan. That kid knew my strengths and weaknesses, and because of my own stubbornness and overconfidence, he handed me my lunch. I had a serious reckoning with myself after that match. It showed me that I could be beaten if I wasn't focused, even by a kid I had previously beaten, and that even if you have the ability, it won't carry you to a win if you aren't prepared and haven't trained to be the best. That tournament was held in Star Valley, so it especially hurt to lose the match in front of our fans and my family.

I regained a lot of focus after that match. I won all of my matches in the state of Wyoming and went on to win the Wyoming State High School Championship. So it looked like wrestling might be a way to help pay for my college education.

Though we came from very modest financial roots, every one of my older brothers and sisters had gone to college. As I entered my senior year of high school, Reynold was already in college at the University of Wyoming, having earned a scholarship from the outstanding work he did in the FFA (Future Farmers of America) organization. Several of my brothers and sisters had gotten academic scholarships and grants. They had put together packages of financial aid and work-study, along with scholarships, to get through college. Most went on to attain graduate degrees.

It was during my senior year in high school that I started to take stock of where I was. When I talked to my academic counselor, I was told that I wasn't "cut out for college. It's just not for you, Rulon." My parents were advised to send me to a vocational-technical school to learn a trade of some sort, because I was more inclined mechanically than academically.

"Rulon is just not smart enough to go to college," a counselor told my mother. She was very offended by that comment, and told the counselor as much.

The counselor also told my mother that encouraging me to go to college would be "setting Rulon up to fail. I don't want to see him get hurt again, because he's been through so many hardships in school." When I graduated from high school, I was only reading at a fifth-grade level.

My mother always taught me how to turn a negative into a positive, which helped me learn to believe in myself. I might fall short doing something, but that would make me better in the future, opening the door to another success. There was no reason to close any doors in front of me simply because I had not aced my way through previous ones. I would learn from every attempt and build from it. So my mother told me to ignore the comment about not being "smart enough" and do the best that I could do, and, somehow, that would be enough. My mother always believed in me, and I always thought about her encouragement when the going was really tough—when I had to study a few extra hours for something that others mastered in a matter of minutes. Somehow, as long as I had that will, I'd find my way.

The high-school academic advisors feared that my learning disabilities and lack of aptitude on some standardized tests were signs that I wouldn't be able to make the grade in college. Once again, I was told I "couldn't do it," which only strengthened my resolve to get myself to college and graduate. I would prove those people wrong and show them I *could* do it.

It was during this "I'll show them" time that I talked

back to my father for the first—and only—time of my whole life. To stay in shape for wrestling, I needed to lift weights and work out at the school after hours. But there were farm chores to be done, and with everyone but me gone off to college or already on their own elsewhere, I had more responsibilities than ever—two or three times as much. Reynold, who was very active in school sports and agricultural clubs, and I had had to pick up a lot of slack a few years ago when he and I were the only two left. It had been that way every time one of the kids left the farm. Now, though, my workload was simply unreal. I knew the chores had to be done, but I needed to work out to improve my chances of winning a scholarship. It came to a head one night when I was getting ready to return to school to lift weights.

"Where are you going?" my father asked me.

"To the school, to work out," I said.

"You have chores," he said.

This had happened dozens of times. But I felt I needed to put my foot down and impress upon my dad how important working out was.

"You want to pay for my college education, fine, then I won't go lift weights and get a college scholarship," I said.

That was the only time I back-talked my father in my life. I did work out that night, but not until about 9:00 P.M., after doing some of my chores, and going home in time to change the pipe. I was exhausted. There were eight lines of pipe to be changed, and each took about forty-five minutes doing it alone. My brother Russell was back in town, and he came out to talk to me.

"You need to work with Dad, to make sure the family

sticks together and the farm survives," Russell told me. I was hurt, because it was just Dad and me, and I had a lot of responsibility on my seventeen-year-old shoulders. I didn't think that was right. I wanted to do the best I could on the farm, but I also felt limited as to what I could accomplish off the farm with so little free time. It was a pretty heated discussion. I ended up finishing the pipe—alone—well after midnight.

And, of course, there were cows to milk the next morning, which by then was only a few hours away.

Late in my senior year of high school, I had a big meet at the Wyoming State Track and Field Championships, taking second place in the shot put and sixth place in the discus. I didn't get back home until 2:00 A.M. Reynold was home for spring break—a lot of other college kids would head south for spring-break fun, but because our parents had no extra money and needed help, most of my siblings came home when they could. Reynold saw me and said there was work to be done.

"Go out and feed the cows," he said.

"No, I'm going to bed," I answered. "I just got back from state."

"So what? I'm on spring break," he said.

I went into my room and went to bed. He came into the room after a minute or two and poured a gallon of water on me.

I got up and went outside for about a half hour just to avoid him, without a coat on, shivering. Then I came back in the house, went to a downstairs room, not my own, barricaded the door, and went to bed. Two hours later, Reynold, realizing I hadn't done the work, busted through the door, and we brawled before I finally decided it was time to go feed the cows.

Even though there was always farmwork to do, day in and day out, sports began to take a front-and-center role in my life toward the end of high school.

During my senior year, I made the all-state football team and even played in the "Down Under Bowl" in New Zealand as part of an all-star football team from Wyoming. Though I considered playing college football, wrestling was going to be the sport that helped me work my way through school, because the only scholarships offered to me were for wrestling. I could walk on and try to earn a football scholarship, but that would've meant paying full tuition up front. And it's hard to gauge how good you are—how that translates to the scale of college athletics—when you are from a rural Wyoming community, where you measure yourself against small-town high schools in a sparsely populated state as opposed to the huge high schools in big cities, where more athletes normally means a higher level of athletic competition.

I had only two offers, both for wrestling at two-year junior colleges: Ricks College in Rexburg, Idaho, and Northwest Wyoming College in Powell.

A series of events made it possible for me to leave for college without worrying too much about the farmwork. Obviously, my father knew the day was coming—and my parents, my mother especially, wanted me to have the chance to pursue a college education, especially since wrestling was going so well. My brother Rollin was planning to come back to take over the farm, and the month after I left for Ricks, he did so. Again, because my parents placed such a high value on education, there was no pressure on me to stay and help the farm survive. My parents could've used what the high-school counselor had said, that I was more mechanically inclined, and justified encouraging me to stay home instead of leaving for college. But they never wavered in their view of the importance of education. And I respect them tremendously for that.

Eight

LEAVING THE VALLEY

A PARTIAL WRESTLING scholarship and a $250 beef scholarship got me into Ricks for my first year. Ricks is in eastern Idaho, just over the border from Wyoming. Ricks had a well-established wrestling program, and Coach Bob Christensen—Ricks College's first national-championship—winning wrestler, in 1964—had a great reputation, and track record, for developing his student-athletes, preparing them for success at four-year colleges both academically and athletically.

Rexburg is another of the strong Latter Day Saints communities in the region—Ricks College is now named Brigham Young University–Idaho, a Latter Day Saints college. Since faith is so important to me, Ricks was a logical place for me to go. And since the only other offer was from Northwest Wyoming in Powell, it wasn't like I had a whole bunch of schools from which to choose.

So I went to Ricks College, because it was close and I

knew about its academic programs. I had a long and cir-cuitous route through Ricks College, even transferring to Utah State for a quarter before coming back to compete as a sophomore and then graduate. It's a good thing I came back, because I have little doubt that had I not ultimately returned to Ricks to see things through, I might have given up wrestling, not to mention failing to seize the incredible educational opportunity I had at Ricks.

College life was a whole new experience; truly seeing women for the first time, socializing with all sorts of people. I started Ricks with a clean slate; no one remem-bered me or knew me as "Fatso" or "Dumbo."

The conditioning program for wrestling was the most intense I had ever been through. At first the amount of running was incredible, including a thirteen-mile run that every team member had to complete—it was to show dedication and commitment, that you wanted to be there. But it was still a long way to run. Coach Christensen wanted us to be mentally and physically in shape and to be a team. I thrived on the challenge. We ran the football stadium stairs, going up and down the stairs twenty times initially, and fifty times by the start of the season. I'd come down those stairs at full speed. The basketball coach at Ricks—Gary Gardner—saw me running one day and said he was impressed that I ran so hard and with "no fear." Gary and I are both related to Vern Gardner, an All-American basketball player at the University of Utah in the 1940s, who later came back and coached basketball at Star Valley High School. So it was nice to have that family connection, albeit distant, while I was at Ricks.

Even though it was grueling, I enjoyed the running. It's always been satisfying to me to complete assigned tasks. As an athlete at the college it was my responsibility to do what the coach said, and running steps was part of Coach Christensen's regimen. I accepted responsibility to follow the rules and meet Coach Christensen's expectations. The times that I failed to do so left indelible marks on my mind.

One day at Ricks, we were headed to a tournament in Washington. We were to leave on a Thursday morning. I had been out late the night before with a girlfriend and had missed my alarm to get up that morning. It was late when I finally woke up, so I jumped on a bicycle and nearly flew down to campus to catch the bus. I was late, and Coach Christensen let me know it. He had a big, long right index finger, and when he shook that finger in your face to make his point, you knew he was serious. He went off on me for well over ten minutes. I went to the back of the bus and was visibly upset for the entire twelve-hour ride. I had let him down, disappointed him. It was an honor to be on his team, and to disrespect my coach by showing up late like that was something I would not let happen again. Even the guys on the team felt bad for me. Hours into the ride, one of the guys went up to Coach.

"Coach, Rulon is in the back of the bus crying," he said.

"Let him cry," Christensen replied. "It's his lesson to learn."

It was a good lesson.

I ended up having a very good freshman year at Ricks, finishing up with a 50–5 record. I made it to the National Junior College Athletic Association Tournament. In my national semifinal match, the referee called me for stalling, which made me angry because I didn't think it was a fair call. So I got a bull run at my opponent, who did the smart thing and took advantage of my momentum to throw me on my back just as time expired. I had made the mistake of letting my emotions get the best of me, and it took away my chance to win the National Junior College Championship. I remember walking off the mat and crying with my mother, who was also in tears. I spent the rest of the year thinking about the lessons I could take from that event.

While I was getting older and learning lessons, I still raised some heck. As the first semester of college ended, my brother Russell loaned me his Ford Tempo. One night, with two or three buddies in the car with me, I went zipping around Star Valley.

On Main Street, next to the movie theater, is a little alley. When you come out of it, you can go right, or jump a little curb and go left. Three or four times, I came out from the alley, hitting the curb each time because there was a snowbank piled up on it. When I'd hit it, snow would go everywhere. We were having a blast and didn't see any other cars on the road at all. When we tired of the snowbank and were parked in the high-school parking lot, a police car came up behind me, lights flashing. The police officer, Mike Hansen, who is now the police chief, told me to get out of the car.

"Am I in trouble?" I asked.

"What have you guys been doing?" he asked.

I didn't know what to say. We had definitely been

messing around, but I don't think we were speeding or anything serious.

"I'll tell you what you were doing, because I was sitting in my office, which faces that curb you kept jumping," he said.

Uh-oh.

"I've got you for jumping that curb—that's reckless driving," he said.

I didn't know if I was going to get a ticket or what. For sure, I'd be in trouble at home.

"I'm going to have to take you down and put you in jail," the officer said.

"Jail?" I asked.

He nodded, asked me to turn around, and put handcuffs on me.

I thought to myself, "I am so busted."

He looked at the other guys. "You fellows are going to have to call someone and get a ride home, because I have to impound this car," he said.

Oh, my gosh, impound Russell's car!

Then the officer looked at me and started smiling. "I'm just joking with you," he said.

He unlocked the cuffs. "I'm not going to arrest you or put you in jail, but you shouldn't be out here messing around on the streets. It could be dangerous. And you guys are going to have to go back and get those blocks of snow out of the street."

"Yes, sir," I said.

His point was well taken: I should not have been driving so recklessly. It was potentially dangerous. I apologized for my behavior and said I'd never do it again, and

I kept that promise. That was an important lesson for me, because I realized that if I made mistakes, I'd have to be accountable for them, even if I thought I was just "goofing around." I was also fortunate to have Mike Hansen as the teacher of that lesson, because he knew he had scared me and made his point, but he also believed in me, that I'd learn from it and not repeat it.

I was also finding my way, and my place, in my faith. I thought about it more, in no small part because Ricks is a Latter Day Saints college, so the entire academic and athletic programs are intertwined with the Mormon Church. In our religion, a mission is an important part of faith, and life. Several of my siblings had done missions, and the experience, I was told, was amazing. With what I was up against academically, it was looking more and more like a mission wouldn't fit into my schedule. After my freshman year, I talked to my coach about it. He gave me an interesting perspective on my mission.

"Your mission might well be the sport of wrestling," Christensen said. "You will be able to express what the Church means to you and how it has helped you through wrestling. It will allow you to reach people in the same ways being on a mission reaches people."

With a renewed focus and better grasp on the school-work, I wanted to end my career at Ricks on the best note possible.

To stay on track to graduate, I had to take classes in the summer. I took the tougher classes, like anatomy then, when I could really focus on just the one subject. The Ricks faculty didn't make it easy on me, but they were flexible and encouraging. Professors helped by reading questions to me and doing little things that made it possible for me to have a chance to demonstrate what I had learned.

After finishing wrestling my freshman year, I ended up transferring to Utah State for one quarter. However, I quickly realized that veering off my path at that point wasn't going to solve anything, so I returned to Ricks, more determined than ever to abide by Coach Christensen's rules and be a leader on the team. I got stronger and learned more on the mat, and started my sophomore year as one of the most dominating heavyweight wrestlers in the junior college ranks.

Going into Christmas break of my sophomore year at Ricks, I was undefeated for the wrestling team. But I was in a car accident and ended up with stitches in my arm, a thigh bruise, and a few other nagging injuries. My missed training time would put me at a disadvantage. I was undefeated entering the holiday break, so the injuries that would keep me from competing in peak condition the second quarter also ended up hampering my bid for a perfect season: I lost at a tournament in Washington to Jeff Thue, a Canadian wrestler who took the silver medal a year later at the 1992 Olympics when he lost to American Bruce Baumgartner for gold.

I also missed some schoolwork, which is really hard on someone like me who has difficulty keeping up as it is. I was in danger of falling behind in a religion class.

Brother Keller, my religion teacher, put things in perspective for me. He told me to work on the classwork when I could and that as long as I kept trying, made satisfactory progress, and completed the course, I would be fine.

I met most of my academic goals, and by focusing on my training, I had an outstanding season, going 42–1.

At the National Junior College Athletic Association Tournament, things went much better, until in the final I tore a ligament in my right elbow. My opponent also broke my nose. This time, though, I kept my emotions in check—didn't bull-run him or anything stupid—and wrestled a technically sound match. I won the National Championship to finish my college wrestling career on the highest possible note.

Just like my senior year in high school, however, I had had that potential for a perfect season—to go undefeated. But again I hadn't prepared correctly for one situation that arose in one particular match, and I suffered a loss. It would be my goal for the years to come to achieve that perfect season, a goal I wouldn't reach until the 2000 Olympic Games, where only one wrestler—the one who went undefeated—would win the gold medal.

Nine

ON MY OWN TWO FEET
IN THE HEARTLAND

AFTER GRADUATING FROM Ricks in August 1991, having taken another session of summer school, several four-year universities were recruiting me to wrestle for them. I liked Oklahoma State, Brigham Young, Nebraska, and, of course, the University of Wyoming, from which several of my siblings had graduated. Because it was our home-state school, it was everyone's goal to be a Wyoming Cowboy.

But I was still trying to find my place in the world, and I was easily distracted, mostly by personal issues. I chose Nebraska, even though it probably would've made more sense to go to Wyoming or BYU. I decided to go to Nebraska partly because of the higher caliber of wrestling. Nebraska had a great wrestling program, and their coach, Tim Neumann, was widely regarded as one of the best in the business. I'd be able to focus on improving my wrestling and achieving self-knowledge within a terrific program.

Coach Neumann won my heart when he came out to Ricks to recruit me. I was living in a trailer during my sophomore year, and I was having some really bad plumbing problems. When Coach Neumann came by, the trailer's sewer pipe had clogged and had to be repaired. He rolled up his sleeves and helped me fix this nasty problem. It really impressed me that this coach literally would get "down and dirty" in such a situation. His blue-collar work ethic and commitment to helping someone in need made a strong impression on me.

When it was time to leave for Nebraska, I had taken a break from conditioning and my weight had become a big issue. I was over 340 pounds and had to get down to 280 to compete. A big part of the problem was my summer-time job, delivering pizzas. If someone wouldn't pay or accept the delivery, our boss told us to take the pizza back and throw it out. Not me—I'd eat the whole thing on the way back to the store. I'd go through several pizzas a night. I didn't have much money for food, so the pizza was something I really looked forward to, but eating all those carbs and fat every night created a weight problem. I put on sixty pounds in just a few months of working. Coach Neumann barely recognized me when I showed up on campus. Great, here I was, barely setting foot in Lincoln, and I had already disappointed this man, a coach who was giving me a great chance.

So I started working on losing the pounds as soon as I got to Nebraska. I lost almost forty pounds during my biggest weight-loss week. Obviously, that's not healthy. Ten or even twenty pounds is very doable and realistic for me, but forty pounds was just too much. At the same time, a 340-pounder losing twenty pounds would be like a 150-pounder losing maybe ten pounds. So I could, and had to, lose more weight.

Before starting classes at the University of Nebraska, in the state capital of Lincoln, I met with an academic advisor. I wanted to be a teacher and was excited at the idea of wrapping up my degree in two years.

The journey would be far longer than that, I quickly learned.

During that first meeting, I learned that I couldn't be admitted as a "regular student," because my junior college grade-point average of 2.5 wasn't high enough and I didn't have enough "good credits"—credits that would transfer and count toward my degree at Nebraska.

"We just can't allow you in," the woman told me.

They ended up putting me on what is called a "letter," sort of a probation, though because I wasn't a student yet, it wasn't a formal probation. What the letter did was give me two semesters at Nebraska— during which I'd be eligible to wrestle—to get good grades and credits.

Coach Neumann met with my academic advisor.

"Rulon is just not smart enough to be here," she told my coach.

"He wants to learn, and he's actually quite bright," Neumann told her. "He'll make it through, no matter what it takes. He's a hard worker."

Still, it didn't look like I was going to last long at Nebraska. The first test I took had twenty questions, and I answered four within the allotted one-hour time period. The good news was that I got all four right; the bad news was that I missed sixteen questions—the ones I didn't answer—so I had a 20 percent grade: an F.

The teacher called me into his office and we talked. We went over the subject that the test covered, and he was surprised to learn how much I really knew and understood.

"I can work with you," he told me. I failed that class, but the teachers had me tested, at which point they diagnosed my learning disability, something I had been through before in Star Valley schools. The advisors steered me to a tutor, with whom I worked long and hard hours. I couldn't believe that the University of Nebraska was so difficult, so advanced, an entirely different world than Ricks College. I was in for another huge challenge.

It went that way for most of my classes. I showed promise, but keeping up with the reading and taking tests within the scheduled time frames was always difficult. The tutoring program at Nebraska is first-rate. No one ever "gave" me any answers or allowed me to cut a corner or cheat. Every step of progress I made was hard-earned, and I credit a lot of it to the tutoring program.

Coach Neumann worked hard just to get me admitted into school on "the letter." We had a heart-to-heart talk about the challenge I'd have to face. I had shown up grossly overweight, and Coach Neumann was ready to go to bat for me. An amazing man.

"Just give me a chance," I told him. "If you give me a chance, I will pass. I will succeed. All I'm hoping for is a chance."

Another curve was thrown at me almost immediately, though. It turned out that I hadn't completed the two years of high-school algebra required as a basic math requirement at Nebraska. I spent hours on end on math, with a tutor walking me through the steps. It was an amazing process, and I learned more than even I thought I was capable of in what was a very difficult subject for me. Nebraska's athletic-academic department was very supportive of me, providing me all the tutors I needed. Never once did my tutors cross the line, but they always went that extra mile, which in my case was pretty standard—I always needed that extra mile. Because I was willing to go that distance every time, the tutors appreciated my effort and gave willingly of their time.

While being tutored in algebra, I enrolled in a basic mathematics class, Math 101. The stuff in that class just blew me away. I started out all right, but as the semester wore on, I began to struggle again. That meant more hours with the tutors, who again bent over backward, demonstrating patience and understanding. My academic advisor called me toward the end of the semester.

"How did you get into Math 101?" she asked. "You're not even supposed to be in there—you're not at a high enough level yet."

"This is a class you told me to take," I answered.

"No, I didn't," she said.

"Yes, you did."

Whether or not she had told me to enroll in the class, I was making the most of the opportunity and wanted to prove it to her.

I pulled out my class report and papers. I had a solid B in the class. Her eyes opened wide. She looked at me, then back at the papers, and shook her head.

"Is this a big deal?" I asked her.

She set the papers down and leaned back in her chair.

"I didn't think you'd be able to pass, much less earn a B," she said. "If you can pass this class, it overrides all the other math work you'd have to complete."

That meant no more basic algebra, which was fine with me. Though the math got harder at the end of the semester, I pulled a C-plus in Math 101. I was pretty bummed to have just missed a B, but I was done with all the basic math requirements.

Once I had enough credits to get off the letter and declare a teaching major, I had to take a Pre-Professional Skills Test, the PPST, to be admitted to the teaching college, and I was low on everything. A student had to be medium to high in math, reading, and writing to progress in the teaching program and ultimately earn a degree. I'd have another chance to take the PPST, and I would retake that test later on with drastically different results. But at the time, I was put into a university program for students with disabilities. Again, as much as I felt let down by a handful of people in the teaching college at Nebraska, the people in the university's program for students with disabilities were phenomenal. The books were on tape, so I could listen to them on wrestling trips. The university took good care of students with disabilities. They allowed me time and a half to take tests and provided someone to read some of the questions to me.

"It's not about what you know, but what you can decipher," one teacher told me. I carried that explanation of my condition with me to the end of my academic career.

*　*　*

My first year of competing at Nebraska was the 1991–92 school year. It turns out that my goal of a perfectly focused wrestling season would have to wait. Due to a lot of external factors in my personal and academic life, I lost my concentration on the wrestling mat. I didn't handle the pressure very well. I was dealing with the academic hassles of transferring from Ricks. Working with algebra tutors to fulfill the basic math requirement was taking its toll on me.

I took low placings at a few tournaments that I should have won. I lost to wrestlers I never should have lost to, under any circumstance. That year, at the National Duals in Ann Arbor, Michigan, a wrestler from a small college pulled an upset over me. As a Big 8 (now Big 12) Conference wrestler going against a lower-level competitor, I should have won. It was a reminder that if I didn't have my focus, I could lose to anyone, just as, conversely, if I was properly prepared and focused, I could beat anyone.

After the National Duals, we had a dual meet with the University of Michigan. Coach Neumann held me out of that heavyweight match because of how I'd performed at the earlier duals. That hurt, but it was the right decision. Coach Neumann was big on accountability and consistency, and though I was exceeding my goals academically, I wasn't doing my best on the mat.

The guy who replaced me for the University of Michigan dual meet lost. That cost us valuable team points—and in my view, I was the one who cost us those points, because I hadn't worked hard enough to earn my spot for that match.

In February we were headed across Nebraska on Interstate 80—tracing the route of the Mormon Trail—toward my home state of Wyoming, for a meet at the University of Wyoming. That bus ride to Laramie, Wyoming, was a turning point in my wrestling season, and my life. I realized how much I missed Wyoming, my friends, my community, and my family. I remembered the work ethic that had carried me through school in Star Valley and on to Ricks College. My mind cleared on that van ride, and I realized what I had to do. As we crossed over into Wyoming, at the town of Pine Bluffs, I knew that to keep Wyoming close to my heart, in the future I had to represent myself, my family, my church, and my home state better. I had to be more disciplined with my weight, focus better in every practice, and wrestle my best in every match.

At the meet in Wyoming, I really took it to a very good Wyoming wrestler, Phil Cogdill, who was from the southwestern community of Kemmerer. Coach Neumann saw what he had long been hoping to see in me.

"You just destroyed that guy!" Neumann told me. "See what you can do? See what you are capable of? Do that every time!"

During that Wyoming trip, my mind and soul had opened up. My commitment to be the best was like it had never been before. Physically, I started beating up guys in every match. But beating them physically was not enough; now I had to destroy them mentally, the key to winning. I was on a roll. At that point, I finally became a year-round wrestler, something necessary to be the best and compete for the NCAA Championship.

With a late rally, I finished my first Nebraska season at 24–10–2 and qualified for the NCAA Championships. At the tournament I lost the match that would've gotten me into the quarterfinals, which are important because the top eight finishers gain All-American status. Still, the season was something to build on.

At the end-of-season wrestling banquet, Coach gave out the Granite Awards, a distinction that singled out wrestlers who could always be counted on, who got the job done and rode out the adversity they had to tackle. This could be as many or as few as the coaches deemed worthy of the award, but in my first year I recall them giving out about a half dozen. I didn't get that award and I was devastated, because I realized I had let down my coach, my team, and myself that year. For so long I had prided myself on not getting tripped up, not losing focus, not letting anyone down. But I hadn't been very successful at all that. At the time, I thought that my efforts hadn't been noticeable to the person most responsible for bringing me to Nebraska, for giving me a chance to excel in school and at wrestling: Tim Neumann.

As the 1992–93 season started—my senior year at Nebraska and my final year of athletic eligibility—I committed myself to being the best in the country. Heading into the 1993 spring semester, I was ranked number two in the nation. We had an impressive team performance at the National Duals that year, and I used a late flurry to defeat Iowa's heavyweight to help our team finish third at the meet. That was big, because I had let the team down at Duals the previous year with a loss, and this time the meet was in Lincoln, so our own fans were there. It was an important performance for our program.

I knew if I continued to progress, I'd be able to battle for the heavyweight title at the NCAA Championships.

I ran up a 34–5 record that season. This time I made it through the NCAA quarterfinals, guaranteeing an All-American finish. But I fell short of my goal of winning the championship or even making the final match. I finished fourth in the nation, losing in the semifinals, a great improvement over the previous year, but it was still not what I wanted: an NCAA title.

At the year-end banquet, I was recognized for having the most takedowns that year, a rarity in the heavyweight class. More important, I had earned one of the coveted Granite Awards because I had been strong for my team all year long and could be counted on to be a good teammate and consistently high performer. That meant a lot.

Still, because I didn't win the NCAA Championship, I felt like I had "left something on the mat" at Nebraska, and I vowed that when—not if—I was in that situation again, I'd make the most of it. I'd meet all expectations.

And maybe even something more.

In the spring of 1993, I went out for the football team at the University of Nebraska. In college, you get five years to play four years of any sports, and since I had competed all four years of college—two at Ricks and two at Nebraska—I could play football for a year if I made the team. The Cornhuskers, known simply as the Huskers to those in Nebraska, are the state's pride and joy. Nebraska has no professional major league teams, but several minor teams. So the Huskers are the big draw. I wanted to test myself , to see if I had what it took to play football at that level. I had left high school believing college football was in my future, only to career away from the sport at Ricks College.

Boy, was that a time for football in Nebraska.

Head coach Tom Osborne was gearing up for back-to-back national championships in 1994 and 1995. Coach Osborne, a man whom I hold in high regard, went on to become a U.S. Congressman (and soon could be governor). He gave me permission to try out for the team.

That spring football season was unbelievable. I was put on the defensive line and quickly learned that practices were incredibly intense. Every play was competed at a Super Bowl level. The hitting was intense, the execution simply amazing. But I was used to the constant drilling of college wrestling practice, so I found the pace of football practices boring. Football was slower; you'd explode for a few seconds but then have a break.

The offensive line at Nebraska, which would gain legendary status and be called "The Pipeline" for its efficiency and dominance, included several future NFL players, including Zack Weigert and Brendan Stai. I was quick for my size. I was strong, too, but those offensive linemen were absolute beasts, three hundred-plus pounds of solid steel, honed and firmed in the Nebraska weight program. I was occasionally quicker, but never stronger than those players. If I were quick enough to get into the right position it wouldn't matter, because those guys knew where to go and they could hold the position once they got it.

In one practice, I had beaten Weigert on a play and was feeling pretty good about myself. On the next play, I learned why Nebraska was so good: they always had the other guy's back. If you beat one guy, you had beaten all of them. They took it personally, and they took it out on you. On the next play, Stai caught me coming in—they didn't make mistakes often, but they never repeated their mistakes—and took me out. I had never seen a group of players who epitomized the team concept so thoroughly. They were like brothers. *You beat my brother? Then I will beat you the next play, and the ones after that.* That mentality gives me a rush just thinking about it. Someone having your back like that must be a pretty awesome feeling.

I believe I could've played at Nebraska, maybe in a reserve role. In fact, I believe my wrestling skills, combined with my arm strength, would have made me into a very good offensive lineman.

But they had too much talent at every position. Christian Peter was the reigning king on the defensive line, and he was very tough. The defensive ends, called "rush ends" at Nebraska, were headed for the NFL; guys such as Trev Alberts were phenomenal players. Right before the Red-and-White Game—a spring game that has drawn sixty thousand-plus fans seeking a preview of what the fall holds—I went in and met with defensive coordinator Charlie McBride.

"What are my chances of getting some playing time?" I asked Coach McBride.

He sort of shrugged his shoulders. "Well . . . well, we'll have to reevaluate you every day," he said.

"But what are my chances?" I asked.

"Well. . . ."

In that moment, I knew I needed to stick with wrestling and try to compete at the U.S. Nationals—which include both college and postcollegiate—as a freestyle wrestler. Though it would've been incredible to be a part of that special group of football players and coaches at Nebraska, I had a full plate already with finishing my academic requirements and with wrestling. By then my eligibility was up at Nebraska, but I was moving toward becoming more involved in USA Wrestling. To be honest, just earning playing time with that talented group would've been a full-time job and required a different kind of training program than what I was doing for wrestling.

The irony is that once my wrestling eligibility was done at Nebraska, it would appear that there was little reason for me to keep wrestling. I hadn't won the NCAA Championships, so I wasn't one of those who was tagged by USA Wrestling as someone to join its elite-level, international program. At the same time, I had made huge improvements during my final year and a half at Nebraska, especially after just starting year-round training a couple of years earlier, something all of the other wrestlers had been doing since high school, or even before that. My feeling after I was done competing at Nebraska was that I hadn't reached my full potential, and was just starting to get really good at wrestling. I still had the hunger and drive at a time when a lot of my teammates, and other college seniors everywhere, were getting burned out on the sport and were ready to move on to whatever was next in their lives.

Getting to know those guys on the football team was the real highlight for me. Meeting guys like John Parella, who'd go on to a long NFL career with, among others, the San Diego Chargers, Oakland Raiders, and Buffalo Bills, made it worthwhile. Parella, who is from Grand Island, about ninety miles west of Lincoln, was a standout wrestler in high school. One day at football practice we started talking wrestling and decided to spar a little bit, so I grabbed him and took him down. He was a great guy, an awesome player and person.

Years later, after I won the gold medal in Sydney, one of the football coaches, Ron Brown—another first-rate person—was in Utah, where we ran into each other.

"Hey, why didn't you ever try out for our team?" Brown asked. I explained to him that I did, but that it just didn't work out.

"Obviously, you made the right choice," Coach Brown said. "But let me tell you, what you did in 2000 inspired a lot of Huskers."

During the summer of 1993, I received an interesting invitation. Done with my college eligibility, I was focusing on school. USA Wrestling was trying to stimulate some growth in the Greco-Roman program, which was low on numbers and still a relatively unknown sport in the United States. It was an established program in other parts of the world, especially the former Soviet-bloc countries.

So when I was asked to compete in Greco-Roman at the 1993 U.S. Olympic Sports Festival in San Antonio, Texas, I had to find out a little more about it. I had never trained or wrestled in that distinct style, which, unlike freestyle, forbids the use of one's legs for moves or defense.

The head U.S. Greco-Roman coach at the time was Mike Hauck. He was good to me and told me that I had more than just raw ability. "You're a good wrestler, and with your dedication and devotion, you could really excel at this," he said.

I went to the tournament and won it. Several coaches with USA Wrestling thought I had a bright future in the sport; at the very least, I could be involved in the growth of the program.

While in San Antonio, Coach Hauck made some nice comments to other coaches, and in the press sessions, he said, "Rulon Gardner is one of the best athletes I've seen." Taken by surprise, I said to myself, "What? What's he thinking?" Some of the other wrestlers were a bit upset about his comments, but the truth is, I had worked hard. We had done a lot of drills during practice, and I took a lot of pride in finishing with the smaller, faster guys. One drill had us jumping over a bar onto a mat, and I could go as high as the smaller guys. That athletic ability apparently impressed the coach. It felt great to be thought of as a good athlete.

I headed home that summer and took a job at the golf course in Star Valley, doing maintenance and working on the grass and greens. It gave me a break from the academic stress I had been experiencing at Nebraska. Reynold, having taken some time for his mission, was emerging as a conference champion wrestler at Oregon State, after winning the 1993 NJCAA title—a title I had won two years earlier at Ricks. I thought we could train together back home. That would help make us both better, keep me in shape for the hopes I had to compete in U.S. Freestyle wrestling—and keep me involved in wrestling, because I knew how quickly I could both lose focus and get out of shape. Reynold did not give me a reason when he told me he would not train with me, which sort of hurt my feelings. Still, just being on the land, on the farm, and around Star Valley's people helped me regain my focus and motivation. I remembered where I had come from, and how all the struggles through the years growing up had actually been a ladder that I climbed to get to this point in my life.

Because I had schoolwork to finish, I headed back to Nebraska. I wouldn't wrestle Greco-Roman again for more than a year.

Ten

TO BE A TEACHER

WITH MY ELIGIBILITY for wrestling over but two years of school still remaining, I began studying in the teachers' college at the University of Nebraska. I progressed well through that program and learned a lot.

Unfortunately, not all of my interactions with the faculty were pleasant. I occasionally found a lot of resistance from some of the faculty members with whom I dealt as my sprint to the end—a degree—grew into another circuitous marathon. I still get worked up thinking about what unfolded over the next two years.

After several semesters at Nebraska, I had a second chance to take the Pre-Professional Standardized Test, just before the start of the 1994 fall semester. I knew taking the test was very important, because it was probably the final chance the teachers' college had to get me out of their program. My coursework had been more than satisfactory; I had nearly a 3.0 grade point average. I had the questions read to me as part of the aid offered through the students-with-disabilities program. Those people, once again, were extremely helpful, not just in diagnosing learning disabilities but also in finding fair ways to deal with the problem.

The test seemed to go very well. I had done my homework and studied very hard, so my confidence was high.

And when the grades came back months later, I was thrilled to see that not only had I passed, but I had also received "high" marks in almost every category. This, after not getting even close to passing scores the first time I had taken it. I was ecstatic when I called my advisor. I told her my score and read off "high, high" for all the various classifications.

"No, that is not possible," she said over the phone. "That's just not . . . that could not have happened."

I was infuriated. I was holding the paper in my hand as I spoke to her. So I drove down to the advisor's building, parked illegally, and ran to show her. She held the paper in her hand and scanned the results.

"Oh," she said. "That's nice."

To this day, I can't fathom her motivation for never believing in me and not wanting to give me a chance. I understand that coming in I wasn't a student who had a gold star on his forehead, or that I had showed a lot of aptitude that would indicate future success. But Coach Neumann and others in the university had seen enough potential and qualifications from my achieving an associate's degree from Ricks, so I felt like once I was in, I at least deserved a fair chance.

When I gave my advisor the PPST results, she didn't say "good job," or "you've made a lot of progress," or "you worked very hard," or even "congratulations." Just, "That's nice." So many times I had to plead with this woman just to let me take certain classes. I remember asking her to place me in an anatomy class and she had said, "No, I don't think you can make it through that." I did get in, and I did very well in the class. All I ever wanted was a chance.

In spite of her negativity, I was able to learn a lot through the classwork and the tutoring program at Nebraska. I had to constantly work, both academically and athletically. I had to work to keep my weight down and to improve my wrestling technique, and I had to work to learn difficult subjects, subjects more difficult than any I had ever studied before. I had worked hard to get into the best shape, as a wrestler and as a learner, that I had ever been in.

That academic advisor left the university following the semester when I had excelled on the PPST, which is too bad, because I really wanted her to see that I graduated.

I was assigned a new academic advisor, who promptly called me in to talk about what I still needed before I could graduate. I finally was told that only sixteen of my credits—out of sixty-four—from Ricks College had transferred to Nebraska.

"You didn't know that?" the new academic counselor asked me.

"I had no idea," I answered. "That's why this is taking so long, I know now." So instead of being a junior when I landed at Nebraska, I was the equivalent of only the second semester of my freshman year in terms of credits. Time to see what the challenge was, design a plan, and push on through to success.

★   ★   ★

Though my brief summer experience in Greco-Roman had been a positive one, I went back to freestyle wrestling, and that spring I took fifth place at the 1994 U.S. Freestyle Nationals. That fall I was planning on staying with freestyle, the discipline within which I had experienced the most success over the longest period of time, and I believed that with my progress, I would be able to contend for the U.S. National title. In December 1994, as the fall semester was winding down, I got a call from USA Wrestling, offering another chance to wrestle Greco.

They were having a "re-ranking" tournament in Colorado to seed the top American wrestlers in the sport. I finished my spring class in Lincoln—the weigh-ins for the tournament were the next day, so I had little time to waste—and drove the 550-plus miles to Colorado Springs straight through. I got to Colorado Springs that evening, weighed in late, and went to bed early.

I soon realized that the re-ranking tournament was simply another part of the effort to stimulate growth in the sport, and I was recruited for the most part just to add a body, though I had produced well in my first effort the summer before. Still, I didn't know my way around Greco yet—it's a whole different sport, with different techniques, scoring, and moves—but figured this was a good opportunity to see if I could pick it up. It was also a good opportunity to meet people at USA Wrestling and see if there might be more wrestling in my future.

The sport seemed to fit me very well. I made it to the final, where I faced Jeff Green, who would become a good friend. When I won the final, a lot of people with USA Wrestling were impressed. And better yet, since I had won the tournament, I would represent the United States at a tournament in Cuba the following February.

Also on that Colorado trip, I met someone who was important in the sport on the U.S. scene then and would be for years to come. He would become as influential as anyone on my young Greco-Roman wrestling career: Matt Ghaffari, who was the top Greco heavyweight at that time but was working through several major knee injuries before he could compete again.

Matt has a tremendous story. He was born in 1961 in Tehran, Iran. Foreseeing the revolution of the late 1970s and knowing his sons would be drafted into the army, Matt's father used the inscription on the Statue of Liberty as inspiration for his sons. Following those motivational words, he brought his family to America.

By the time I came along in 1994, thirty-two-year-old Matt was the most accomplished Greco-Roman wrestler in the system. Like me, he was a heavyweight. He had been an alternate for the U.S. Olympic Freestyle Team in 1984 and 1988, then switched to Greco-Roman in 1989. He quickly learned the sport and made the 1992 Olympic Team, but couldn't compete to the best of his ability, because he tore knee ligaments in France two weeks before the Olympics—though he still wrestled. He came back four years later, at the 1996 Atlanta Games, where he lost to Russian world champion Alexander Karelin in the gold medal match.

Matt had faced another immovable object in the past, U.S. Olympic freestyler Bruce Baumgartner, who later would bring me to Pennsylvania to train with him. Bruce liked to wrestle with me because he said I had no fear of him. He said he could tell I thought I could beat him, whereas most guys he wrestled were afraid of him. I didn't fear his size, ability, or all the accolades, including a pair of Olympic gold medals. I just liked measuring myself against him, because at the time I was still a freestyle wrestler, trying to make a name for myself in the U.S. National Freestyle program, and Bruce was the best. So Matt and I had that link as well.

Matt gave me a good reference to Art Martori, founder of the Sunkist Kids wrestling club. Sunkist Kids, and other companies, sponsored wrestling programs that allowed postcollege wrestlers to continue, or those in college to have an off-season program and support to continue wrestling. Art, another important figure coming into my life just when I needed him, was a blessing, and the fact that Matt referred him to me shows where Matt's heart was too. Sunkist paid a small sponsorship stipend, something that was important to any wrestler trying to stay in the sport.

"Ghaffari speaks highly of you," Art said.

"I'm a college student, so any support you can give me would help," I said. Art agreed to help, so it was through him that I made my first money as a wrestler—$185 a month. That doesn't sound like a lot, but it is to a poor college student.

I couldn't believe my good fortune; first, my college wrestling career ends and I have all kinds of academic hurdles to clear at Nebraska; then, suddenly, I'm getting paid—though not a lot, then the upcoming trip to Cuba, all to do the sport that I love.

I still remember exactly what happened after that Colorado tournament ended. I was getting ready to go back to

Nebraska to finish my studies. I stopped by the USA Wrestling office to tie up some loose ends, thank them, and let them know I was interested in continuing to compete in Greco-Roman if they wanted me. The officials told me that of course they wanted me to continue; they'd be in touch with me when I returned from the Cuba trip in February early the following year, 1995.

As I was walking out of the USA Wrestling offices in Colorado Springs, I spotted a poster of a sculpted wrestler with huge muscles. It said simply, "Madman!" on it. I said to the person walking with me, "Who in the heck is that?"

The guy laughed. "That, Rulon, is Alexander Karelin."

"He competes still?" I asked, looking at the ripped and shredded muscles.

"Yes," the guy said, laughing. "In fact, he's the best in the world, hasn't lost, hasn't been scored on, has won world titles and the last couple of Olympic gold medals."

"Greco?"

"Yes, Greco. He's a heavyweight," the guy said. "He's in your weight class. No one has touched him."

So I had met both my best supporter and my toughest future opponent in that one weekend in Colorado. Matt truly took me under his wing at the re-ranking tournament. He encouraged me to pursue the sport. He also saw in me the top-level training partner that he needed to challenge him to be a better wrestler. Matt was instrumental in getting me involved in USA Wrestling's Greco-Roman program; that weekend, he coached me on some of the specifics of the sport.

It would be an irony when, four years later, Matt, after

a two-year hiatus, would make a final run at the 2000 Olympic Team, and it was me who beat him—and then beat Karelin, Matt's motivation for coming back.

By the spring semester of 1995, I had only a teaching methods class to complete, and then after a semester of student teaching I'd have my degree. Teaching methods involved going to a local school and observing and learning, and then writing or talking about it back at the university. That is, I'd go to a local school and learn from the teachers, then demonstrate what I had learned for my classmates and professor.

Meanwhile, I was excited about the chance to wrestle in Cuba. The trip would take me out of school for one week in February. So I spoke to the teacher at the Lincoln Northeast High School who I was observing for the teaching methods class, to see if I could miss a week for the Cuba trip and then make up the work.

"Sure," the teacher told me. "That sounds like a good opportunity. A week shouldn't hurt you."

I hadn't been training in Greco-Roman wrestling since Colorado. I could only work out with the freestyle wrestlers at Nebraska, but since I was no longer a member of the team, I had to push myself and try to find someone to wrestle with. Nevertheless, I went to Cuba and won the heavyweight championship, this time against an international field.

It was unreal. Just over a month after returning to a sport I had tried briefly sixteen months earlier, I won a U.S. tournament—a re-ranking format, which at the time I entered, I didn't think was that big a deal—and then claimed the title at an international tournament in Cuba. I went back to the University of Nebraska ready to make up the week I had missed in my teaching methods class.

But a surprise was awaiting me in Nebraska.

Eleven

CHASING MY WRESTLING AND COLLEGE DREAMS

WHEN I GOT back to Lincoln after the Cuba tournament, I was told by my methods professor at the university that I had missed too much of the teaching methods class—a week that I had cleared ahead of time with the teacher at the local high school where I was observing—and would have to come back and complete my studies the next semester, the fall of 1995. Of course, I explained that I had cleared the weeklong absence with the teacher I was observing. Nevertheless, I was told I'd have to take an "incomplete" in the teaching methods class because of my wrestling trip to Cuba.

I couldn't believe that my plans to student-teach and graduate were being pushed back an entire semester because I'd been gone little more than a week, especially since I had received permission from the appropriate person before leaving. She had even offered her support.

My Nebraska professor also said that I had "physically harassed" a teacher about getting the week off for the Cuba trip—the same one I had been observing and who had given me clearance to miss the week.

"How can this possibly be true?" I asked myself. The conversation had been very cordial. Harassment, to me, means intimidation or some sort of confrontation or harsh words. The teacher I had talked to had been very interested in hearing what I was doing, and how establishing myself internationally might even give me a shot to qualify for the Olympic Team in the future. She had not only encouraged me to seize the opportunity, but also said that the trip wouldn't conflict with my studies, that I could easily make up the missed work and classes.

I can only guess that the university professor either knew my former advisor, who thought I didn't belong, or she too thought I was a dumb jock who was trying to skate through the program, and didn't deserve to be a teacher. The way I was raised, if you had a problem with someone, you talked to them and addressed it. In my mind, this was clearly a miscommunication of some sort, because there had been zero harassment. I was completely confused by the two different versions of this incident, between what I was being told and what had actually happened. I mean, I had absolutely no clue. So I called the teacher I had observed and asked, "Did I do something?"

"What are you talking about?" she asked. "Harassment? I don't know where that came from."

I then visited the university professor who had made that claim.

"I talked to the high-school teacher, and she said I didn't harass her or anything like that," I said. "I talked to her and we basically had the same conversation we had before I left for the trip, where she said I could make up the work and it shouldn't slow me down at all."

The professor was furious.

"How dare you contact a teacher!" she exclaimed. "That's further harassment!"

In attempting to resolve the first harassment charge, I had, in my professor's mind, committed another infraction.

So I focused on wrestling—until school the following semester—where I liked the people and was afforded a lot of respect.

Though I'd had some Greco-Roman success—I was ranked number two in the nation behind Matt Ghaffari, once he had come back and was healthy and reassumed the number one spot he had earned before knee injuries shelved him for a while—I decided to go back to freestyle and try to make an impression on the USA Wrestling people. Though I was one of the two top Greco wrestlers, I knew Matt was far and away the best in the country, with international experience and an Olympic silver medal. The only person who had beaten him in a major tournament was that Alexander Karelin guy on the poster at USA Wrestling's offices.

After Cuba, I again trained at Nebraska with the Husker wrestling team, helping out as an unofficial undergraduate assistant as much as I could and wrestling whomever I could. I couldn't have trained Greco if I'd wanted to, because that wasn't part of Nebraska's program. Coming from where I had, and having had success in freestyle over a longer period of time, I wanted to reach my potential in freestyle and see where that took me. Plus, it seemed like freestyle was more glamorous—it was more well known in the United States, and our most decorated heavyweight, multi–Olympic gold medal winner Bruce Baumgartner, was a freestyler.

Then I heard that Ghaffari's hard luck had continued: he had broken his leg. That left the field wide open for Greco's 1995 U.S. Nationals. As the number-two-ranked heavyweight Greco-Roman wrestler, I was considered one of the favorites, though that's hard for me to imagine because I had so little experience in the sport. So I entered the 1995 U.S. Nationals in Greco-Roman. I felt bad for Matt, but I also realized I had an opportunity to compete for the national title.

Entering was the right choice. I won the 1995 U.S. National Greco-Roman heavyweight championship. I had gone from unknown in the sport to national champion in less than a year. I went to the 1995 World Team Trials, which are used to select the World Championship team. I was excited about that, because if I won, I would represent the United States at the 1995 World Championships. The "Worlds" are comparable to the Olympics in the non-Olympic years. It's a big deal.

I went into the World Team Trials feeling pretty good about myself. As the defending national champion from winning the 1995 U.S. Nationals more than a month earlier, I was allowed to sit out as the others wrestled through the bracket, meaning I'd have to wrestle only the guy who won the qualifying bracket. That was Matt Ghaffari, whose leg had healed—after sitting out Nationals—and he was as hungry as ever. Still, no one else in U.S. Greco—I hadn't wrestled Matt yet—had given me much trouble, and I had won both the international tournament in Cuba and the U.S. Nationals already that year.

Boy, did I miscalculate where I was in Greco.

Ghaffari destroyed me in the championship, schooling me in two straight matches in the best-of-three format. He turned me. He threw me out of bounds. He controlled me. I had a lot of natural ability and desire, but I had to improve my technique if I was going to have any future success in this sport.

After getting that grade of "incomplete" in teaching methods, I set out to finish the class in the fall of 1995—another semester of college for which I had to pay. Maybe, because wrestling was going so well, those who were against me in the department just assumed—or hoped—that I'd give up and go away. Maybe they had seen the results, publicized in Lincoln because I was a former Nebraska wrestler, about how well I was doing on the national and international scene—perhaps that could've caused resentment; I just don't know.

I trace the resentment to the attitude toward certain athletes at Nebraska. Football players were above the fray—they are treated as celebrities at the school. I didn't begrudge them that—I was a Husker fan and understood the arduous work they put into their sport and studies. But it seemed to me that because the football players were immune, the so-called minor sport athletes received the brunt of the professors' frustrations about the way athletes were treated at the school. Again, others might have a different point of view. But as things kept unfolding, I realized that several key people had something against me and didn't want me to be a graduate—or even a part—of their teaching college.

I think it goes back to the teachers' college administrators being wary of me from the get-go, believing I didn't belong in their school, that I wasn't good enough. I was more than familiar with that sentiment—I had never been good enough in anything school-related. I wonder, why do we put these things upon each other? Why not offer to help out? Offer some constructive criticism? Show a path that will lead that person to success, help them find a way to overcome their struggles? What could be inside a person to make them treat someone so poorly, setting them up for failure, especially someone who is trying hard, trying to overcoming disabilities?

Certain teachers at Nebraska tried to wear me down, get me to quit, and, short of that, tried to get me to fail. Under any circumstance I can't see what they would have gained from that. If they truly believed I was that far behind or unqualified, couldn't someone have stepped up and specifically told me what I was lacking and offered me some options to reach the level they envisioned?

However, school is so important to my family and to me, giving up wasn't one of the options. I'd keep playing by the Nebraska teaching college's rules and do everything I could to excel, even though I knew certain people were working against me.

That teaching methods class that I had to take the "incomplete" in for the spring of 1995 was very important to me, because I needed an A for a 3.0 cumulative grade point average. In spite of all subjectively graded coursework assigned in that class, I ended up less than one point away from an A.

College professors have a lot of flexibility in deciding borderline grades. I was sure that because I had worked hard and shown so much improvement, the grading scale would slide in my favor. But I got a B-plus.

Had I received the A, I would've finished with a 3.0 grade point average at Nebraska—not bad for someone who was told he would never graduate, told he didn't even belong there. But the B-plus gave me a 2.9-something average. Students holding at least a 3.0 GPA could do their student teaching wherever they wanted, even out of state. Because I had a 2.9, I was at the mercy of the teachers' college officials.

I completed the methods class and learned a lot. While finishing the observing portion of the class at Irving Junior High School, I helped coach the junior varsity and freshman football teams. I found I really enjoyed working with kids. Instead of continuing and doing my student teaching in the spring of 1996, I took a semester off. With 1996 being an Olympic year, I decided to train intensively for a spot on the U.S. Olympic Greco-Roman team. Once again, Art Matori and Sunkist Kids gave me a boost, because in addition to helping me with the stipend and paying for some of my trips to wrestle elsewhere, I could train at their Phoenix, Arizona, facility. I trained in Arizona from January 1996 to the middle of the summer leading up to the Olympic Trials. I enjoyed living and training in Arizona with Sunkist Kids.

Sunkist practices in 1996 were amazing. Wrestling is wrestling—you get better at wrestling by wrestling hours on end, learning technique, practicing it, and getting feedback from coaches. There is weight training and cardiovascular work as well, but wrestling for hours and hours every day does plenty to build strength and endurance. Plus, a lot of those guys in Arizona were among the best in the nation, and some of the best in the world. So I had a lot to learn, wrestling guys who were far advanced—above and beyond me. These guys were twice as good as anyone I had wrestled in college. Training with the best in America, seeing how they worked on the mats and with the weights and took care of themselves provided a huge growth spurt for me as a wrestler, this time in the Greco discipline. For the first time in my life, I was speeding through the learning curve, which only fueled my hunger even more.

I set a goal at that point to make two Olympic teams. At the time, the plan was 1996 and 2000.

Plans change.

Unfortunately, I developed a problem with my leg, a constant pain and occasional stiffness. In wrestling, almost everyone has a nagging injury all the time, so you keep quiet about it until you can't function. This pain was persistent and intense, but I could still practice—though it did affect pushing off and was a constant source of irritation—and I wasn't about to let something stop my march toward a possible spot on the 1996 U.S. Olympic Greco team. From March until June the doctors in Arizona couldn't figure out what was wrong. Then, USA Wrestling's doctor, Bernie Feldman, said he would look at

me the day before the Olympic Trials were to begin.
Feldman had worked with the Chicago White Sox and
was a talented sports physician. He examined me and in
less than a minute determined the problem was a staph
infection.

I was told to elevate my leg. The weigh-ins for the
Olympic Trials were from 5:00 P.M. to 6:00 P.M. that day—
or so I thought. Lying down with my leg elevated, I
received a call at 5:28 P.M. in my hotel room in Concord,
California, site of the Olympic Trials.

"What are you doing?" a USA Wrestling official asked
me. "You have to get down here. Weigh-ins end at 5:30."

I was twenty-two seconds late for weigh-ins and, as a
result, wasn't allowed to wrestle in the 1996 Olympic
Trials. It was a hard pill to swallow.

Even with the staph infection, I had been prepared to
wrestle for a spot on the U.S. Olympic Team.

The next day, I underwent a surgical procedure to
remove the staph infection. I was running "what ifs"
through my mind, but Dr. Feldman brought me back to
reality, as the situation turned out to be even worse after
he had done the surgery and discovered the full extent of
the infection.

"If you had wrestled with that staph infection, even all
bandaged up, it could've killed you," Dr. Feldman. So,
missing the weigh-in turned out to be a blessing in dis-
guise. If I had learned before weigh-ins that it was life or
death, I would've had to scratch. At the same time, had it
been correctly diagnosed weeks earlier, I would've had the
surgery and wrestled with it all bandaged up. How many
shots do even the best athletes in the world get to make

the Olympic Team? From what I've learned, seldom more than one, and I was already in my mid-twenties.

Since I wasn't allowed to wrestle at the Trials, I went back to Wyoming to hang out with my family and friends. Later that summer, I watched Alexander Karelin beat Ghaffari in the gold medal match at the Olympics, with Ghaffari taking the silver medal.

Only then did I realize that Karelin was becoming known as the best wrestler in Greco-Roman history, confirming what I was told at the USA Wrestling offices that day I saw the poster. Karelin lived up to his billing in "live action." He was a machine, physically and mentally. His aura was palpable. He was the "Madman," an absolute beast.

And I wanted a shot at him.

Though it was time to finish up my dealings with Nebraska and get my degree, I thought I could do that without setting another foot in the teachers' college offices. I had enjoyed my time training in Arizona and wanted to do my student teaching there.

I was told, however, that I had to do it in Nebraska.

I had looked around the state and found a wonderful small town in the panhandle of northwestern Nebraska—Chadron, where Chadron State College is located. I had wrestled there twice in the Chadron State Invitational while I was at Ricks, and enjoyed the rural atmosphere and the people. Chadron has a lot of history, with Fort Robinson—site of the Lakota Indian warrior Crazy Horse's death—about twenty-five miles to the south in the town of Crawford, and South Dakota's Mount Rushmore about a hundred miles to the north. Chadron State has a solid teaching program, so I figured teaching in one of the public schools there would be good experience, because with their own teaching college they probably had a lot of experience with student teachers. Plus, it would put me out in a rural community, which was the kind of place I wanted to teach in when I eventually graduated. And I wanted to avoid any further confrontations with the Nebraska teachers' college faculty.

"No, not Chadron," I was told. "You can't pick, because you didn't have a 3.0 grade-point average. That's what you needed to pick your own place. You will have to do it in Lincoln."

I had made some good contacts in Lincoln while I was there. I had been the head wrestling coach at Park Junior High School for its spring-semester wrestling seasons in 1994 and 1995, and had been an assistant junior varsity and freshman football coach at Lincoln Northeast High School in the fall of 1995. So I decided to do my student teaching at Park Junior High School. I arranged everything and was ready to go. Even though I hadn't planned on doing my student teaching in Lincoln, I was excited that the staff at Park had worked with me to set up the program. I called the teachers' college to let them know I was all set up in Lincoln, as they had demanded.

"You can't set it up on your own," I was told. "How dare you set it up? It's our job as professionals to set it up."

I was getting frustrated.

"Every single student I know has set it up on their own. I can't think of one I know who had you all do it for them," I said.

"We will figure it out and get back to you," the advisor said. "Do you have any requests?"

I mentioned that I did not want to do it at any junior high schools other than Park, where I knew I had some allies. High school was where I wanted to be, if not Park Junior High.

"How about at Lincoln High School?" they suggested.

"Fine," I said.

When the call came back, I got neither what I requested nor what they offered. I would be at a junior high other than Park.

So I headed out to Dawes Junior High School. Surprisingly, it ended up being a wonderful experience. The kids were great to work with, and the staff was incredibly supportive and provided valuable feedback. Joe Shandera, a physical education teacher, was one of my supervisors and my strongest backer. As it turned out I needed that.

The boys and girls in one of my P.E. classes were not getting along, with the boys being aggressive and the girls laid-back. My University of Nebraska advisor, "Milt" (not his real name), came out to observe this class.

I had done something for that particular class that I thought was really neat, that I thought would help end the intimidation going on between the girls and boys. I split the boys and girls into teams based on gender for a football game. This worked out well, because there were twice as many girls in the class as boys, giving the girls an advantage in numbers. I would give the girls a chance to prove they were equals and would encourage the boys to respect the girls. The girls played hard and didn't back down against the boys. Though the girls lost the game, they had played with a lot of heart and they won the boys' respect and were even congratulated on their impressive effort. Boys and girls mixing together like that had never happened before in this class.

I was proud that something I had come up with had worked so well. It meant a lot to me, because I know how hard things are for kids who feel intimidated and who simply want to be respected. Even Joe Shandera was smiling ear to ear, which really made me feel good. The only person not smiling was my Nebraska advisor. Milt looked angry when I walked up to him after class.

"What are you doing with this boys-against-girls stuff? Do you want to get sued?" he asked. "This is just not good enough."

"Look at these kids," I replied, pointing to the laughing and talking boys and girls. If he had seen how standoffish these kids had been with each other earlier, he would've grasped just how special this occasion was.

Milt went on to shred everything I did. I had not done a single thing right, in his mind.

Joe Shandera stepped up after a few minutes. I could tell he couldn't believe what he was hearing. He had seen how well things went; he realized something special had happened in that class.

"Rulon, go ahead and go up to class, and let me take care of this," Joe said.

I was sort of shy and felt more than a little embarrassed after Milt had just scolded me in front of some of the kids, and Joe.

"Are you sure?" I asked.

"Yes, you did a very good job," he said. "Let me talk to this guy."

So I gathered my stuff and went up to the classroom.

What happened next was talked about for weeks and months afterward. Joe Shandera told Milt that the class had gone great and that anyone should have been able to figure that out simply by watching.

When I saw Joe later in the day and asked how it went, he said, "I just told that guy how it was."

What he actually did, according to several teachers who witnessed it, was rip Milt up one side and down the other. He schooled Milt on teaching strategies and philosophies. Then he took it a step further and pointed out that he knew that Milt didn't want me to succeed and wasn't treating me fairly. Then Joe called the teachers' college at the university, asked for the dean, and proceeded to rip apart the teachers' college. He told the dean that the college had a bad reputation and that incidents like this only verified how lousy a job they were doing.

Joe didn't stop with the teachers' college. He called other officials at the school, including the university administration. He let them know what the teachers' college was doing wrong, how I had been treated the whole semester, and how I had been treated after the P.E.-class football game as examples of how low the program had sunk in recent years.

It was unreal. Again, I can only guess that Milt had talked to my advisor and to that small pocket of people who believed I didn't belong in the program, and wasn't worthy of a teaching degree from the Nebraska teachers' college. When Joe was interviewed for this book, he corroborated my opinion that Milt's actions were aimed at getting me tossed from the teaching program.

"Rulon was very caring, yet he challenged those boys

and girls to do the best they could do," Joe said. "He used a lot of personal examples, because he had been through a lot of difficult situations on his own. I thought that would make him a very good teacher."

Joe's support was continuous throughout the semester. He was there for every day of my classes, reviewed my lesson plans, and, more importantly, saw how I interacted with the kids. He appreciated that the kids learned valuable lessons from the programs I had designed.

"Rulon and I had a really good relationship—and the work he did for me was really good," Joe said. "The person from the University [of Nebraska] had some pre-judgments about Rulon. I got the impression he had several strikes against Rulon and was looking for a reason to pull him out. I couldn't give that guy one reason for such action, because Rulon continually improved as a teacher from the first day to the last."

That message, though, was lost on Milt. He sought me out after Joe finished with him. Milt wasn't going to be deterred. Since Joe thought the class went so well, Milt turned to my paperwork for the class, which was all mapped out like it was supposed to be—or so I thought.

"This is all wrong," Milt said. "All completely wrong. Your lesson plan should be broken down in thirty-second increments—two per minute, in other words—about what the kids are doing for every thirty-second increment of the forty-five-minute class."

On Milt's final observation day, he was walking down the hall to check in at the office, as all visitors must, when another teacher on staff, a woman from Great Britain, came over to Milt.

"I would like to see you, sir, teach my class the way you are proposing," she said. "Because I know that is not possible."

Joe encouraged me to go ahead and follow the instructions Milt had given me, to do the paperwork the way Milt specified and do my best. Joe's message was important: even though Milt apparently didn't know what he was doing, he was the one in charge of my student teaching. My ultimate goal was to pass the student-teaching program, and in order to do that, I had to do the work the way he wanted it done. I wrote out the thirty-second increments the way he told me to, and at the end of the semester we sat down again.

"Rulon is adequate," was his final evaluation.

With Milt, I couldn't even plead my case or get an honest answer as to what I did wrong or right. It was an amazingly frustrating time for me, mostly because I knew I was doing good work, doing it the right way. I watched other student-athletes do their work, and I was a cut above—I had been told this by others. Yet the football player in my class could do no wrong. He'd come into class and joke, do whatever he wanted, and got great grades. The preferential treatment was ridiculous.

School had been difficult for me from the first day of grade school; I knew what it was like to be a student. And I thought—no, I *knew*—I would be a good teacher. When I got to Nebraska, I knew my calling was to be a teacher. I could challenge the bright kids to push themselves even more, to expand their horizons. I could take the kids in the middle and get them to reach for that next level, encourage them to become standout students. And, of course, I could relate to those who were behind academi-cally—and felt left behind emotionally—because I was that kid, and still am in no small part. I had many teachers over the years, both good and bad, but I learned from every one of them. I learned from the good teachers what works, how compassion and patience is as essential as the schoolwork itself. I learned from the bad teachers what not to do. I felt I had a lot to offer public education, and a big part of that was offering myself.

As it ended up, I finally got my degree. During that last year or so, every time someone put me down, I strength-ened my resolve to complete the program. To have a great educator and person like Joe Shandera to study under was probably the biggest blessing I could have hoped for at that point. Had I remained under the thumb of that pocket of faculty that wanted to fail me, I would've continued to bang my head against the wall.

There is no doubt that I was greatly aided by some wonderful people at the University of Nebraska, teachers who were willing to help me manage my disability and overcome the challenges it presented to me. On the other hand, there's equally no doubt that those who had it in for me would've run me out of the program if they could have. They didn't, though, because I believe, in the end, if you are willing to jump through enough hoops and willing to complete all the coursework at the level required, char-acter will come into play.

I will always believe that in life we should at least give ourselves the opportunity to try the things that are impor-tant to us. That might mean failing, but we should insist on having the opportunity to try, even if others try to kick us to the corner. When I won the gold in 2000, I made a big swooping movement with my arms, as though I was throwing something to the wind. I actually was thinking of several teachers at Nebraska, and the other naysayers along the way, who had tried to get me to fail or quit.

I look back at Nebraska and wonder what that small group of people had against me. I believe it was because I was an athlete—and not a football player, because those athletes were treated with special care, from my observations. At that point, there were no longer that many athletes in the teaching program—I can count on one hand how many non-football athletes were in the program, so maybe those teachers who were so difficult for me to deal with had a "dumb jock" belief about athletes and thought I didn't belong, didn't deserve to be there.

So, in the end, I became a teacher not because of the Nebraska teachers' college, but in spite of some of its members. I remain indebted to those teachers and tutors who did help me: graduating from college with nearly a 3.0 grade point average was a huge accomplishment for me. No matter what the future holds for me as a teacher, I will never treat any student the way that hanful of negative people treated me. It was not constructive or productive, and even now, looking back with a clearer mind, it was just plain mean. They completely underestimated me. When I got my degree in the fall of 1996, it was like winning an Olympic medal.

Because I believed in myself, they weren't able to keep me down.

Twelve

HEROES

WE TALK ABOUT heroes and role models a lot these days. I think one of the big reasons we talk about them is because our primary role models, parents, are often on the go, hoping daycare staff can raise their kids or that teachers can fill the void. That's not fair to the teachers, but most of all it's not fair to the kids.

My primary role models lived under my roof while I was growing up. On a daily basis, my father and mother set a course of hard work, integrity, and character. My parents, brothers, and sisters were those I learned the most from, and they were those who knew me best, my personality, my strengths, my weaknesses and goals. Meanwhile, my secondary role models were teachers and coaches, people with whom I had frequent contact and who took the time to get to know and care about me.

I remember that big flap about Charles Barkley saying, "I'm not a role model." I think he had a good point, because pro athletes—while they should set a good example—aren't going to be able to affect kids on a daily basis. The role model has to be someone who the child knows, and, in turn, that role model has to know the child. An effective role model is not a person a child sees on a television show, in a game, or on a commercial. It's someone the child actually knows, someone the child can watch to see how they carry themselves on a day-to-day basis, not just during a two-hour game.

At the same time, I do believe in heroes. One person I only briefly met, but who I consider to be a hero, is Pat Tillman. When I was training in Arizona, I met Pat, who had played college football at Arizona State University and was set to make a bigger name for himself in the National Football League. I met Pat for only a minute, but immediately I knew his character was very high. When 9/11 happened, Pat and his brother drove to Colorado to enlist in the army. They drove to Colorado so no one would know what they were doing. Pat didn't want attention for doing something he was called to do, defending this great country by serving in the armed forces. He knew the fundamental rule of doing something good— that if it's good, you never need to tell someone it is. Pat Tillman let his actions speak for him.

Pat was willing to sacrifice his multimillion-dollar contract in the NFL, along with the high standard of living that comes with being a professional football player, to serve the country he loved. He felt he had to give something back to his country. He didn't just go into the service, either; with a college degree, he could've gone in as an officer and joined a branch that wasn't on the ground or near the fighting. Instead he requested assignment to the U.S. Army Rangers and worked in covert operations, which he did in Afghanistan.

He ended up giving his life for this great country.

We don't always remember that whether the members of our military agree with our government's policies or not, they serve that elected government and are sometimes put into harm's way because they are duty bound. I think back to all the heroes from World War I and World War II who are sometimes forgotten by the current generation of Americans. All of those soldiers who had the guts to defend liberty at Omaha and Utah beaches in Normandy. All of those soldiers sent to remote areas of the world, places many Americans could never find on a map. They had so much love for this country that they were willing to die for it. I worry sometimes that we no longer adequately honor our country, or the principles that have made it possible for us to attain our high standard of living.

Pat Tillman, like many other men and women, was willing to give up everything he had to pick up a rifle, go to Afghanistan, and hunt down Osama bin Laden and his network of terrorists. He was willing to give up the enthusiastic roar of eighty thousand people every Sunday to do a thankless job, where not adulation, but death could come around every corner, over every hill.

Dave Draney was another of my heroes. A Star Valley native, Dave was several years older than me, so I only knew of him growing up, though I did get to meet him when I returned to Star Valley for a visit in 1994. Dave was an outstanding athlete who came back to Star Valley to become a teacher. Before terminal bone cancer set in, he had become an elite-level track and field star, breaking all kinds of school and state records in the triple jump, long jump, and high jump. He went on to college at Brigham Young, where he was an excellent student. When the cancer was diagnosed, he had six tumors. He endured sixteen surgeries.

In spite of the toll that the cancer and the treatments took on him, Dave Draney never backed down. He kept teaching as long as he could after graduating from college, fighting through the pain just to help kids learn to make better decisions for themselves. He lost his leg to cancer, but kept trying to the very end to make Star Valley—and by extension, this country—a better place for the future. I believe every kid who came in contact with him will be forever influenced by his courage, discipline, and determination. His spirit will live on long after his death.

When I was back home working out in 2003 in the Star Valley High School weight room, I saw the picture they had put up of Dave Draney. Underneath it is printed, "Never give up."

I remember I once asked Dave if it was hard to give up competing. After all, he might've been able to try out for the U.S. national team. I wondered if he almost regretted competing at all, since he had had to stop with the knowledge that he still had more to give.

"I had a chance," Dave said, "and I made the most of it. That's all I can ask for."

That's all I ever asked for, all anyone can ask for. I hope lessons like this, from people like Pat Tillman and Dave Draney, are remembered forever.

But it scares me that the Pat Tillmans, Dave Draneys,

and veterans of America are already fading from our nation's collective memory, that after a few years the name won't be recognizable, and more importantly, that their actions and lessons will be lost and forgotten. They will always be heroes to me.

Every member of my family, and every teacher and coach I had, was a role model to me. To the special ed teachers who bent over backward to help me push myself through a class, to the coach who saw an ounce of potential in me and helped me turn it into a pound of success, I'm forever grateful.

Thirteen
THE ROUTE TO 2000

FEBRUARY 14, 10:30 P.M.

The cold was consuming me. No doubt in my mind I was now in this for the long haul. Life or death. Sudden death. Overtime. Think about it: the bout of my life, this one for my survival.

But the cold. I had been cold before, freezing at times. But never had I been as frozen to my core as I was now.

Severe hypothermia sets in from 92 to 86 degrees body temperature. The shivers come in waves and are violent, unlike the pauses that come with the first dip of about two degrees in body temperature. Your body is in serious trouble at that point, because your muscles cannot burn enough glycogen to counteract your continually dropping core temperatures, causing your body to slow the shivering to try to conserve what glucose is left. Muscle rigidity—stiffness—develops because of the lactic acid and CO_2 buildup in your muscles.

At 90 degrees, your body shuts down all peripheral blood flow and reduces both your heart rate and breathing rate. In effect, your body goes into a sort of hibernation. Between 90 and 86 degrees, you pretty much stop shivering, and you begin to lose muscle coordination, leading to confusion, irrational and incoherent behavior, and an inability to walk. You may also lose your ability to maintain posture. Finally, at 86 degrees, your body is in a state called "metabolic icebox"—you may be alive, but you appear to be dead.

From 86 down to 82 degrees, you become semiconscious and move into a state of stupor as your pulse and respiration rate decrease. You also run the risk of a heart "event"—such as a heart attack or heart fibrillation.

You become unconscious once your core temperature dips to between 82 and 78 degrees. Your heartbeat and respiration are now very erratic. The medical community says that at 78 to 75 degrees you will experience cardiac and respiratory failure, though your "death may occur before this temperature is reached."

After I was found on the morning of February 15, 2002, my body temperature registered in the lower 80s, and then mid-80s, when it was taken at the hospital in Idaho Falls, where I was airlifted after the initial stop at Star Valley Hospital.

But your body has amazing built-in mechanisms for dealing with illness, injury, or trauma—for example, shivering to warm itself up, or going into a coma to deal with a head injury. Doctors, as incredible as they are, *can't account for what makes your body react in certain situations, nor can they explain how your mind recognizes certain things and adapts to fight the illness or rehab the injury on its own.*

Sometimes our minds take us to a place we never imagined we could go. No one knew exactly where I was—obviously, or they would've found me. Until sunlight, it was just me and my faith. I was in the middle of what most people would consider to be "nowhere." I had been there before and stunned the world.

Now, I'd have to beat the odds again.

In 1997, I trained hard and prepared to travel the globe, putting in the time and entering all the tournaments necessary to make a name, and a place, for myself in the sport of Greco-Roman wrestling.

It's important to note that I began to work with USA Wrestling coach Steve Fraser—another man, another coach who would shape me during this early, critical point in my Greco-Roman wrestling career. As a wrestler, Fraser won the United States' first gold medal in Greco, at the 1984 Olympic Games in Los Angeles. Coach Fraser and I have an outstanding relationship. While a big part of it is based on our mutual love of wrestling, we also enjoy a healthy and fun competition between us. Coach Fraser is so competitive, it's almost unreal. We'd have friendly bets on everything you could imagine, though most were feats of mental or physical strength. In early 1997, we were in Poznan, Poland, for the 1997 Pytlasinski Grand Prix, a post-1996 Olympic tournament where wrestlers started sizing each other up for the 1997 World Championships later in the year. When we landed in Poznan, the wagering began immediately. Coach Fraser's bets at this time were based on guys carrying each other, sometimes it would be how far we could make it, sometimes it would be how quickly we could make it to a particular destination—the cab, or something—while carrying another U.S. wrestler. This went on for the entire trip.

The 1997 Pytlasinksi Grand Prix was an important tournament for me; it was where I won my first major international championship. With Matt Ghaffari in retirement (he later would come out of it), the top heavyweight spot for the U.S. Greco team was wide open. Right after I had won the championship there in Poznan in the tourney's final match, Coach Fraser decided it was time to start the wagering again. I was supposed to carry Kevin Bracken, an accomplished 138-pounder, back to the hotel. I was tired and sweaty, but Fraser had dropped the gauntlet in front of the whole team, and given the gathering of testosterone and machismo around me, I had to pick it up. So I looked at Bracken, thought about the distance to the hotel from the tournament site—I would guess almost a mile—and got ready. At the last second, Coach Fraser called the bet off. He said carrying Bracken was too easy. He'd pay off the bet—$150—only if I would carry a heavier wrestler back to the hotel.

Dan Hicks, our 215-pound wrestler, and Fraser had been going back and forth. Fraser saw a way to involve Hicks and, in his mind, probably win the bet. Hicks, obviously, is a much bigger guy than Bracken.

I'll let Dan Hicks tell the story from here: "The day of the finals, it was just unbelievably hot outside. Rulon had been in the finals and won, and everyone was going nuts for him because he beat this big German, and this really put Rulon on the map, because he hadn't had that big breakout win yet and this was it," Hicks said. "Coach Fraser, as usual, was ready to issue another challenge, not even ten minutes after the match, just as we started to leave back to the hotel, which was probably almost a mile away on these old sidewalks. But in the heat that day, it wasn't going to be comfortable. Many of us had wrestled that day, and Rulon had just finished his match, the final wrestling match of the tournament, the heavyweight championship.

"Walking out, he accepted Fraser's challenge and was getting set to pick up Bracken. But then Coach pointed to me and said that was the deal. Rulon was drenched in sweat and probably pretty dehydrated from just wrestling, not to mention hungry. So Rulon picks me up and we walk out of the competition venue. It was just brutal. He was soaked, and I was sweating pretty good, too. I got on piggyback, and he hardly could hold me. Because he was so wet, I could barely hold on—I had my feet on his thighs and was strangling him around the neck just to stay on.

"I'm thinking we won't make it to the end of the block. Everyone else realized Rulon and I had bit off more than we could chew, and they were laughing, congratulating Fraser on his impending windfall. All of a sudden, Rulon said to me, 'Just hold on,' and just takes off, trucking down the road with me on him. I could feel Rulon was hurting, but he wouldn't say a word, wouldn't give Coach the satisfaction. Coach Fraser kept trying to trip him, or would bump into Rulon say, 'Oh, sorry, didn't see you there!'

"Remember, these were friendly bets among people who cared for each other, but the way things work among athletes (Coach Fraser is a former athlete) is that pride is at stake, and that means a lot more than money. It was over 90 degrees, just nasty weather to be exerting yourself in, especially after just wrestling at a major international competition. The Polish people on the streets looked at us like we were crazy, this huge sweaty guy laboring with this 215-pound guy on his back holding on for dear life. Finally, we got to the building, and Rulon was just screaming to fight back the pain. Coach Fraser said the bet wasn't over, that he had to take me to our rooms upstairs—this would've been on the eleventh or thirteenth floor, so we had to ride up the elevator. Rulon just gritted his teeth and waited. Someone was holding the elevator for about ten minutes so it wouldn't come down, maybe at Fraser's urging. I was just holding on with soaked arms around Rulon's dripping neck. We bumped into the wall by the elevator and Coach Fraser jumped at us, 'You can't lean on walls!' he yelled.

"Finally, the elevator comes down and we get on. Coach Fraser hit every button on it, so it would stop on every single floor. We finally got to the door, and I was about to get down. 'No way,' Fraser said. 'You have to be *in* the room.' What Coach Fraser didn't know was that this Wyoming farm boy had been through situations like this his whole life.

"Coach Fraser or someone had our bags, and our room keys had mysteriously disappeared. Finally, after another five- to ten-minute wait, someone came through with the room key. Rulon was just dog tired, but he got a lot of respect that day as a wrestler, and for that incredible ride he gave me to the hotel. I would say that, overall, with the delays at the elevator and finding the elusive room keys, the trip took an hour. Rulon showed a lot of strength, but a lot more mental toughness. You could see by the look on Fraser's face that he thought Rulon had something special at that point. And Rulon gave me half, seventy-five dollars, because, first of all, that's how Rulon is, but he also knew I had been working hard just to stay on his back!"

My training for this, Coach Fraser couldn't have known then, had been carrying the calves to the barn across slick fields, though Hicks was the weight of *two* calves. Hicks didn't kick, squirm, and bawl like the livestock—he was a pretty good passenger.

I don't think I ever carried Dan Hicks again. He's the kind of teammate you want, though—the tough guy who will gut things out and never let a teammate down.

I gave Fraser a chance to get even in Arizona, where I continued training after the Poland trip. I slapped $150 on the table and bet that he and his son could not eat ten of these spicy-hot "suicide" chicken wings, apiece. His fifteen-year-old son, a hot-food freak, did it no sweat, didn't even blink. I admired the kid as he picked up the seventy-five bucks and told his dad, "The rest is up to you." Coach Fraser gutted it out, sweat trickling down his temples as he ate the last one. This was back when I was struggling financially; $150 was a lot of money to me. But it was money I had won from him in Poland carrying Dan Hicks, so it was only right to give him a chance to earn it back. And when I saw his face after that last wing went down, I knew that he had earned it back, or would later that night, when he dealt with the heartburn that had turned his face beet-red.

On another trip that year, on the way home from Europe, Fraser challenged me to keep my hands above my ears from the time we took off in Poland until we landed in Chicago, about an eight-hour flight. Since he felt this bet was extraordinarily difficult, it was a one-sided wager—it would cost me nothing if I lost, but he'd pay me if I won. Coach Fraser was sure I'd have to go to the bathroom or something, but I waited it out, even getting the person next to me to feed me my in-flight meal. My hands were killing me and my deltoids were numb, but I made it through the first leg of the flight. I made it more than four hours, until the in-flight movie started. The lights were turned down on the flight, and with only a few hours left, I momentarily nodded off, and my hands came down. Even though I quickly snapped out of it and threw my arms back up, I was too late: Coach Fraser had seen. I heard him calling out, "Rulon! I win! I win!"

Those bets were fun, but they also built up a sense of camaraderie among USA Wrestling team members and coaches. They provided good distractions from the long hours of travel and were a constant test of mental, and sometimes physical, endurance and toughness.

After the Poland tournament, it was time to focus on the upcoming 1997 World Championships.

Once again, though, I had to deal with a serious injury. At a pre-Worlds tournament in California, the Concord Cup, I was wrestling Cuban Hector Milan (220-pound gold medalist at the 1992 Olympics), and he snapped my arm in two places, including the radius.

So I went to the World Championships two months later in 1997 with a broken arm. One of my matches was against Alexander Karelin. It was there in the semifinals that I was introduced to his famous move, the "reverse lift." In this signature move, Karelin picks up his opponent like a sack of potatoes. He starts "on top" with the opponent on the bottom. Karelin then turns so that he is facing the opponent's legs, not his head—thus the term "reverse." So he picks up the opponent around the waist, gets the opponent's legs up in the air, and throws him with brute force. It is an impressive move to watch—fans are in awe of the sheer muscle it takes to do it, but it is very dangerous for the wrestler who is being thrown, because a wide array of back injuries is possible as he sails over Karelin's head and crashes, usually back first, onto the mat. The opponent's feet are over his head as the body sails through the air; it's quite a spectacle. Karelin used that move to throw me three times during the match. Twice I landed on my forehead, and once on the back of my shoulders, because I arched my back so he couldn't get me on my back to pin me. But I lost 5–0.

I also lost to the guy who broke my arm, Hector Milan, leaving me in fifth place. Still, I believed fifth place at the 1997 World Championships was a step forward, considering the broken arm. That injury kept me from doing the best that I otherwise could have, so I saw reasons for optimism.

In 1998, I went to the U.S. World Team Trials. My arm, which I never allowed to fully heal, was getting worse and required medical attention. Matt Ghaffari had come back after taking more than a year off, choosing to train at the Olympic Training Center in Colorado with former Russian/Soviet coach Anatoly Petrosyan, who told Matt, "If you can't beat the Russians, join one—me!" Matt's whole focus was to beat Karelin.

Matt and I wrestled for the spot to represent the United States at the 1998 World Championships. I made some mistakes in that match, and my arm hampered my wrestling. Matt beat me, earning the spot on the team. Even so, I knew that I was wrestling at a high caliber, high enough to compete with the best national and international wrestlers.

Karelin continued his dominance in the heavyweight class, defeating Ghaffari, who settled for silver, as he had in 1996 at the Olympics.

Finally, I realized that I needed to be healed and healthy if I was going to make a run at making the 2000 U.S. Olympic Team. I gave my arm three months to heal, keeping it taped up. In the fall of 1998, I wrestled Karelin's understudy, the number two Russian, Yuri Patrikeev, at a December tournament in Sweden, breaking one of my ribs in the first thirty seconds of the match, and losing in a wild match—I believe the score was 13–10 or something like that, a high-scoring match, and Yuri beat me by three points. So once again I was injured. In my next match following the loss to Patrikeev, the broken rib led to another loss, this one to American Corey Farkas in overtime. I became very frustrated, but would not let my injuries stop me.

A week later, I flew to Finland and won the Banta Tournament, broken rib and all. Heading into 1999, I felt things were falling into place, especially if I could stay healthy. I won a tournament in Cuba and came back to the 1999 U.S. National Championships feeling good about my chances.

Working my way through the draw, I faced Dremiel Byers in the final. He had beaten Ghaffari to get there. We had a very good match, working each other over. I got the upper hand when I took Dremiel to his back with what is called an "arm bar." But he screamed out in pain, and the referee, fearing I'd broken Dremiel's arm, blew his whistle. I got only one point, which I thought was unfair, especially since I ended up losing to Byers in overtime with his patented throw, the straight body-lift. In a foreshadowing event, Dremiel asked me to come to Athens, host of the 1999 World Championships, as his training partner. I did, and it was a lot of fun, and though I wasn't competing, it was still a learning experience. Dremiel took sixth, and Karelin, as usual, won the gold, defeating a familiar face, Cuba's Hector Milan, who had broken my arm—in the Championship final.

Though Matt Ghaffari and Dremiel Byers were still in the way, my Olympic dream was alive heading into 2000. I focused on being the best wrestler in America, no easy task given the number of talented heavyweights in this country. No matter who represents the United States, we always seem to finish among the top five or six in World and Olympic competition. So I had to be the best in America before I could think about anything else.

"What will it take for me to be number one?" I asked Coach Fraser.

"Stick to your game plan, don't lose focus of who you

are and what you are doing," he said. "You're good enough to be number one. Don't change a thing."

It was important advice, because it reinforced what I really did believe—that I was following the right track. Everyone around me could see I had talent in the sport and was making progress, so that was an affirmation to stay the course and keep believing in myself and what I was doing. I won the "Belt Series" again, given to the U.S. wrestler who does the best nationally and internationally in a given year. In fact two "Belt" awards are given out—one for freestyle and another for Greco—not by weight class, just one Belt Series award for each of the two wrestling disciplines. So here was my paradox; I'd have these great seasons overseas, and then come home and lose to Ghaffari or Byers—which made my international accomplishments less important, because if I couldn't beat these two guys, I wouldn't be able to represent the United States at the Olympics or World Championships.

Yet I finally came through and beat Ghaffari 2–1—Ghaffari had beaten Dremiel in the semifinals—at the 2000 U.S. Nationals. That was a boost for me.

Again, though, it looked like I had to take two steps back after the big step forward. Not long after Nationals, I was working out at the Olympic Training Center in Colorado Springs. We had new mats, and once they got wet from wrestlers' perspiration, it was like practicing on an ice rink. I was working with a partner and slipped, falling into a complete split.

"That's kind of weird," I thought to myself. I can do the splits front and back because I am flexible. But I can't do them down the middle. And there I was, doing the splits

The Gardner family, Thanksgiving, 1978, just days after my father got out of the hospital, and days before the family barn burned down. (Front row, left to right): Marcella, me, my father Reed, my mother Virginia, Reynold, and Ronald, who would pass away the following year. (Back row): Diane, Russell, Geraldine, Evon, and Rollin.

A photo of me showing a heifer cow at Dairy Days in Afton, at age 7.

From left to right: me, Diane, and Reynold. We're showing cattle during Afton's Dairy Days.

(Above) A chance to compete and escape farm work: Football, my junior year for Wyoming prep powerhouse Star Valley High School. Sports gave me a chance to prove myself and to build strength and cardiovascular stamina at more than 6,000 feet above sea level.

(Left) Home from school and back to work: Here I am feeding calves, one of our family's most important daily duties.

(Left) At the 1997 World Championships semifinal match, Russian Alexander Karelin used his trademark "reverse body lift" to score on this throw, and to defeat me 5-0. I arched my back when he threw me to prevent landing on my back and getting pinned—the problem was, as you can see, that I would land on my head. I was thrown three times in this match, twice arching and actually kicking myself in the back of my head as I was thrown.

Hauling hay with my father on the family farm in the summer of 1989, after my senior year of high school. The beauty of Star Valley and the feeling I got from working on the farm are hard to duplicate anywhere else.

I am getting ready for the gold medal match in 2000. Walking in front of me was Alexander Karelin, my opponent and arguably the most dominant Olympic athlete in history, and all I could think about was wrestling my best match.

Holding on for dear life: Against Karelin, if I had let go of my grip here, in the clinch, I would have let the gold medal slip away. I held on and scored a point—the only point in the entire match—from the "inferior position."

Determination: The chiseled Russian didn't have the high altitude lungs I had developed on the family farm in Wyoming. And though you could never count out the three-time defending Olympic champion, as the match wore on, I was able to wear Karelin down.

After the 2000 Olympics, I had the opportunity to wrestle around with some of my heroes. Here I am with Garth Brooks at the Touch 'Em All Foundation dinner.

(Above) Welcome home! I couldn't believe the thousands of people who were packed into my hometown of Afton for a parade following the "Miracle on the Mat" in Sydney in 2000. I have always maintained that I won for everyone in Star Valley, and the people turning out to share it with me is a priceless memory that still gives me goose bumps. (Photo © Ravell Call/Deseret News 2000)

(Below) Thanks again: The day of the parade, I broke down when I realized I had the love of my family and friends, and an Olympic gold medal—my dream came true. God bless America. (Photo © Ravell Call/Deseret News 2000)

I was overwhelmed by all the kids who perhaps saw in my story that their dreams could be achieved with the right attitude and hard work. (Photo © Ravell Call/Deseret News 2000)

Off we go in a U.S. military helicopter: One of the most amazing experiences I had after Sydney was visiting the brave men and women who serve our country in the Armed Forces. Olympic athletes represent our country in sport, while those in the Armed Forces protect it and give us the amazing opportunities that a free society affords its citizens. I'm grateful to all members of our military.

Seeing stars: I was so impressed by the bravery of these men and women who defend our country that many times I asked for their autographs.

Say cheese! Here I am sharing my experiences in a school in Japan for American military children.

It was a big deal: The first non-Japanese sumo champ, Akebono, dwarfs little ol' me during a trip to Japan. He is an inspiration and shows us all that anything is possible.

Bring it on: Here I am training two weeks before the 2001 World Championships with workout partner Matt Lamb, in Des Moines, Iowa.

I wrestled against Hungary's Mihaly Deak-Bardos for gold at the 2001 World Championships in Greece. (Photo © Gary Abbott/USA Wrestling 2001)

(Right) After winning the 2001 World Championships I was struck by emotion. I could do nothing but fall on my knees and thank God for the strength to win the gold medal and prove that Sydney 2000 wasn't a fluke. (Photo © Gary Abbott/USA Wrestling 2001)

(Below) Here I am on a U.S. Navy ship in Japan with training partner Matt Lamb, who went on many trips with me to help me train and stay in peak condition. I'm grateful to those who sacrificed to help me achieve my dreams.

(Above) In this picture taken in December 2001, I am kneeling on the snowmobile that I will be lost on just two months later. I would be in a fight for my life.

(Left) Standing on top of the mountains west of Star Valley, which can be seen in the background.

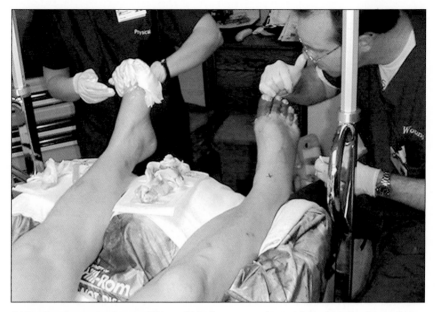

Right after my rescue, I was told I would be fortunate to keep either of my frostbitten feet. At that point frontal amputations seemed imminent. I'd be lucky to walk again. Wrestling, I was told, wasn't even in the picture.

Being coached by the best: 1984 Olympic champion Steve Fraser and U.S. Army head coach Shawn Lewis, coaching me at the 2004 Olympic Games. (Photo © Gary Abbott/USA Wrestling 2004)

Overpowering Poland's heavyweight in a pool match in Athens. (Photo © Gary Abbott/USA Wrestling 2004)

(Top Right) Going after Iranian Sajad Barzi in the bronze medal match in Athens with my taped injured right wrist. (Photo © Gary Abbott/USA Wrestling 2004)

(Right) Pushing off with my damaged, frost-bitten feet while executing a gut wrench at the 2004 Olympic Games in Athens. (Photo © Gary Abbott/USA Wrestling 2004)

(Below) After 27 years of wrestling, I had a chance to salute the crowd for a final time as a wrestler, comforted by Old Glory. (Photo © Gary Abbott/USA Wrestling 2004)

Leaving the shoes: A wrestler who retires takes his shoes off and leaves them in the center of the mat, symbolizing his departure from a sport to which he gave years of his life. I have the opportunity now to put the shoes on as coach and mentor to future Olympians. (Photo © Gary Abbott/USA Wrestling 2004)

A final moment on the podium: Winning the bronze medal at the 2004 Olympics in Athens was a moment of great pride for me. No, it wasn't the gold medal that I was hoping for, but considering the incident that nearly killed me, then a motorcycle accident and a dislocated wrist, I was able to exceed a lot of expectations. (Photo © Gary Abbott/USA Wrestling 2004)

down the middle on the slick new mat. A burning sensation ensued, and I pulled my legs together.

I had torn a groin muscle. To this day, I still have scar tissue in the muscle from that severe injury.

The injury happened right before the 2000 Pan American Games in late June/early July, so there was no slowing down, no looking back. I won the Pan American Games even though I couldn't push off with my left leg, which was still swollen. I had baseball-size lumps on the back of my leg; I hadn't realized it, but I had torn the muscle all the way through to the back of my leg. I don't think I was even 75 percent for that tournament, but it was important to go. The win was a boost, as I beat the Cuban who had beaten me twice at the 1997 Worlds, Hector Milan.

So going into the 2000 U.S. Olympic Trials, I was riding a competitive high—I had also won the Cuba tournament, along with several others—but I was limping, literally, with the groin injury.

Since I had won Nationals, I had a bye at the Trials until the finals. Likely Ghaffari or Dremiel would emerge from the bracket, to face me.

Because I had beaten Ghaffari once, I no longer had any mental blocks when I had to face him. Ghaffari had to wrestle his way through a mini-tournament; it was Ghaffari and I who would battle for the berth on the Olympic Team.

The finals format is best two out of three. Ghaffari had a move called the "backbreaker." The backbreaker is literally what it sounds like: Matt gets on top of his opponent and grabs the guy's head—imagine a steer wrestler, how he yanks the animal's head to turn it back—so with

Matt's arms around the guy's head, he leans back, and that puts all the pressure on his opponent's back. Either the opponent goes down with the motion and basically submits, or his back can be seriously injured.

Regardless of Ghaffari's arsenal, I was prepared for anything and everything, and I beat him in the opening match, reversing him before he could use his backbreaker move. In the second match, he kept trying the same move. I kept my arms out to prevent it and was leading 1–0. Somehow in that second match, I was called for a caution, and he received two points to win the match 2–1. I felt like he didn't earn that victory—that was a "gift," in my mind—and I wasn't happy about it. I was even more fired up when I looked across the mat at him as we prepared for our third and final match, the one that would decide who would represent America at the 2000 Olympic Games in Sydney.

Ghaffari was laughing—actually laughing—and having a ball with a couple of other guys, just minutes before we were set to wrestle the final match.

"He's not even worried about this match," I thought to myself, my temperature rising. "He thinks life is grand, so confident. He is sure he is going to win. No way I'm walking out of here a loser to him."

I took him out of bounds five times in the third match before I got a single point, beating on him relentlessly. Time wound down and then ran out on Ghaffari. His run had been incredible, but it was over. He had lost to Karelin twenty-two times in a row and wouldn't get what he wanted most—a final shot at the Russian at the 2000 Olympics.

I was representing America and, in particular, Star Valley, Wyoming, in the 2000 Olympics. I was representing everyone who had milked cows during morning darkness, carried calves across muddy fields in the evening, moved pipe for hours on end, or baled hay until there was no more. It wasn't just me going to the Olympics.

It was all of us hardworking folks of rural America.

Beating Matt Ghaffari at the 2000 Olympic Trials was a good feeling, because he was always sort of my mentor, and then my nemesis in Greco-Roman. But when you close one door, another is always in front of you, and this one was ten times as big.

I did what I always did when something big—good or bad—happened: I went home to Star Valley to be among those who love me, as I gathered my thoughts and focused on my next challenge. I loved to go home and see my two dogs, Bo and Tie, chow-husky-retriever mixes.

My second day home, I was sleeping at 10:00 A.M. My brother Russell came in.

"Did you hear?" Russell asked.

"Hear what?" I replied.

"Your dog got hit this morning," Russell said.

Bo had been hit by a truck driven by a family friend. The accident had happened in front of our house. Those dogs are the closest things I've ever had to children. Anyone who has ever lost a dog can understand what it feels like: like you've lost a family member. Bo was the sweetest little dog, and I had raised him since he was a six-week-old puppy. He was my baby; I took care of him and loved him for all I was worth.

Bo's body had been taken by my father to a place we call "the junkyard," a place where dead animals were usually taken for safe disposal. We went down and picked up his body, then headed up into the mountains and had a little funeral. I found a fitting place across the river and buried him near Dry Creek, a couple of miles up the hill from my house. After I had dug out the hole and placed my pup in there, Tie walked over and, as he always did before he went to bed at night, circled until he found that right spot. This time, he circled and lay down right next to where I had just buried Bo. I still have Bo's collar, and I think about that wonderful dog often.

There wasn't time to grieve, because the Olympics were coming up quickly, just after some pre-Olympic annual meets. I needed to train as hard as I ever had.

People around Star Valley seemed to think it was a neat thing that I had made the Olympic Team and would represent America. But no one really knew what it meant— or what was possible. So some folks thought it was no big deal. More than one person said, "It's not like he's going to win a medal or anything," or another favorite, "It's not like the whole world's suddenly going to know who Rulon is now."

No one imagined anything big happening.

Except me. And my coaches.

The Star Valley community helped raise money to send my family to the Olympics. I, on the other hand, had to go to Europe and wrestle in some pre-Olympic events.

And if no one was thinking about me making a mark at the Olympics, then my performance at the Russian pre-Olympic tournament gave them every reason to believe I wouldn't even be a blip on the radar.

I had hoped to have another match against Karelin at the Russian Podubbny Tournament. He was there, but he wasn't wrestling. Instead, Yuri Patrikeev, the young, strong bull of a man, would wrestle. Because he was so young, Yuri didn't have Karelin's resume. But he was strong and quick, and definitely on his way up. There's no doubt that if Karelin hadn't been able to go to the 2000 Games, not only would Patrikeev have gone, but he would have been one of the gold medal favorites.

I made it to the finals, where I would face Yuri, who was wrestling extremely well. When I entered the arena for the championship, which was just outside of Moscow, I saw Karelin, who was hanging out with several of his friends and compatriots. I had wrestled well to that point, though I can't say if I had caught Karelin's attention or not.

On the mat, I tried to be particularly aggressive with Yuri.

That was a mistake. A big one.

I got caught leaning, and Yuri hip-tossed me.

And then pinned me, eighteen seconds into the match.

That was the first time I had been pinned since junior high.

I can only imagine what people in the wrestling community, and in my community back home, were saying—things like, "He can't beat even the number two Russian? How can he think about beating Karelin? Or any of the other top Olympians from other countries?" I was having those same thoughts as well, but had to put it behind me, learn from it, and get focused.

At that point, I threw everything out the door. I came back to America with 100 percent dedication, and I wasn't going to let this thing pull me down: I was going to let it motivate me.

I had to put the Yuri match behind me, had to use it to get better. I had grown up wrestling one way, and one way only: all or nothing. That match against Yuri drummed it into my head that I had to develop some mat strategy. I had to be willing to slow down. I knew I couldn't wrestle to someone else's strengths and simply will my way to a win; that much, Yuri had taught me. I had to pace myself and wrestle each match with the idea of becoming the best. I should have beaten Yuri in that match, no doubt about it. Instead, I beat myself. I took myself out of any chance of winning the match by playing right into Yuri's hands.

Though lying on my back in Russia, with only a month to go before Sydney, wasn't a good feeling, it did strengthen my resolve. And it made me much angrier. The loss to Yuri was a turning point in my wrestling career. I had made a dumb mistake, but I was smart enough to learn from it.

I came back to America more motivated and more focused than ever on what I needed to do. Everything came together as I worked toward my goal: an Olympic gold medal. A bronze would be nice, and a silver nicer. But you don't go into a tournament hoping for anything but first place. So that was my goal.

The workouts at the Olympic Training Center in Colorado Springs were relentless and exhausting—yet exhilarating.

We'd have group matches—me against a group of four or so wrestlers. We called it "shark bait." I was the bait. I would stay in the middle, and they'd come in and tear me up. One teammate would come after me, then a fresh team-mate would come in, and again and again, until I couldn't stand. The lung capacity that I had built up through nearly twenty years of farmwork, day and night, at more than six thousand feet above sea level, was getting even greater. Everyone supported me, sure, but they all wanted a piece of me, too. I was the Olympian, and they had wanted that spot. This was their chance for revenge.

And their energy fueled me.

I'd last twenty minutes in those sessions, and I did get roughed up a little bit, but I enjoyed them. Though I was the "bait," I was constantly on the attack, dishing out as much as or more than I'd take in, because I knew it was making me better, going after those guys one after the next. I learned something different from each one of them; each of them had a particular strength and a strong move. Those sessions prepared me for every opponent I would face at the Olympics.

We had some intense training camps. Dremiel Byers and Corey Farkas were especially beneficial as training partners. These are guys who would have legitimate shots to medal in any international match they entered. Byers was a national champion, and a World Championship placer, in his own right.

There was no doubt that when I stepped on the mats in Sydney, I was wrestling for far more than myself: I was also wrestling for my family, friends, community, team-mates, and, of course, my country.

Fourteen

JOURNEY TO GOLD

FEBRUARY 15, 2002, 9:10 A.M.

A loud noise came over the hill, a thwack, thwack, thwacking noise.

Finally, a helicopter. I had expected snowmobiles, but a helicopter would do just fine.

This horrible experience was coming to an end. The last part of this journey—getting to the helicopter, which touched down perhaps forty yards away from me—would not be easy. I couldn't walk, because of both the deep snow and my frozen feet, so I had to crawl, something I had done on the wrestling mat many times to get out of a hold, or simply when the whistle blew and I was on the bottom and my opponent was on top, trying to prevent any movement by me.

And then it hit me: since LifeFlight was here, that meant everyone knew I had been lost all night in the Wyoming wilderness. People would be talking about my mishap.

"Oh crud, now everyone knows I was stranded," I said to myself as I leaned forward and started crawling toward the helicopter, as someone inside it came toward me. I had to do a "military crawl," an eight-point crawl, where I was on more than just my hands and knees—I was on my forearms, legs, feet, everything.

But the more important thought was that I was going to be saved. All those times in the middle of the night when my body was shutting down, when hope was as lost as I was, were coming to an end. And though people in town—and, I'd soon learn, around the country— would learn about my adventure, I was going to live

I was happy just to be alive.

As we prepared to travel to Australia for the 2000 Olympics, I had other things to deal with.

My groin muscle was still torn, so I didn't have the strength I wanted in my legs. I wasn't able to squat properly, which eliminated a lot of our key weight-lifting exercises from my workout. But I did have mental toughness, focus, and a resolve that nothing would sidetrack me.

The USA team flew to San Diego to be processed for the trip to Sydney. From there, we flew to Canberra, where we stayed and trained at the Australian Institute of Sport.

As we stepped off the plane on September 10, 2000, Fraser gathered us.

"You guys have put in the devotion, you've been dedicated," Fraser said. "Now it's time to take care of business." At a pre-Olympic press conference on September 16, U.S. coaches were asked who could be an athlete to surprise the world, and Coach Dan Chandler answered that that would be our 213-pounder, Garrett Lowney. "The coaches agree the guy who has progressed the most has been Lowney," Chandler said. "He expects to win whenever he steps on the mat." Garrett confirmed that a day later, announcing he thought he could medal (he did, winning bronze).

The first day there, the team's competitive juices were flowing, so much so that a game of Frisbee football almost turned into a series of fights.

We were ready to rumble. It got so physical that during one of the skirmishes, my training partner on the trip, Corey Farkas, turned his ankle. Corey is a top-notch wrestler and our workouts were important; I needed them to stay in top shape and to remain sharp. Since Corey couldn't wrestle me, I had to have lighter-weight guys double- and triple-team me—shark bait again—to stay in shape. Dave Surofchek, a 220-pounder, had come along as a training partner for our Olympian in that category, but I also needed to train with Dave because of Corey's injury. One training session in Australia, I was going after him hard, and he went for my head. But I got him in a headlock, took him out of bounds and to his back, where I could've really physically hurt him. The intensity was so high, I had to let up before I broke the guy's neck.

I would have wrestled whomever I needed to in order to stay sharp, be it my coach, or my brother, or even one of my sisters! (who collectively claim to this day to be undefeated against me! . . . Talk of some matches that should be "under review.")

Though we were in Australia, we didn't go to Sydney until the day before the Opening Ceremonies. So the first time I put on the nice Team USA warm-up suit was the day of the Opening Ceremonies.

I was excited, meeting these superstars of sport, though several brushed me off. I'm this big farm boy from Wyoming, someone these guys had never heard of. I realized that. One who was really nice was Alonzo Mourning. I knew he had the reputation of being a tough, physical basketball player (I like to picture myself that way on the basketball court, too, a picture that would almost end my 2004 Olympic dream). Anyway, when I met Alonzo and asked to have my picture taken with him, I said, "Just be gentle, Alonzo," and we enjoyed a laugh.

The Dream Team basketball players pretty much kept to themselves. Most of the Olympic Team members were like myself, toiling at some level of obscurity, staying out of the national spotlight, and working odd jobs to make ends meet. Granted, some Olympic athletes made decent livings, but in wrestling it was a month-to-month existence for pretty much all of us.

We went in to the Opening Ceremonies as the U.S. Olympic Team. But the television cameras focused on the Dream Team when it entered and cut to a commercial before I was able to get on TV, a disappointment for everyone back home. I thought that would be their one chance to see me on television because of the time difference and focus on the major sports, so I was disappointed that they would miss seeing me.

Soon, though, I'd make it up to them.

The wrestling tournament draw at the Olympics was a very odd scenario. It's random, meaning past accomplishments have no bearing. I had a good draw, not having Karelin, the Hungarian, Bulgarian, or Cuban—the favorites—in my pool, and wouldn't see any of those established wrestlers until the medal round, if I made it there.

I realized I was on the opposite side of the bracket from Karelin, the greatest Greco-Roman wrestler in history. That meant, to face him we'd both have to reach the final—only there, for the gold medal, would we encounter each other. I looked at Karelin when we were in the arena at the same time, but he didn't look at me; I'm sure the thought didn't cross his mind. Not losing ever in the Olympics and reportedly not being scored upon in more than a decade, he probably wasn't worried who was placed anywhere in any bracket. It caught my attention, but quickly I turned my focus to my first opponent, a physically strong wrestler, Omrane Ayari, of Tunisia.

That match wasn't a much of a problem, as I controlled the tempo and took my easiest win of the Games 7–2.

My second match, I felt even stronger. I faced Haykaz Ghalstyan of Armenia, and I dictated every aspect of the match, shutting him down 6–0. Right before that match, I watched Karelin in action. Karelin had his way with big Mihaly Deak-Bardos of Hungary on the very same mat. Rather than suffer through a humiliating and occasionally painful reverse throw, Karelin's trademark move, Deak went to his back and Karelin pinned him. I noticed that Karelin wasn't really being tested, his endurance was hard to measure, because he hadn't been pushed in his matches—he pinned his opponents, or they didn't attack. We both still had a "pool" match left the next day—and I was about to wrestle Italian

Giuseppe Giunta in a matter of minutes—so I doubt Karelin had given me any thought.

I wrestled Giunta mostly with technique. He wasn't as big as me, but he was strong for his size and so quick that a mistake would cost me. He is a very strong wrestler who doesn't make a lot of mistakes, but I was able to take him down for one point and get another point off a turn-around. So entering the second period, I was up 2–0. At that point, the match turned into a sort of street fight. I probably needed that let's-get-nasty and down-and-dirty kind of brawl at that point. Giunta had come up from 213 pounds to heavyweight, which explains his quickness. So I worked on him and held my 2–0 lead. But if three points aren't scored, the match goes to overtime. He put his hand in my singlet and hooked it—an illegal move—and took me out of bounds. It made me mad when the referee gave him a point and said I was "fleeing my opponent." But I was able to keep the 2–1 lead and win, sending me into the medal round.

In the semifinals—with no medal assured, as I'd have to win at least one of my next two matches to take even a bronze—I knew the matches would be much tougher. There wouldn't be any multiple-point wins or 6–0 shutouts. From here on out, a mistake meant the end of the road. My semifinal match was against Juri Yevseychyc of Israel—originally a Russian—who looks just like the guy on the Mr. Clean bottle.

My chances didn't look good midway through the match. He scored a point in a clinch when he made me break my lock. I started attacking him harder to try tiring him out. He squirmed away and pulled me off balance, taking me down out of bounds for another point, and I trailed 2–0. My coach, Steve Fraser, encouraged me.

"Don't freak out!" he said. "Frase" is animated to begin with, but at this moment his eyes were open so wide he looked like a cartoon character. Who was freaking out here, I wondered, me or Frase?

"Be patient," he whispered. "You're wearing him down. He is gassed."

I knew that if I was going to come back, I had to open things up. I locked Juri up and carried him to the out-of-bounds line, because I wanted to make sure that if I threw him, and he caught me, I'd still get points. When I threw him, his momentum carried him all the way to the floor, headfirst. Since I was so committed to finish the throw, I too went out of bounds and was only a step from the wooden floor off the mat when I finished the throw. When I threw him, I had spun out of control and had hit hard. But Juri, it would turn out, had hit harder, and suffered a mild concussion in addition to a cut on his chin.

"You've got him," Fraser said. "Focus. Look at him; you broke him."

I was actually seeing stars at that point, I was so wound up—do I actually believe what Fraser says at this point? Absolutely.

With two minutes left, down 2–0, we continued to attack each other and, at the referee's urging, stayed in the middle of the mat.

The last 120 seconds of the match took a long time to play out. Juri looked very tired, and in order to sneak a bit of rest, he kept pulling at the tape on his chin, causing his cut to bleed and forcing the ref to stop the match. I was getting frustrated.

With just over a minute left, I scored my first point on a takedown to close the gap to 2–1. We came back to the center, and I scored another point when Juri was cautioned for not being aggressive—it's called "fleeing a hold." Since I was attacking, I got the point, tying the score at 2–2. So we went to overtime.

"You're going to win this match," Fraser said. "Keep the pressure on, but don't make a mistake. He's wiped out. He's gonna get called for passivity."

For the first time ever in my career, a caution was called in overtime—on Juri. I had worn him down and he didn't have anything left. I had Juri in an underhook; he barely could stand up. At that point, physically exhausted, he stopped wrestling, the ref penalized him with a caution, and I picked up the point—and the 3–2 win.

Fraser remembers this from the match against Juri: "That was a big match," Fraser said. "They [match officials] wanted the Israeli to get in the final against Karelin. I don't know exactly why, but they thought they would make sure Karelin wins—that stuff happens in wrestling. I just know that the Yugoslavian official wanted Rulon to lose. It's just a part of the sport, a part of the game. You have to not only fight to win the match, but you have to fight the politics. Midway through the second period, Rulon was completely dominating the guy. The referee was calling them out of bounds before they were even out of bounds, because if a guy is chased out of bounds two or three times, they get penalized a point for fleeing. The referee was trying to protect this guy by blowing his whistle early. But Rulon got the Israeli gassed, so much so that the guy was falling on himself. I knew it was only a matter of time before he fell completely. The guy was dead on his feet. That was a great victory. That was a big match for our country too, because the win guaranteed us a medal, at least a silver."

The win over the Israeli put me in the gold medal match against Karelin, who already had made the final. Making that match meant I'd get at least a silver medal. A silver medal! But wait, why not a gold medal?

Wow, I thought, a gold medal, that would be unreal. A farm boy from Wyoming beating the best-ever in the world for a gold medal.

Wouldn't that just be something?

Fifteen

THE MIRACLE ON THE MAT

I WAS FOCUSED as I prepared for Russian legend Alexander Karelin and our gold medal match. A victory for Karelin would give the Russian a fourth straight Olympic gold medal. Both IOC President Juan Antonio Samaranch and former U.S. Secretary of State Henry Kissinger were on hand to present Karelin's gold medal, the only time of the 2000 Games that Samaranch would award a medal. The presence of such dignitaries told me, the coaches, and everyone else on my team—everyone in the stands, even—that they believed this match was a foregone conclusion. The most celebrated and most decorated wrestler of Olympic history, Russia's Alexander Karelin, would get his gold medal from the brass.

I actually was offended. I'd had a lifetime of being overlooked, underestimated, and denied attention. If I let this go, it would be just another of those memories. No. Not this time.

Yes, making that match against Karelin meant I'd get at least a silver medal. But I didn't care about silver. In fact, silver would be worse than not medaling at all, I told myself, especially considering all those times—high school, Ricks, even at Nebraska—that I lost one match that kept me from a perfect season or NCAA championship.

Me being here right now, in Sydney, on this mat—this was the Olympics to me, not the favorites who repeat their world title from the year before, or the names we see year in and year out. It is one person rising to the occasion, someone we have never heard about. He might be a swimmer from a little-known country just finishing a race, a ski jumper from a snowless country just landing a jump. Or maybe, just maybe, he's an unknown farm boy from a tiny Wyoming town barely visible on most maps, beating the most dominant force at the Olympics—summer or winter—for the past twelve years.

I knew how strong and focused Karelin was, yet I didn't buy any of the hype that he was superhuman. I had carried cows across icy farm fields. I had survived my brother's death and our barn's burning. I had gone to college, and graduated, for crying out loud—don't tell me about long odds. My optimism might have outrun my ability several miles ago, but my faith and my dreams are still mine to do with what I want. I also knew that if I was going to accomplish my dreams, and be successful, it meant winning this match, no matter who the opponent was.

I kept focusing on what was working for me. My upbringing. My faith. My family. And my country. Add to that the fact that Karelin had to wrestle three times that day, and I only had to wrestle twice. It had been reversed the day before, with me wrestling three matches, and Karelin two. I felt like my matches had been tougher, though, because Karelin's mystique wore guys out before they even met him on the mat. He hadn't been pushed, at least not consistently, in any of his Sydney matches. I don't know if it was his physical or mental dominance, but I felt that his path to the final match had far fewer obstacles than mine. My obstacles had made me stronger: I had seen every move, every attack I could've imagined. I knew Karelin hadn't been attacked like that, hadn't had to wrestle to survive like I had, hadn't had to rally from a one-point deficit in the final minute of a match as I had. Those moments had made me better, stronger, and more prepared for this match. Plus, Karelin couldn't have been as mentally prepared for me—or at least not as ready as I was for him—because he had seen me struggle as recently as the semifinal match.

Before the final, I had an hour to rest. I went back to a United States Olympic Committee hotel room where we could go relax. I was by myself, because no one really knew who I was—yet.

"What a fun place to be," I thought to myself as I considered where I was, the atmosphere, the surroundings—and what was at stake. Almost everyone else was counting down the time to Karelin's final coronation as the best ever in this sport, arguably the most dominant athlete in Olympic sport history. Not many people even knew it was a Wyoming farm boy who was left in his path.

When I got to the room, the first thing I did was call my friends back home to let them know I was in the final.

Everyone already knew, but hopes weren't that high because Karelin still stood in the way.

Just three years my senior, Karelin was a legend, and his reputation was boosted by fans and writers around the globe. Our sport was not often mentioned in the Olympic preview editions of magazines and newspapers, but when it was, Karelin was always the focus of the story. *Time Magazine Europe* thought Karelin was a lock for gold in Sydney, illustrating his mythical status with a story about how he carried a five-hundred-pound refrigerator, alone, up eight flights of stairs and then adding: "Humans have even less of a chance against Karelin, 32, a super-heavy-weight Greco-Roman wrestler who has won gold medals in each of the past three Summer Games. In fact, the Siberian native has never lost in international competition. His streak extends 13 years, an astounding record. No wonder Karelin is a 'bogatyr'—a folk hero—in Russia, where he represents his home town in the Duma (the Russian parliament) and holds the rank of colonel in the customs police."

The wrestling Web site GrapplersWorld.com wrote that Karelin was in a class all by himself heading into Sydney: "A horror fiction writer could not conjure up a more imposing human being. With looks any Holly-wood director would kill for, Karelin is the real deal. No man in the history of wrestling has owned the sport like he has, and no man has made cowards out of otherwise supreme athletes like he has. There is simply no way to verbally capture what Karelin can physically do to his opponents. From his unbelievable training regimen to his reverse body lift, he has a lock on the Greco-Roman

heavyweight division with no signs of ever relin-
quishing it."

Trying to nap, I thought about all of this. When a
friend called fifteen minutes before I had to return to
the wrestling arena, I decided to stay awake and get
focused.

I thought about how this was almost too good to be
true. I thought about what could be: Rulon, I asked
myself, what if. . . .

Yet, I had to wrestle *Alexander Karelin*. I should have
been overwhelmed, but I wasn't at all.

I walked back for my match. The roads were crowded,
almost jammed with people, but I walked alone and probably looked like just another American tourist, carrying
my gym bag, wearing shorts and a T-shirt, looking for the
next buffet. In fact, I was looking so ragged that I probably
looked like a bum. I saw a carnival and a bunch of people
along the harbor near the city park. For some reason, that
struck a chord in me: a carnival. Chaos and fun. Wild
rides. As I crossed the final street, a thought entered my
mind and I began to smile.

"You know, I could beat this guy," I thought.
"Wouldn't that be a carnival? A wild ride?"

After walking in through the athletes' entrance, I had
to be escorted back to the wrestling area. I had gone from
thinking I had a chance to actually thinking I'd win. If
that happened, everyone but Secretary Kissinger and President Samaranch would join me in orbit.

"If I can go out there and do everything right, I can be
successful," I said to myself. I had convinced myself I was
going to win. I honestly and truly believed it. I didn't

express it publicly, but inside myself, I knew I could open up a whole new world.

I laced up my wrestling shoes and went to work out with my wrestling partner. Prematch workouts get your heart rate up, warm up your muscles, and put you into the right frame of mind to compete. Corey Farkas was still hobbling, but the pushing back and forth got me going.

Corey, a U.S. Air Force sergeant in "real life," asked, "Rulon, what are you going to do after you win the gold medal?"

I thought to myself, "I don't know." I thought about my childhood, being made fun of, laughed at, all those times I didn't know what I could actually do.

I knew Corey was just trying to boost my confidence, but I couldn't answer the question—I'd thought about only the win at that point, not about one millisecond afterward. First, the win. I sort of shrugged and walked toward the mats to finish getting ready.

The freestyle weigh-ins were going on and there was wrestling on three mats. There were still four weight classes to wrestle before Karelin and I would battle for the gold medal.

Forty-five minutes before the match, I was still getting warmed up and had broken a sweat. I wanted to make sure I had every base covered and was prepared for anything.

Karelin showed up late and just hung out for a while. He watched the matches going on, showing little emotion or interest.

In the previous matches, both at the Olympics and World Championships, he had started warming up a half hour before the matches. Not until ten minutes before our match did he stand up, and even then it was only to do a few arm stretches.

"He thinks this is no big deal!" I said to myself in disgust. He didn't know it, but he had a fight on his hands.

Of course, why should he have thought anything else? For Karelin, the only edge he needed was mental, as he had shown time and again during his thirteen-year unbeaten streak.

Dan Chandler came up to me. "Look at Karelin—he's nervous!" he whispered. "He's scared about what you might do to him."

Chandler's a great guy, coach, and friend, and though I'd give him a kidney in a heartbeat, at that moment I wouldn't have bought a used car from him. I shook my head and thought, "Yeah, whatever—Karelin's not scared of anything."

Karelin might have looked nonchalant, but he didn't look scared.

Then America's wrestling legend, the great Dan Gable— one of the most accomplished U.S. freestyle wrestlers, along with Bruce Baumgartner, and one of the coaches of this team—came over to me. We have a running banter because he's freestyle, which allows the use of wrestlers' legs for moves and attacks, and I'm Greco-Roman, which doesn't.

"Hey, Rulon," Gable said, "you haven't been saying things you shouldn't be, have you?"

"About your ankle-biters? No way," I said smiling. Then again, he could've been talking about my comments at our precompetition press conference on September 17, when I had said, "I'm not here for second place, and I'm not here on vacation."

Gable moved closer to me. I don't know if he gave me any kind of chance—it's hard to say, because he knows what legends are made of, and he knew I was a stranger to these fans as much as Karelin was a conquering hero. Still, because I was on his team, Gable shared his thoughts with me. The tone of his voice told me he believed in me. Dan Gable believed I was going to win this match if I wanted it bad enough. Since I believed I wanted it bad enough—well, you can make the conclusion.

"Don't give him too much respect," he said, eyeing Karelin. "You wrestle your match. Do everything you can. This is his last Olympics. That means you have an opportunity to do something no one else ever has. This is for you. And for your country."

I could've climbed the wall of the building after getting that pep talk from Dan Gable.

Karelin still wasn't really taking the match seriously—that much is certain. Another Russian in a different weight class was going for a medal, so Karelin watched that match, and then he watched the ensuing medal ceremonies, almost oblivious to our upcoming match, and to me.

Finally, officials called us over to a staging area, and it was just Karelin and me in a small area that was 15 feet by 12 feet. He stretched his shoulders and neck and walked a little bit. I was running around. I looked at Karelin, and he sort of rolled his eyes as if to say, "Let's get this over with."

Later, some would say that Karelin was at the end of his career, that he wasn't at his peak. But know this: he was ripped with muscle—the kind of guy you'd see in a bodybuilding magazine. He was lean and had that stare—and he hadn't been beaten or even scored upon in Sydney or the previous World Championships, or the previous Olympics in Atlanta in 1996, or the Olympics before that in 1992 in Barcelona, or in Seoul in 1988, so why anyone would question this match, or his resume, is beyond me.

I looked around. The cold war had ended, but this was still *Rocky IV*. This was Rocky, from a hardscrabble upbringing and circumstances, against Ivan Drago, the big powerful Russian whose mere presence left his opponents quaking in their boots.

"You're okay," I said to myself. "Stay focused. Do your job."

The last time I had faced Karelin, he had beaten me 5–0. Three times he had used his famous "reverse lift," where he uses brute strength to lift his opponent from behind, and throws them like a sack of potatoes. Twice I landed on my face, arching into the throws instead of ducking my shoulders, so I'd face-plant into the mat. The first time, my feet came up and kicked me in the back of the head.

Today, I vowed to myself, it would be different.

For other wrestlers, you have a game plan on how to beat them. Karelin had never been beaten, so there was no tried-and-true formula where you could say, "Hey, he lost this match doing this, and lost this one this way to get pinned."

But in that 5–0 loss to him, I had made some mental notes. I couldn't be scared, and I had to compete at his level. Going out scared would get me beat. If I believed I had a shot to win, I *would* have a shot to win. Was that realistic thinking? Probably not. But this much is sure: I hadn't yet wrestled my best match against him.

He was going to get everything I had.

My concern right before the match was simply to keep a good sweat going. The room was so cold, and the officials wanted us to take off our warm-ups long before we went out on the mat. If I lost my sweat and went out there with dry arms, Karelin would get a grip and throw me. He's so physically strong that he could have picked me up, tossed me down, and pinned me. So I worked up my heart rate to keep a sweat.

We were introduced to the crowd. He was the reigning world champion thirteen times over, and a three-time gold medalist. There was no roar, just polite, respectful applause. This was the master going to work. An artist in front of the easel for the last time. An unbreakable record about to get cast in stone.

Karelin chatted with the Finnish referee, who also spoke Russian. Since I didn't speak Russian, I had no idea what they were saying. And I didn't care. I focused only on my positive affirmations. I had come a long way. Though Karelin's physique is very, very impressive and mine might not be, I did have the lungs of someone raised at six thousand feet above sea level in the Wyoming winterland. I had to be willing to commit myself 100 percent to doing what it takes to beat him. The guys he had beaten—in other words, everyone he had faced—either hadn't done that, or the critics were wrong in saying Karelin was no longer the dominating force he'd been for more than a decade.

There was a pause—had they forgotten my name? Then, the silence was broken. A lone voice started the chant, "*U-S-A . . . U-S-A.*" Other voices joined in, a little louder, "*U-S-A, U-S-A!*" Louder still—when had all these Americans come in?

The public-address announcer finished announcing the Russian legend, and then he said, "From the United States, Rulon Gardner."

"*U-S-A! U-S-A!*" The walls of the building were shaking, or maybe, just maybe, it was only me. The hair on my arms was raised. I could've run a marathon. "*U-S-A! U-SA-! U-S-A! U-S-A!*"

I started to get emotional and even felt my eyes start to water. I'm a proud American to begin with, but now, in this one moment in time, I *was* America. They were calling my name still, "*U-S-A . . .*"—that was for me, representing every single citizen who proudly calls America home.

"That's what Karelin really needs to see—tears running down your cheeks," I scolded myself. "Come on, Sunshine. Toughen up. You are representing the Stars and Stripes. Think of the military personnel who have died, and all the ones from home. Think of what your country stands for. You're representing your country against Russia and 'their' world champion. Have some pride! Come on, Sunshine. Fight!"

"*U-S-A! U-S-A!*"

My veins surged with energy, and with anger. I was mad at the world, even my own country members who had bad-mouthed the very American things I love so much. If they didn't like our country, then they didn't like me. If they had been there that day, I'd have taken them all on, too.

A proud, fired-up American was standing there, looking as out of place as one could imagine. I saw Secretary Kissinger, on hand to bask in a Russian's glory. He wouldn't. Not if I had a say in it.

And I did have a say.

Karelin and I looked at each other. His stare was piercing.

I wasn't scared. Neither, of course, was he. I knew I had to tire him out and be aggressive. If I started out half-hearted or unsure of what I was doing, I'd surely lose. Half of his work is smelling the kill, and the rest follows. He wouldn't smell one whiff of fear in me, I knew that much. Yet I couldn't be so aggressive that I'd get pinned like I did against the second-best Russian at the time, Yuri Patri-keev, the month before.

Time to go for gold.

When the match started, I fully expected that I would lose the first passivity, because—while it could go either way—I knew that Karelin would get all borderline calls. That didn't mean he'd get points, it just meant that the referee would give Karelin the choice to be up or down, and he'd take up, to set up his patented reverse lift. We scrambled and were pretty even, but as I expected, I was put down.

"No big deal," I thought as I went down. "You've pre-pared yourself mentally for this. Go down and defend."

Karelin got a pretty good lock on me and got me par-tially up, but he couldn't finish me. Those watching thought I had a good defense, but it was really a horrible defense, because all I was trying to do was get him fatigued.

But it was working.

After the three-minute first period, we were scoreless

as we headed into the second and final period of regulation. The referee flipped the coin, and Karelin got the toss, so he was allowed to lock me up first in the clinch before the action resumed. He put his arms around my torso.

The crowd chanted, again. I had stayed in the match longer than anyone had thought. Surely, the dignitaries were squirming in their seats.

"U-S-A! U-S-A!"

Karelin got this awesome lock on me, really had me good. He could have done whatever he wanted with me, I thought at first.

He didn't.

Still, I had to get my lock. "Action, blue!" the referee called out to me. "Either lock up or I'm going to call you for delay."

Okay, the Finnish ref speaks English. If I couldn't lock up, Karelin would get a point.

The match almost ended at that point when I locked up with the worst lock I could have ever gotten. But I had no choice; either I locked up or I didn't, and if I didn't, he would get two points. Since Karelin hadn't been scored on in a decade, my chances of coming back from being down 2–0 in the final period wouldn't be good. There are politics in this sport, as in any, and I'd have to score at least four points to get even one or two—I knew that for a fact. I couldn't fall into a 1–0 or 2–0 hole.

So Karelin clearly had the advantage. While Karelin had a better lock, he didn't push it. At that moment I believed he didn't want it bad enough; if he had, he would've pushed it and tried to throw me. I realized he believed that only time stood in the way of a win, not me.

"Work! Work!" I chided myself, out loud.

I had to take a chance and scramble. I knew if I could keep him from scoring for one minute, I would get a point, since he had to score—the rule in the clinch is the guy who gets to lock up first (Karelin in this case) has to score, so if he didn't score or didn't take me out of bounds, he'd get a caution and I'd get a point. But that minute, held in that terrible lock, felt like forever.

I had to hold on to my lock, even though he had me halfway out of it. I knew with the inferior lock I had, I would lose the match if I didn't go for it. But I had to neutralize the position. Clearly, Karelin thought I couldn't hold on. I knew I would have to improve my position in order to keep him from scoring. I tried to get my underhook higher—above his underhook. I tried and tried, but couldn't do it. I was working hard and struggling. Perhaps he sensed it.

Twenty seconds into the lock, we got into what I call a little death spin. Against Matt Ghaffari at our Olympic Trials, I beat him in the clinch by putting my left leg inside his legs trying to get underneath his hips. Realistically, when you do that, you should get launched on your head. I tried it on Karelin, expecting him to bring me up and go for his throw.

"Work!" I yelled at myself. "Work!"

Karelin didn't react.

He let me alter my position, thinking he could just keep me under control. We were in a bit of a stalemate, so I decided to take a chance. Being fully committed to beating this guy meant I had to take a chance—now. If there is a time in your life where a decision made within a fraction of a second can change things . . . well, this was my moment.

I took a little underneath jump so I could readjust, so I would be in a position to score by neutralizing his position, forcing the official to give him a caution and awarding me a point. On the other hand, my biggest concern was to not get taken down, and to not let him get me in a position where he could throw me with the reverse lift. I had to keep him neutral. Because his lock was not great this time, I knew I could force the issue, maybe even by breaking his lock. I had equalized him up to that point. He wouldn't win from this lock, I knew for sure.

Suddenly—inexplicably—it was slipping away for Alexander Karelin. I kept holding and squeezing. Something was wrong on his end of it. I held harder. Tighter. I held on as if it were for my life.

His lock started to slip. For a fraction of a second, he had unlocked his hands to get a better grip. Immediately, I unlocked, because I knew if he got a better grip, he would have me and he would throw me.

But the referee saw only my hands break and was ready to award points to Karelin. Another referee, off the mat, said he couldn't make the call, because he didn't see it. The third referee was getting ready to raise his paddle to give Karelin the advantage. Finally, another referee asked to see the video to determine who had unlocked first— Karelin or me.

With the match stopped, the referees huddled and looked at the tape. I had a sinking feeling, because European refs rarely gave the call to Americans.

Amazingly, after watching it on video from several

angles, they saw where Karelin had broken his lock first. *I* knew Karelin had broken first, so it was only a matter of the referees making the right call.

And they did.

"Caution, red!" the referee said. Karelin and I both looked at our singlets hoping to see blue.

"U-S-A! U-S-A!"

Only I was wearing blue.

A point went up on the scoreboard for USA.

The crowd had hit jet-engine decibel levels. I don't know if it was shock or they realized that something *just* might be going on here, but there was a sense that one of those Olympic history moments might be happening before their eyes. "Do you believe in miracles?"

When you hit a point of disbelief, you sit silently in shock, you run away, or you yell at the top of your lungs. All I heard was yelling.

And that was fine with me.

I felt good, because I had a point, but the match was far from over. Yet I knew that if I didn't allow Karelin to score, I would win the match.

"I have five and a half minutes to finish this match off," I thought. I've never run from a match. I've never given up on myself, and I wasn't about to start. When I started to get on top of Karelin, I wiped the sweat from my face to get my focus back to the mat, away from the scoreboard.

"Stick to your game plan," I said to myself. "You're ahead, but you don't stop."

I didn't want to make a mistake and let him stand up, which would give him a point. I knew because of Karelin's skill and reputation that he would take every chance to score if there was a borderline call—there's a little bit of figure skating in our sport in that regard. For so long it had been Karelin breaking his opponents' will, wearing them down mentally and physically. He had always been in control.

Not now. Not against me.

I held on through the end of the second period, and since three points hadn't been scored, we went to overtime, where I continued to dig. I didn't get him as tired as I wanted to, but I used other tactics to control the match. Karelin was doing things totally out of character, such as grabbing at my head. No one had tried that before.

I kept attacking, knowing I needed to display some offense and continue being aggressive, to avoid getting penalized for passivity and to keep him from going on the offensive—he had won many matches against guys who got "deer in the headlight" looks and waited for however he decided to attack next. I had to stay in his face, because I wanted him to know that I wasn't backing down and I wasn't afraid of him.

Just a few moments into overtime, I realized something crucial: Alexander Karelin hadn't prepared for this situation.

You can't take a crash course the day of the final exam, even if you have aced all the tests up to that point. Facing adversity suddenly, you cannot develop a game plan on the fly. I was sticking to my game plan and wasn't backing down. Karelin no longer had a game plan.

I was put down twice more into the starting position in overtime, but Karelin couldn't score either time.

He was getting frustrated. It was at that moment that Karelin himself realized he hadn't prepared for this situation. Worse for him, I was reading his thoughts as he tried to figure out to how to fix this unforeseen circumstance. We were both drenched in sweat, but only I was about to bathe in emotion.

"U-S-A! U-S-A!"

My conditioning was setting in; my high-altitude lungs were allowing me to hold on. I was better prepared than Karelin, and both of us knew it.

But he was still dangerous. I kept working and working him. His body had nothing left and was telling him, "Sorry, you've cashed in everything. You didn't train to come from behind to win."

He needed a shortcut, but the only way he'd get one was if I made a mistake, and I wasn't about to do that. If I made an error, it would leave the door open for him.

The door was shut. And barred.

Three more times he came at me, and three more times I beat him to the contact. Each time, he was surprised. In the last thirty seconds, I kept getting in his face, taking nothing for granted. I could feel from his movements that he was starting to doubt himself, starting to lose strength and confidence. My resolve was only growing. I knew no matter how tired I got, he would be more tired. In my mind, I believed that he was suffering twice as much pain as I was.

With eight seconds left in the match, Karelin put his hands on his hips, and his head bowed.

The thirteen-time world champion and three-time Olympic gold medalist had just conceded victory.

The noise in the arena was deafening, yet all I could hear were the audience's roof-raising chants of "*U-S-A! U-S-A!*"

The clock expired, and the referee lifted my hand.

After the ref let go of my hand, the first thing I did was make a throwing motion. I was throwing away all the negativity over the years, all the times of being told I was stupid, fat, or incompetent. The only thing the naysayers had been right about was that I was different.

Had I believed any of their discouragement over the years, I wouldn't have made it to this moment.

"Doubters and naysayers, this is for you!" I cried to myself.

I almost had to pinch myself in order to gather my thoughts. I worried that FILA, our sport's governing body, would still find a way to give the match, and the gold medal, to Karelin, would find a way to end his career the way everyone had thought it would happen.

I knew I was living proof that anyone could achieve his or her dream if they were willing to put in the work and sacrifice. Then, in a split second, I remembered how heavyweight wrestlers are thought of as big, clumsy, and uncoordinated.

So I did a cartwheel, and then a forward roll.

Still, it had not quite sunk in—I had beaten the unbeatable legend. My coaches ambushed me and gave me an American flag, which I held up proudly. Coach Fraser knew this feeling, having won Greco-Roman Olympic gold in 1984 in Los Angeles. But this was still a new feeling for our country, because mine was only the third gold medal the United States had ever won in Greco (Jeff Blatnick won the second gold, also in LA during 1984).

Coach Fraser later explained for this book how he had felt about my chances heading into the Karelin match: "The first time Rulon wrestled Karelin was in 1997," Fraser said. "Karelin lifted him three times, in midair, and didn't really 'get him' until the last time he threw him. The first two times, Rulon defended against that reverse lift and throw like no one else had. He arched and landed on his face instead of landing on his back. It's painful, but also hard to do, because you know you are going to have your face smashed into the mat. Plus, it puts a lot of pressure on your back. He did that the first two times Karelin lifted him. Finally, Karelin got him and won the match. But Rulon gave him a match. Rulon had improved a hundred-fold since 1997.

"Rulon had to wrestle a perfect match—completely work to his strengths—and had to capitalize on Karelin's weaknesses; and he had to beat the officials. The officials were not going to let Karelin get beat. That may sound kind of strange, but it's true. To beat Karelin not only was a fantastic feat man to man, but he had to beat everybody else, the 'officials' and the system, FILA. Thank God, the right call was made—after they had made it incorrectly in the clinch, and they went to the video, which clearly showed it was Rulon's point . . . I had seen too many times through the years, they blatantly gave the call to Karelin no matter what, not just in clinch situations, but anywhere guys were close to scoring on Karelin.

"He had three chances on top of Rulon, and Rulon stopped him three times," Coach Fraser said. "One of our strategies—which I credit to Rulon, which he had to execute—was to tire Karelin on the mat. We noticed he'd go to his reverse lift and the common defense for the guy on the bottom is to turn the body hard into it, and Karelin has a counter when people do that. When they turn too far into it to defend the reverse lift, Karelin runs into them and knocks them onto their back. It's not a spectacular thing, but it serves the same purpose of getting guys to their back, and he pins them with that. What we decided to do with Rulon was to not defend so hard that way, which would allow him to knock into you with the follow-up move. Give him a shot at reverse-lifting you, but don't turn the hip in to defend it. Rulon did it perfectly. He countered by moving more around the 'corner' as opposed to turning into him and setting up Karelin's counter.

"It was a tenacious fight the whole way through, and since there has to be three points scored in regulation—and it was 1–0 at that point—it went to overtime. In the overtime with them on their feet, I could see Karelin getting tired, but he was still in it. It wasn't until thirty seconds or so were left in overtime that Karelin glanced at the clock, which was near our corner, to check the time. I had never in my life, in so many years of watching him, seen the look of desperation and defeat on his face. He looked over and it was like he was saying, 'Oh, no, thirty seconds,' and he was so tired. He hadn't accepted he was going to lose, but he knew he was in deep trouble.

"I thought Rulon had a good chance to beat Karelin at the Olympics—I had thought that for a couple of years. Again, it's one thing to say that—because Rulon had to do all the preparation and then execute in the match—so it's another thing to do it. So I don't think I'd go so far as to say I predicted it, but I truly did believe Rulon could beat him . . . I don't know what everyone else thought—I can't speak for anyone else but myself—so I don't want to sound like this great prophet, but I knew Karelin could be beat, if Rulon wrestled the right match against the guy. Rulon still had to do the things needed to beat him. I think the fact that Rulon went ahead of him and won the clinch and went ahead 1–0—not that that would bother Karelin, because he had been behind before—what was really the shocker for Karelin was that he was behind someone with Rulon's capabilities: the conditioning that Rulon had is what shocked Karelin. Most heavyweights wrestle slow and methodical. That's not Rulon's style. Karelin's not used to that high-tempo, fast pace. That's what won it for Rulon, the fact that he could stop Karelin's reverse lift and keep a high tempo that got Karelin tired and kept him from doing anything."

When I came off the mat after having beaten Karelin, the Cuban, Turkish, and all of the other wrestlers from other countries came running up to hug me. No matter who slays Goliath—a prior medalist, a contender, or even a cow-milker from Wyoming—everyone wants to embrace David. It was more than just the win; the entire journey represented a great deal to them. Turning adversity into success, on the biggest possible world stage.

We went back in for the medals presentation. From the top step of the podium—the gold medalist spot—I leaned over to Karelin and whispered in his ear. "I just want to let you know that you are the best wrestler who has ever been," I told him. "You are the best. You are the man, and you always will be. I thank you for the opportunity to wrestle you."

As shocked as the world and the media were, no one was more shocked than Karelin himself. Except, maybe, me.

Samaranch awarded me the gold medal, and I watched the Stars and Stripes, my country's flag, be hoisted first. Later, people pointed out that I appeared to struggle with the words to the "Star Spangled Banner," but that's not true. It's my favorite song, and I know the words by heart. I was struggling with what had just happened, how many obstacles I had overcome to reach an impossible goal. I actually thought this was a dream—too good to be true—and I had to catch myself from extending an arm to touch Karelin's head and make sure this was happening. I looked down and saw the back of Karelin's head.

"He's down there and I'm up here," I thought to myself. "That means I beat him!"

After we were awarded our medals and started to step down from the medal stand, Karelin looked over at me.

"You are very good wrestler," he said quietly. It meant a lot, that acknowledgment.

He nodded his head and said nothing more.

The IOC's drug control people took us for testing and again I saw Karelin. I didn't know what to say, and I had a feeling that no matter what I said, he didn't want to hear it. His life had changed; instead of going out of on top— he's still the best ever, by record and accomplishments— he faced the desolation of a career-ending loss. The plan was for him to go down as the best of all time and with his streak alive, not to go down in defeat.

I was blind to the fact that my life was going to

change. In a few hours, the sun would rise in the United States and America would learn about the improbable series of events that had rocked the sporting world Down Under.

I talked to several media gatherings. I said a bunch of stupid things about the stars lining up—as if I had any idea about astrology! The moment just hadn't sunk in yet.

At the postmatch press conference, I fielded more than a hundred questions, many about my background, which I was proud to share with the reporters—about Star Valley, Wyoming, our huge family, and the farm. One of the reporters, though, asked me if, as I entered the Olympics, I thought I could beat Karelin. The truth is, I never thought about beating Karelin. I thought only about preparing for each match. I trained hard and focused on things I could take care of, or I'd never have made it to the medal round. So if I were even to have the chance to battle Karelin, I had a lot of hurdles to clear first.

Dan Chandler ran with me out of the media area.

"Coach, what just happened here?" I asked.

"Rulon, I have no idea," he said, and slapped my back.

Sixteen

Who Am I Now?

MY FEET WERE *soaking wet and I was shivering.*

I hadn't slept in twenty hours, and I had no idea where I was. I shook my head and sat up in the water.

Trying to get up, I nearly fell. The water was unbelievably cold, and the shivering was getting worse. My body hurt from head to toe.

I was in the bathtub in my room at the Olympic Village in Sydney, Australia.

"Come to Sydney to catch hypothermia?" I jokingly asked myself after waking up from an hourlong nap in the bathtub.

But what was I doing here? During an hour in the tub, I had dreamed that I had beaten Russian legend Alexander Karelin to win the gold medal. Carefully, I got out of the tub. Every body part hurt, and I could barely move my legs. I wrapped a towel around myself and dried off with two other towels.

"If it's true that I beat Karelin, the gold medal will be sitting on my bed," I told myself.

I hurried out to my room, and there it was on the bed: the gold medal for winning the heavyweight championship at the 2000 Olympic Games in Sydney.

The special ed survivor, finally, was as good as gold.

As the first twenty-four hours after the match unfolded and America caught up with what had happened at 3:00 A.M. Mountain Time, things started to blur. I talked to more and more media, yet the requests for more interviews were coming in at the speed of light. I went to a USA Wrestling party at a venue right next to the Olympic Stadium and visited with everyone. They were going nuts. Seeing all my friends and family so happy was really cool. KSL, the TV station out of Salt Lake City that had come to follow me, did a twenty-minute interview with me that night. They flew around the world to follow me, one of the bigger longshots at the Games—what a sell that must've been to the person who signed the expense check! The least I could do was give them all the time they needed; I knew it was their station that my neighbors in Star Valley would be watching.

I went to track star Michael Johnson's Olympic party at Sydney's Planet Hollywood, and then did an interview with CNN. I went on the radio with ESPN's Dan Patrick— it was in the early hours of the morning in Australia, but it was daytime in the United States, where Mr. Patrick's radio show was being broadcast. That was a lot of fun.

At 5:30 A.M., I headed back to my room to go to bed. After falling asleep in the bathtub, I woke up and realized that what had seemed like a dream—what was too good to be true—was reality.

My plan had been to go back to America the next day. But I was told that I might be the flagbearer for the Closing Ceremonies. The flagbearer is chosen by athlete vote and they had voted for me. What an honor. That flag means so much to me. Carrying it in my hands and leading our team into the Closing Ceremonies was both a responsibility and a privilege.

All that went through my mind as I picked up that flag and led our team in for the Closing Ceremonies was, "U-S-A! U-S-A!"

Beating someone who can safely be called an Olympic legend changed my life. I did appearances on TV talk shows with Jay Leno, Rosie O'Donnell, David Letterman, and even Oprah. Leno was phenomenal, the nicest guy you could ever imagine, in addition to being really funny. I think Oprah is a great example of success and determination, a wonderful model for every person who has aspirations of reaching great heights through hard work.

Letterman was a little different, and I feel bad to this day that we parted less than friendly. They flew me to New York to do a "Top 10" list about the perks that go along with being the Olympic heavyweight gold medalist and beating a legend. I found some of the listed items offensive, like one about how I'd get "longer lap dances." I wasn't about to say those things and embarrass my family, friends, and church, not to mention the younger kids who looked up to me. I don't want them saying they want "to win a gold medal so I can get lap dances." I know it sounds like I'm on a podium preaching, but being someone's "monkey" is selling out, and once you do something like that, it's never forgotten. I know my mother would've been very disappointed in me to see me saying those words on TV—knowing full well that I hadn't written them and they weren't my beliefs—but I would've been even more disappointed in myself.

So I had them change or modify a couple of the items. I heard that Letterman was not happy with my decision, and I wasn't able to talk to him. That was a disappointment, because I've enjoyed his show for a long time, but I had to be true to myself, and my faith, first. It really wasn't a hard choice. I had done the *Tonight Show* the night before, and had been told that people seldom do these two shows "back to back," because they are competitors for the same audience. Maybe that could've been part of the friction. I just thought it would be fun to meet Mr. Letterman. He's got a place not all that far up the interstate from Star Valley in Choteau, Montana. Maybe we'll go fishing sometime when he's out visiting the Treasure State.

Rosie O'Donnell was great. She called me a "cutie-patootie" (yes, that would be the first time I'd heard myself referred to that way) and gave me a wave runner. As an avid outdoorsman, that was a great gift. I did the Jim Rome radio show several times. Other regional television and radio interviews and appearances came by the dozen. The print requests were even more numerous than that. I did a magazine shoot with famed photographer Annie Leibovitz, who has put an image to some of the most significant aspects and people of pop culture. I was photographed with the beautiful and intelligent Katie Couric. In the photo, I held her up over my head.

"I hope I'm not too heavy," she said, with a smile.

"Oh, please, I wrestle three hundred-pounders for a living," I replied. She was just adorable, and could not have been nicer. One of the neatest parts about this media whirlwind was meeting a lot of interesting people. Even though I was getting to meet famous people, I wasn't meeting them as a fan, I was meeting them on a level field; I was able to talk to them as though we were regular people, asking them questions, answering theirs. Yeah, I had done something on a world stage that was televised around the globe. But I wanted everybody to see that I was just a regular guy, a lot like the majority of people who never appear in TV or the paper, whom I admire so much for their hard work and dedication.

One of the highlights of the whole experience was returning home to Star Valley, to a parade attended by thousands and thousands of people who came from Afton, all the surrounding Star Valley communities, and as it turned out, from across Wyoming, and even out of state from Utah, Colorado, Idaho, and several other states, I was told.

At the parade, I talked to people who had driven hours to come see me. I saw a group of kids approaching me, and they didn't look familiar.

"Where are you guys from?" I asked.

"We're from Rawlins" (a town almost three hundred miles away in central Wyoming,) one of them said. "A bunch of us drove over."

You have to be kidding me, I thought, that's more than a four-hour drive. Having people do that for you is very humbling and touching.

The media did a lot for me in publicizing my win over Karelin and telling my story to the public. I ended up getting a lot of good, in-depth coverage. There's an irony about the media and how it deals with athletes: athletes often complain that the media is too negative or writes slanderous things about them, doesn't quote them correctly, or focuses on things the athlete doesn't want to talk about. In turn, the press gets frustrated with athletes who have rubber-stamp answers to questions. That makes the reporters' jobs harder to do, because they can't keep writing the same old thing over and over again. Athletes who speak only in clichés or not being completely honest make for boring and repetitious stories. I was fortunate because I really had no prejudices going into my dealings with the media. I talked to the press like I would anyone else: here's me—the good, the bad, and the ugly. Here's what happened, here's my opinion about what happened. That was it.

To be honest, I didn't have a lot of prepackaged answers, because I hadn't been interviewed a lot before the Sydney Olympics. But I had been raised to tell the truth and be pretty open, so I just shared stories about how I grew up, what influenced me, and how I built on everything to reach this apex. I even heard some fellow athletes say, "The media loves you." The truth is, I never had a problem with the press in any aspect. Some of the questions were ones I had heard before, but many of the reporters asking these questions weren't at all the other interviews, so they either had not heard the answer I had given, or wanted to hear the answer themselves. I respect reporters who want firsthand information, because quoting from some other reporter's story often leads to inaccuracies. If a reporter had not heard the original discussion, he or she would not know what the atmosphere had been like during the interview. Was I in a hurry? Had I just been talking about a friend who had recently passed away? Had I been in the euphoria of a win? Of course, I don't have to deal with the media every single day like pro athletes do, so maybe that familiarity breeds a contempt that I don't have any understanding of. After all, I'm involved in a sport that usually gets most of its attention only every four years.

When I won the gold medal and beat Karelin, that was the peak of the mountain in a lot of people's eyes. It was like, "What else could he possibly do now?" Star Valley, my hometown, Afton, and I enjoyed the post-Olympics honeymoon while it lasted. Every news account of my gold medal win mentioned the farm boy from Star Valley. The town reveled in the attention. We were on the map—our hardworking, blue-collar lifestyle; our no-excuses, here-are-the-cards-you-were-dealt-so-do-the-best-you-can mentality. I was, and am, very proud to be from the Star Valley of western Wyoming. The land and the people and the lifestyle all shaped me into who I am. I can imagine no other place like it on earth.

It is my hometown.

The people, the land, the lifestyle—it all helped shaped me, and it all defines me still.

It's important to note that I would still be the person I am whether I had won a gold medal, or taught junior high school, or coached a wrestling team. I've always wanted to take the lessons I learned on the farm, take the work ethic and values I absorbed from my family, my community, and my church, and make a positive contribution to society. I will carry those lessons and values with me wherever I go, whatever I do.

After the 2000 Sydney Games, the *Tonight Show* did something really neat when Jay Leno had me on the show. The *Tonight Show*'s producers put up a direct satellite link to the Star Valley High School gym; a big part of the town turned up to voice their pride in what we had done in Sydney.

It was the best feeling—not just the fact that the town was proud of me, but also knowing that they were being recognized for what they were and how they lived. It touched me deeply that they were proud of my accomplishment, but it meant more to me to see our blue-collar lifestyle—a lifestyle that feeds America and much of the rest of the world—receive well-deserved attention. Even with that brief attention, I still think Star Valley is one of the best-kept secrets on earth.

After an incredible post-2000 Olympic Games honeymoon period, my hometown area of Star Valley and I struggled to come to grips with my celebrity.

Soon, too soon, the talk around town became, "What could he possibly do next?" That got my attention.

I compare it to a football player coming out of a small town and becoming a successful big-time college player. The town embraces the player, and he's the poster boy for all that is great about the community. Then the player makes it to the NFL and becomes rich and successful. The town starts to feel left behind and some bitterness emerges. Yet the reality is just the opposite: the townspeople have done plenty with their lives, raising a family, contributing to their community. The football player simply took a different step, met the next challenge, and moved in a different direction.

Though I know it evolved over time, it still seemed that suddenly I was "Rulon Gardner, the Olympic wrestling champion" and not "Rulon Gardner, Wyoming farm boy from Star Valley." The truth is, I was both of those people rolled into one. As a consequence of getting a lot of media attention, my name became more familiar and sometimes the press no longer mentioned my hometown. It seemed to some that it was all about Rulon Gardner, not about Star Valley. It never changed for me or for those who really knew me, those who really supported me.

Still, I was surprised to see some backlash, even some that was reported in the media. Stories about how some in Star Valley were ready for me to be out of the spotlight and be a "normal person" again. I never asked to be well known, and I certainly didn't have any say in how the media referred to me.

So becoming suddenly famous was a hard thing for me to make sense of. Don't get me wrong; I enjoy it. But growing up almost friendless, being picked on for being "dumb" or "fat," left me alone a lot of the time. Although I wasn't allowed to go to dances or parties, I was never invited to them either. My schoolmates didn't ask me to come to their sleepovers or to play in their yards. Even if

I couldn't have accepted, it would have been nice to be asked. Except for Rick Johnson, I think people liked me because they wanted something from me. It's difficult for me to accept that some people didn't see anything in me to like until I came home with an Olympic gold medal.

When I returned to Star Valley after Sydney in 2000, several people looked me up or sought me out to apologize for the bullying they did to me growing up. While forgiveness and reconciliation are important, I wondered what made them wait until after I had won a gold medal to bring this up? Why not when I was in college in Ricks and was back in Star Valley regularly? Why not when they saw me around town in the summer when I was back from Nebraska? It seemed so odd to me that they would wait until I was in the spotlight to come to me to tell me how sorry they were for calling me "Stupid," "Fatso," and "Dumbo," or for doing mean imitations of how I read, or cruelly teased me for being big. Did my winning an Olympic medal suddenly make me worthy of being in their world? Were we suddenly equals because I had been on the *Tonight Show?* What was the motivation? Don't get me wrong; I like the idea of healing and burying the hatchet. But it would have meant a lot more if they would have sought me out when I was in high school, or maybe back from college, and said, "Hey, what I did to you was wrong. I'm sorry. I hope we can put it behind us." Because whether they realized it or not, I came back the same person I had been when I lived in Star Valley and while I was in college. Apparently my stature post-Sydney had made me more worthy of being treated like a human in those people's eyes.

* * *

As I was growing up, girls never showed any interest in me and guys didn't want to be my friend. People ask, "Well, what did you like to do then when you were younger?" My answer is, I liked to milk cows. It was a chore that I was good at and it helped the family. It was a skill, something I could get better at. It was also solitary work that allowed me to develop a great imagination, so I didn't always miss having friends around. When you're out there milking early in the morning or changing pipe and you're by yourself, you daydream. I never dreamed I'd be in a situation like this, writing a book after winning a pair of Olympic medals, appearing on national TV, becoming a spokesman for my sport. Not having friends to bounce ideas off of meant I had to pull myself into a shell and focus deep within myself and think about what it would take to reach my goals. While I am grateful to Star Valley for mobilizing and donating—very gener-ously—to help send my family to the 2000 Olympics, it's awfully hard to forget that until that time, I was just the dumb, fat kid from the farm.

When you achieve something out of the ordinary in the public's eyes—when you break the shackles of expecta-tions and achieve your dream—you are placed on an astoundingly high pedestal. Role-model status comes with it, and for reasons I've already mentioned, I was never comfortable with that. However, I'm flattered to be seen as a resource, or as someone who fought through adversity to reach a seemingly unattainable goal. I'm happy that people see strength in me, because it came directly from my parents. If you want to talk about adversity, talk about my parents trying to raise nine kids on a small family farm, dealing with situations they couldn't control, from the weather to the up-and-down farm economy.

So the circumstances, the attitude, and the support surrounding my run to make the 2004 Olympic Team was definitely different "back home" in Star Valley than what it had been leading up to the 2000 Games. To be honest, at times it hurt to hear negative comments.

My ultimate goal is to return to Wyoming and grow older in Star Valley, enjoy the people who helped shape my life, came to our aid when our family barn burned, and were our neighbors. Those people knew me before all the fame and attention came, and those people will remain my friends for the rest of my life. I enjoy that time back home. And the reality is, that not much has changed, because we have the common bond and values that such a rural, family-oriented upbringing instills in us. To this day I'm still amazed how many people in Star Valley cared about me, showed up for the parade in 2000, and kept me in their thoughts when I was stranded. Having that kind of upbringing has kept me grounded when I needed it the most—not everyone back home knows that, because they weren't there with me at times, but that is the truth. My circle will be completed once I am back home, for good, living contentedly among the people who have known me the longest.

Seventeen

VALIDATION: DEFENDING THE GOLD AT THE 2001 WORLD CHAMPIONSHIPS

WINNING THE 2000 Olympic gold medal meant I had climbed an incredible peak. While I realized the importance, and significance, of beating the "unbeatable" Alexander Karelin, I had no illusions about the next peak, which loomed just months away in 2001. That peak might not be higher than the one I was on, but it was steeper. The 2001 World Championships would feature several wrestlers who had not been in my pool at the 2000 Olympics. These were wrestlers who wanted a shot at me, to prove, at least in their minds, that it could've been them battling Karelin in Sydney.

Some strange things happened after the Olympics and before the Worlds. I began to learn public-speaking skills and, to pursue commercial opportunities, I relaxed my wrestling and training programs. My wrestling skills fell off considerably. Consequently, I had less than impressive results at several 2001 Grand Prix events. I was beaten twice in my first post-Olympic tournament in Hungary, once by Mihaly Deak-Bardos of Hungary, and then by the top Ukrainian wrestler, Georgiy Soldadse.

Later that year, at the Polish Grand Prix, I had a pretty good draw. The event itself was held on the grounds of a castle—an amazing setting. The ground wasn't even, so if you took a step, you lost your balance on the mats, which had been placed in the grass yard. Deak beat me again. I wasn't sharp, and the pack behind me was hungry to get a piece of me. I knew that if I was going to defend my Olympic gold medal by winning the 2001 World Championships, I'd have to get back up to speed, and in a hurry. I returned to the Olympic Training Center to train with even more passion than I did leading up to 2000. Between appearances and speeches, I trained on the road, got in the gym late at night or early in the morning. Whatever it took.

I learned from those early 2001 tournaments that I was not used to being the favorite. In school, I had always been the slow one, the big, plodding kid. In high school, I didn't win the state wrestling tournament—wasn't even the varsity heavyweight wrestler—until my senior year, so I never faced the pressure of repeating. In two-year junior college, I didn't win the National Junior College Championship until my second year. And at Nebraska, I never made it to the NCAA finals. While I did have several U.S. national titles under my belt, this was something different. This was as big as it got, and, as the Olympic champ, I had a target on my back.

So I'd have to be the best I could be. Which meant being better than I'd ever been before.

Even better than I had been in 2000.

* * *

I was really looking forward to September, when the World Championships were to be held in Patras, Greece. The event would be a nice precursor to the 2004 Olympics, which were to be held in Athens.

But then September 11, 2001, changed America and the world.

I was in Fort Wayne, Indiana, studying and attending a training class for speaking engagements. Someone told us about what had happened while the class was being held. I turned on the news. I was shocked and hurt. I'm from a conservative area in the West, where the flag is still flown proudly and being an American is something we take a deep pride in every day. We say the Pledge of Allegiance with pride, pray in school, and while we're not always in agreement with what the government does, we're of the belief that it is a government for the people, by the people—which means us. We root for American teams whether we like the players or not. And we don't like U.S.-bashing from other countries. September 11 shook me, like it did everyone, to the core. It was an attack on every American, our way of life, our children, our families and friends. It was an attack on our Founding Fathers, on the soldiers who have served bravely in both just and questionable wars, on schoolteachers and doctors, ranchers and farmers, everyone.

I ended up giving a speech that night in Fort Wayne. It was very emotional, but I thought it was important that as many Americans talk to other Americans as possible, that we reaffirm our love for our country and support for one another. Being the leading nation in the world leaves us open to cheap shots from those who won't meet us face-to-face. We had to pull together to even survive this thing, much less try to make sense of it all. The world was in a dangerous moment, and healing would take a long time. In the interim, we had to lean on one another, as Americans have done over the centuries in other crises, from the Revolutionary and Civil Wars to the Depression and the World Wars.

The 2001 World Championships obviously, and rightfully, were postponed and shifted to the back burner. The event was rescheduled for December.

Many aspects of life changed after 9/11, travel arrangements being one of the foremost. The head of security for the United States Olympic Committee was Larry Buendorf, a former Secret Service agent who is very bright and who had assembled an incredible staff. Larry and his staff made sure that all we had to worry about was wrestling.

"We'll handle everything else," he said, and we knew he meant it. The Secret Service, like other similar agencies, has a specific job—protecting Americans. In the Service's protection might be Democrats or Republicans, but it doesn't matter: they are all Americans. The agents would take a bullet to save a president they'd never vote for. They do it because they are citizens of the United States, because it's their job, and to live in this land of freedom and liberty means there are some who have to step up—the Secret Service, the troops, the police—and be willing to give their lives to protect that freedom. Soldiers might not fully agree with the policy they're charged with carrying out, yet they put on their boots and helmets, and with a patch of the flag on their arm and the American ideals in their heart, they do what they are told.

Postponing the 2001 Worlds gave me a little more time to heal from the injuries I had already suffered after the Olympics. Just like in 2000, when I wrestled with a badly torn groin muscle, I was dealing with various ailments. On the road with my training partner, Matt Lamb, I broke my right index finger at the knuckle during a practice match. Then, at a wrestling clinic in Pennsylvania, we were on a cold mat, which made the surface harder than usual, and I partially separated my left shoulder, which is my main shoulder for throwing. Wrestling with another training partner, I broke a rib in my back. I was getting ready to throw him, and I thought, "Wait, don't hurt yourself," so I flipped around and landed on my back, with his fist under me, breaking the rib. At Worlds, the doctors said they couldn't do anything about my hand, and nothing for my shoulder, but they could deaden my rib so it wouldn't hurt as much

So we went to Greece, and I had a lot of American pride in my heart. The events of 9/11 provided me with patriotic inspiration. I already had plenty of motivation. I had to prove that 2000 was not a fluke. I had to validate myself against pool opponents as well as medal round opponents.

Before 2000, I could go to weigh-ins and bracket draws relatively unnoticed. That all changed at the 2001 World Championships. Everything was different. All eyes were on me. Some of the wrestlers were really nice and congratulated me on my upset of Karelin. Others weren't as happy. Some, especially those from Eastern-bloc countries or from former parts of the Soviet Union, took my win over Karelin as a personal affront, an attack on their way of life and on Karelin's reputation as the greatest Olympic wrestler ever. Their attitude didn't bother me; I wanted to face every one of the best four or five wrestlers in the world. I was ready for the draw.

And I got exactly what I wished for—the toughest draw I could've imagined. Coach Fraser said it "could not have been tougher" if the tournament officials had deliberately drawn it up. In the six years I'd been competing internationally, I'd never had a draw anywhere near as tough as this one. Of course it was a random draw, so there were no politics involved. Like I said, I wanted the toughest road; it's where I do my best work.

So bring it on.

In my pool were two of the best in the business. Israeli Juri Yevseychyc had been a medal favorite on many occasions. When I faced Juri at the Olympics, he had been ahead of me 2–0 before I rallied late to beat him 3–2.

The other top wrestler in my pool was Georgiy Soldadse, the Ukrainian, who was very familiar with Karelin and was a staple on the world scene.

While I wanted to win every match at Worlds, and thus be the world champion, I always wanted to win by wrestling my best in every match. I didn't want to give up points. I didn't want to lose my focus for even a second. I didn't want to make any mistake that would cost me a point, the match, or the championship. Since the World Championships are not held during Olympic years, a gold medal here, in effect, would be repeating as world champion.

I opened the championship with Yevseychyc. Though it was tight, I kept control of the match and won 3–0.

Next up would be Soldadse. As part of that former Soviet system, Soldadse, I was certain, had an axe to grind.

Coach Fraser felt similarly: "The match that I was most nervous about, besides the Russian, was the Ukrainian, the guy Rulon wrestled second, because that's a tough, tough guy and very good wrestler, who hasn't gotten a lot of recognition, because he hasn't won the Worlds yet—but he's right there."

I could sense a heightened excitement in the arena when Soldadse was introduced. The crowd knew this was his chance to validate his successful career and to avenge his former countryman's stunning loss to me in Sydney. But I was very tightly focused, and once again I pulled out a 3–0 win.

I made it out of my pool, and then all heck was ready to break loose.

A revenge match, a chance at redemption, whatever you want to call it—the quarterfinal matchup placed me against Russian Yuri Patrikeev, Karelin's successor. This was the same guy who pinned me—in just eighteen seconds, the fastest pin I'd given up in my entire career—two months before the Olympics at the Russian's own tournament. In fact, a lot of people thought Patrikeev would have had the best chance at gold in 2000 if Karelin had been taken out of the equation. My own feeling was that Patrikeev could harbor no realistic ideas of replacing the legend until the legend decided to step aside. Karelin had been a mentor, or at least the wrestling role model, for Patrikeev for at least a dozen years. What better way to prove he was more than an understudy than to repeat his winning performance over the guy who knocked off Karelin?

In other words, Patrikeev had strong motivation to beat me. He had everything to gain, and nothing to lose.

Though Karelin had long overshadowed Yuri on the world scene, Yuri was still considered one of the world's best wrestlers. He learned and used all the little wrestling "tricks" that were outside the rules but not often called. He had started using an illegal move called "knee taps"—using his knee to bump and thus lock his opponent's kneecap, making the opponent less mobile because the knee is locked straight. The match started and, too quickly, I was down 1–0 on a passivity call. I needed to throw him to get back in the lead and take control of the match. I wanted to make sure there was no question in the officials' eyes, so I took a double underhook, which would work to my advantage against Yuri, who is a smaller wrestler, but more agile and quicker—and stronger. I picked him up to throw him, but I didn't rotate my back through the move. He retained control and was up 3–0 at that point. The world title was slipping away.

I was put down in the *par terre* (French for "on the ground"). In the *par terre*, the wrestler on top tries to turn the wrestler on the bottom, so my goal was to not get turned. I tried to stand up and should've gotten an escape point. I thought the referee had made a bad call. I was infuriated. I wasn't getting points I deserved; Patrikeev was getting points he didn't deserve.

So I decided to start attacking him. There were only seventy-five seconds left, and he easily could've stalled the remainder of the match, especially if the calls had kept going his way. I moved in, got a body lock on him, and threw him pretty hard. He landed out of bounds.

Once again, I was given no points. I could not believe it. Just over thirty seconds were left in the match. The crowd was going wild. All the of the "Russian support staff"— who looked pretty shady, and very tough, I might add— were smiling ear to ear. Karelin was to be avenged, and I was to be shamed.

I'd thrown him twice and should've been in the match, at least within striking distance. Yet I had no points, trailing 3–0.

So many things were going through my mind: my own personal pride, of course, but I was also thinking about everyone who had believed in me, from my coaches and teammates to the people back home in Star Valley, across Wyoming, and throughout the United States.

Even though I didn't get any points for throwing Yuri, he had felt my fury. He had landed pretty hard on his head, and he looked shaken. He sort of stumbled back into the mat. I body-locked him again and threw him a third time. This was not as good, technically, as the previous two throws, but it was still a solid throw.

As I threw him, I felt something in him give as he hit the mat—his spirit or will, I don't know. Nothing gave in me; I was ready for more.

But Yuri didn't move after that third and final throw. He sort of grabbed at his head as I continued, with my momentum from the throw, to move on top of him and pinned him. Down 3–0 thirty seconds earlier, the ref pounded the mat to signal the pin as a stunned look appeared on Yuri's face.

I had won.

It felt as good as it had felt winning the gold in 2000,

especially to come from behind like that—Greco matches are often decided by a single point, and coming back from three points down is rare—against such a great wrestler as Yuri.

I knew the Russian wrestling machine had focused completely on me, that their number one goal was to beat me at that tournament.

I ran over to Coach Fraser and jumped into his arms. He stumbled, but managed to congratulate me.

Coach Fraser recalled that match several months later: "When he wrestled Patrikeev, the atmosphere was so intense," Fraser said. "All of the former Soviet countries wanted their revenge, and they all knew Patrikeev had pinned him the year before. The mood reminded me of the whole Caesar kind of thing. Before the match, a lot of people expected the Russians to get revenge for beating their hero, their legend. Sure enough, every close call went in Patrikeev's favor. Rulon couldn't get a break. And Patrikeev was the real deal, this young, strong, good-looking guy. Rulon gets behind 3–0, and things got interesting.

With about a minute and fifteen seconds to go in the second period, they were battling tough, and Rulon needed to score because time was running out. Rulon got this look on his face I will never forget. That look told me 'This guy will not beat me.' Rulon ended up challenging Patrikeev to the Russian's strength; Patrikeev's best position is the body lock, from which he throws people—that's what he used to throw Rulon the year before, a hip throw from a body lock. Rulon goes to the body lock not once, not twice, but three times. On the third time in the body lock, it was like things shifted into slow motion as Rulon took him from the body lock and pitches this guy onto his back with this spectacular throw, with Patrikeev crashing onto the mat, his feet fluttering, and Rulon then sticks him. It was unbelievable. I have never seen anything like it in all my days. Using the Russian's own move against him with all those Russians there, at the World Championships, with Rulon defending his title—and having everything to lose—against the guy who was the last to beat him the year before."

There were a whole bunch of tough-looking Russians traveling with the team. The head of the Russian group was a guy named "Neva." It's no secret that the Russian mafia was a driving force behind the country's athletic programs after the fall of communism. I had seen many of these men in Sydney. I knew they probably didn't think too much of me. Neva had an intimidating presence about him, sitting behind the scorer's table during the whole match. When I finished hugging Fraser and went off the staging area, I hit a big set of doors. There, right outside the door, facing me head-on, was Neva. He bowed his head and shook my hand. I knew this was the guy who, more than anyone else, wanted to see me defeated for ending Karelin's reign in Sydney.

"Wow," I thought, after shaking Neva's hand, "that was pretty weird."

In the semifinals, I met another wrestler from the former Soviet bloc, Sergei Moreyko of Bulgaria. Moreyko is another of those wrestlers who has been on the scene a long time and who has represented the sport and his country very well. There's a reason that entire region has five or six of the top Greco-Roman heavyweight wrestlers, year in and year out: they understand the sport, practice it hard, and are all unbelievably strong.

Moreyko is a taller wrestler, about six-foot-three.

"Moreyko was largely viewed as the second-best wrestler in the world during Karelin's last few years as the top-ranked heavyweight in the world," Coach Fraser recalled later. "He was constantly second to Karelin and was widely considered the next world champion."

Again, it was a chance for a wrestler from Karelin's region to take me down and get revenge. Only now it wasn't just revenge for what had happened at the 2000 Olympics, but also for beating the young up-and-coming Russian bull, Patrikeev, in the quarterfinals.

It didn't matter. I was just as hungry for the championship now as I had been at the beginning. We started in the clinch, and I could already feel myself taking control of the match. He put a little pressure on me but left himself open—a mistake. In a sport that often comes down to one point making the difference, you have to seize every opening. I was able to throw him to his back and pick up three points. There were still two minutes left in the match at that point, so I kept the pressure on and held off his attacks for a 3–0 win.

"The Moreyko match was funny, because Rulon, who doesn't usually use the body-lock move, used it again in that match to win," Fraser recalled.

I was in the championship match.

And since irony seems to find me at just about every turn in my life, who would I face in the final? Mihaly Deak-Bardos of Hungary, who already had beaten me twice that year. Deak had a lot of momentum built up, both from falling short at the 2000 Olympics—where he had it in him to medal, I believe—and from his two prior wins over me.

Deak looked good and very strong at the 2001 Worlds. During weigh-ins earlier in the week, I was a little uncomfortable, because for the first time I was the favorite—I was no longer flying under anyone's radar. At six feet, one inch, I'm the shortest wrestler by far in my weight class, by a good two or three inches. Deak, who speaks very good English, had seen me kind of looking around at the weigh-ins.

"I guess I'm the little guy," I said to Deak.

He looked at me and broke into a smile.

"Yes, but you have the Olympic gold medal," Deak replied. He was professional and respectful, a worthy opponent and a good representative for our sport. He had made it to the final of the 1997 World Championships, where he lost to Karelin 10–0. So he had faced the pressure of the finals before, and he was ready for this match.

Neither Deak nor I could score in the first period. In the second period, Deak had the "lock" on me and was chasing me around and around. I circled and got into good position, and just as I was getting near the out-of-bounds line, I pivoted and backed myself in, pulling him. He dragged his foot to the out-of-bounds line. I was upset I didn't get at least a point, because I had control of him and he was fleeing, not wrestling me. I should have been awarded a point, because Deak was backing up, not attacking, and thus should've have drawn a caution and one—the point going to me. But I stayed with him, attacked him, and pulled out a 2–0 win in overtime.

I had won the 2001 World Championship. Any questions about the legitimacy of my 2000 Olympic gold were answered. Any doubts about my ability to be the best in the world were erased.

Coach Fraser says the 2001 World Championship was the most difficult, but also the most satisfying, of my accomplishments under his tutelage. "Rulon winning the Worlds in Greece was an even bigger feat than winning in Sydney, in my opinion," he said. "Sydney got the publicity, and beating Karelin was huge. But for Rulon to come back at the 2001 Worlds and have the toughest draw possible— the five top heavyweights in the world—was amazing. After that, he was truly the man. I had coaches calling me after that, telling me again and again how the 2001 Worlds title was even more impressive than the Sydney gold medal. Rulon's never been afraid of a challenge. He could've sat back and skipped the 2001 Worlds, or he could've even retired. But his attitude was still that he'd wrestle anyone, anytime, any place."

The 2001 World Championships, however, proved costly to Coach Fraser. Here's how he told the story: "This is kind of a funny thing, and I don't want to make Rulon sound bad, because it really was done in the spirit of our competition with each other, which is really a lot of fun for both of us," he said. "Before Sydney, I gave Rulon an incentive: win two medals, at least one of them gold—one medal at the Olympics and another at the 2001 World Championships—and I'd give him this Rolex watch that I was given by Domino's Pizza for some success I had when I worked for them (as an area manager overseeing several regional stores) before coming to USA Wrestling. Rulon is a big watch guy, he has something like twenty of them. So he beats Karelin, and on the way home from Sydney on the plane he comes up to me, 'So, this means I get the Rolex, right?' I looked at him and laughed. 'No, I said two medals. One has to be gold—so you've got that one out of the way,' I told him. He sort of nodded at me and said, 'You know, I'm going to get that watch.' I said, 'I hope you do—because I want that medal for our team at Worlds.'

"So we're in Greece for the 2001 World Championships, and he's beaten Patrikeev, and then Moreyko, so he has Deak in the final for the gold medal—repeating as world champ, in effect, because Olympics are our World Championships every quadrennial. Rulon already had gone through his main warm-up. There were about thirty minutes until the match, and he was stretching, just staying warm and loose. He calls over to me, 'Coach Fraser, come here!' I think he wants to talk some last-minute strategy or something, because Deak had beaten him twice that year. We knew Rulon was going to get Deak's best shot, because Deak had to view this as his best shot at finally winning a gold medal at Worlds, plus he has the incentive of knocking off Rulon, who, of course, had beaten Karelin to win the gold at the Olympics. So I get over to Rulon, and he says, 'Hey, I'm in the final, right?' I look at him and I say, 'Well, yeah, obviously, this is the final.' He starts smiling, 'How's the Rolex?' I just started laughing. I joke with people that Rulon went for two years with nothing on his mind but getting my watch, and that's why he won the 2000 Olympics and 2001 World Championships!"

Coach Fraser gave me the Rolex, and I gave him two watches of mine in return. However, in 2004 after he helped coach, guide, and inspire me to come back, I gave him back the Rolex, because he earned it and deserved it.

Eighteen

MIRACLE IN THE MOUNTAINS

I HAD HEARD *about hypothermia all my life, simply because of the region in which we lived. Mild cases of hypothermia were not uncommon for those who worked on farms. Part of farm life simply involved getting wet and working in the cold, and then "being smart" and getting inside or at least warmed up before you "caught your death of a cold."*

What I didn't know, as my body temperature dropped several degrees on the night of February 14, 2002, was that when the body temp goes lower than 98.6 degrees, involuntary shivering begins. Though you can walk, complex motor functions can become difficult.

I didn't know that from 95 down to 93 degrees, it gets much more serious, as you become dazed and lose coordination, especially in the hands. Soon, as slurred speech and violent shivering set in, you become unaware of how truly cold it is.

No one would need to tell me that ever again.

* * *

Twenty-five degrees and sunny; a perfect winter day to head out on snowmobiles to the Cottonwood Lake area, about seven miles south of my hometown of Afton.

At about 1:00 P.M. on February 14, 2002, Danny Schwab, Trent Simpkins—both are neighbors and friends; Danny is a half dozen or so years older than me, while Trent was still a teenager—and I headed out to the Bridger-Teton National Forest, through which begins the Salt River. Just about everyone who passes through the region falls in love with the high peaks, the winding valleys, and the rivers and streams that snake through the countryside.

At about 3:30, Danny, who knew the area well, headed back into town for his daughter's basketball game. Danny, as usual, had a survival pack with him, with matches, flammable gas used to start a fire, and a small shovel that could be used to create an emergency shelter. Neither Trent nor I had such a kit.

We also had no idea that either of us would need one, even though neither one of us was at all familiar with the area we were sledding (another term for snowmobiling) in that day. Sure, I had lived around here all my life, but there are still patches of wilderness I'd never explored. It was one of the reasons why this promised to be an exciting day.

I wanted to try an aggressive climb up Wagner Mountain, but I couldn't make it all the way to the top. So I opted instead for a nearby mountain, which was also substantial. At that point, Trent and I separated as I headed off on my own to look for some more aggressive routes and absorb the incredible scenery on such a fabulous winter afternoon. We agreed to meet up in the next half-hour or so and head back together.

When I started out to try the second mountain—after the Wagner climb had failed—I thought I was looking at a pretty easy climb. There was a pretty safe trail to get to the top, with the reward being a spectacular view. I made a couple of cell phone calls near the top, including one to Danny. I wanted to make sure he had gotten into town with no problems.

"I'm on top of the world," I told Danny. I've felt on top of the world before—beating Karelin, graduating from college—but in a pure, literal sense, if there is a view better than the one I had that day, I have not seen it.

We went through our plans once again for the evening. After his daughter's game, we would all meet up and head to a nice restaurant in Jackson, Wyoming, a popular skiing and vacation spot.

After putting my cell phone back in my bib snow overalls, I looked at the shining sun. I was wearing three layers of clothing. I had left my coat at the base of Cottonwood Road. So I had on a T-shirt, sweatshirt, and fleece pullover, but no winter coat. I didn't wear a coat, because I didn't plan on needing one; we were going to be back in town before the sun was even close to setting. I had a couple pairs of gloves, both made for lighter winter weather, such as this day. I wasn't planning on doing outdoor work, so the gloves weren't waterproof or heavy-duty.

I hit the throttle as I tried to get up to the very top of the mountain. On my first attempt, I was close, but got stuck. I turned my snowmobile around. I was close again on the second attempt but got stuck in about the same area.

The slope I was on was actually quite treacherous, despite my earlier assessment. The sled was positioned such that if I couldn't turn it, the slope of the hill would pull me downhill, where I ran the risk of hitting some trees. So both times I headed back down the hill, I used extra caution to avoid the trees and to avoid losing control of my snowmobile. Suddenly I realized I had burned out a belt in the engine. I was still on the slope at that point, so I had to be very careful changing the belt. It was a very steep quarter-mile drop from me to the river below.

After I changed the belt, I spent about ten minutes riding around, looking for Trent. I searched throughout the area where I had left him and any trails indicating he had been in the area. I decided to drop back down into the valley, careful to avoid the trees, and try searching down a gully near the head of the Salt River. At that location, the Salt River is a little stream with a series of water holes leading straight to the headwaters of the river.

I didn't think Trent was in this particular area, but the snow was beautiful and undisturbed—virgin snow, so the adventurer in me wanted to enjoy it. So I decided to ride a little bit more and I headed farther down the gully. Since I couldn't get the snowmobile through the deep powder covering the slopes of the gully, I thought I'd try to follow the stream.

When I reached the head of the stream, I noticed the water holes were larger, about five feet across. Since the way I had entered this area—a steep descent—was not an option for a way out, I felt that if I kept following the water, I might find an exit to this valley. So I thought I could push some snow into a sort of ramp and ride across the water—basically jumping it—and get to the snow on the other side. The banks were high on both sides of the stream, about four feet.

I took some time to pack snow around the side of the water hole, so I could avoid going into the water. I was halfway around the small pond when the sled, which was at a dangerous angle three feet above the water, dove downward, broke through the snow and ice, and went into the water.

As the snowmobile went into the water, I jumped off. I looked at the sled and saw there was water up over the seat. I had to make a choice at that point: get the sled out of the water, which meant getting myself wet, or wait several hours for help. At the time, it was an easy choice: I knew I could get the sled running again once I got it out.

Unfortunately, this wasn't the wave runner Rosie O'Donnell had given me.

The sled's rear end was now completely submerged. I stepped into the water, soaking my boots and legs up to my thighs. I had to reach down, putting my torso, upper arms, and of course my hands in the water to lift the snowmobile, which was made that much heavier by the cold water.

"Great, now I'm wet," I said.

I knew that I had made a critical choice at that point, because once I was wet, I had about an hour to get out of there before hypothermia set in. Any longer than an hour, and I could be looking at a bad situation, even death. I pushed the snowmobile out of the river and then pulled on the front skis to get it up onto the bank. The effort to get it out was a strain, and I could feel the effect of the hard work in my muscles.

"Good thing I won't be out here much longer," I thought to myself, as I looked at my soaked legs and arms—and hands.

While I was thinking about what to do next, I felt my body begin to shiver.

I still had a second water hole to clear to get across the stream, which I hoped would lead to a way out, and was faced with the same situation: a high bank on each side, with a drop to the water in between. To my great relief, the snowmobile started up.

My approach to the second water hole wasn't successful, and the sled ended up in the drink again.

Once again, I hauled it out of the water.

I was thinking, "No big deal. Uncomfortable, and not what I would do if I had to do it all over again, but no big deal."

My plan was to get the sled running, head out of the gully, and then ride the ridge back up to either find Trent or at least back to "civilization." But I just couldn't get to that ridge on the snowmobile because of the water and the fact that the terrain in that direction was so steep. I thought perhaps I could hike back to the top and try to get my friend's attention.

"Nah, you're tough, you can do this," I thought. "You're going to make it out of here. It's not like it's life-threatening or anything."

I searched for and found what I thought was a different route out of the gully. It wasn't as steep as the areas I had been in, but it was still a tough route. The spot I was aiming for was about four hundred yards up the mountain. I made an educated guess about the route, but quickly realized I wasn't going to make it, because the hill was too steep for the sled and too deep to hike through on foot. The light was just beginning to fade; I knew I had to stop, reassess my situation, and come up with a new plan.

I decided to give up trying to get up on the ridge from where I was. Instead, I went farther down the gully and spotted a path where I could ride until it came out. But a few yards down, I saw another opportunity to climb onto the ridge. I had only about twenty feet to start my run up a twenty-yard incline that was very steep. I didn't have the energy to scout it out and make sure there wasn't a cliff on the other side. I accelerated, shot over the top of the hill, and came out just fine. I worked my way through the trees, toward a small opening on the ridge. But as I rode up the side hill, I saw there was a cliff at the top and realized I could not get out going any farther in that direction because of the steep drop on the other side. So I turned around and headed back in the direction I had come from, but could not find any escape in that direction either.

I decided I'd just have to ride the gully out. Eventually, I figured, I'd end up in Smoot, a nearby community. First, though, I had to negotiate the steep sides of the gully. It wasn't going to be easy. The first option was to try inverted, basically straight down fifty yards. That wasn't a good option, though, because there were so many rocks along the cliff. Another option was to back up and work the sled to the right. The slope was still about an 80-degree angle, but I thought if I could control the slide of the snowmobile down the hill, I would get down safely and could then find a good route out.

But the angle of the slope was too steep, and sliding the sled proved to be too difficult. So I started straight down, holding on to the sled with my right leg, my left hand on the brake, my right hand on the throttle, and dragging my left leg behind to slow me down.

The sun that just minutes earlier had been warm was now fading and it was getting dark. I was dragged straight down about forty yards or so, but was fortunate enough to slow down at the bottom.

"Okay, what's next?" I asked myself. All I could see were two streams at the bottom of the gully. Once again there was no way to get out.

Heading south, I reached another substantial mountain, so I turned east, following the river. The Salt River's general direction is south, so I decided to follow it as far as I could.

I looked around for the best route. I would have to cross two streams to reach an open area about twenty feet on the other side. This was a wide valley that came together, narrowing by the yard, at the two ponds, about eight feet deep and four to five feet wide. I thought about my best option. I thought if I hit the pond edge hard enough I could jump it—at worst, I might have to submarine the sled a little.

I came across the snow and hit the bank. Gravity pulled the sled down onto the snowbank, so I tried to pop a wheelie, trying to stay on top of the snow. That slowed me down so that I got only about three-quarters of the way across the water hole. When the sled went into the water, I fell in up to my knees. I got myself out and pulled the sled out again. At several points during this time, I checked my cell phone, but I couldn't get a signal while down in the valley.

At the second water hole, I again tried to push the sled across, but, even though I accelerated for the second jump, I didn't make it. I fell off the sled into the water for the fourth time. However, I was able to push it through to the other side of the bank.

Behind me was the big mountain, Wagner, so going back that way wasn't an option. I could go only farther down into the canyon. Since finding some days-old snowmobile tracks earlier—which gave me hope—about four or five inches of fresh snow had fallen, so I could no longer see the tracks, couldn't tell what direction they had come from. I stared harder at the last track, but with the snow, could make out nothing.

Because of the narrow confines along the river, I had to work slowly and carefully, going south. The Salt River was filled with snow and ice, so I worked the sled along the spots that looked like they would hold. I saw some more tracks.

"Someone has been here," I thought. "So I will be able to get out, I just have to follow their tracks."

I headed south, following the snowmobile tracks. But the trail ended and doubled back.

"How did whoever made these tracks get out?" I asked myself.

I assumed that if I kept going, I would pick up the tracks again, maybe in a few yards. I headed over a hill, at the bottom of which there was a four-hundred-yard-wide meadow. As I headed west across it, the meadow shrank smaller and smaller. There were a lot of great spots for snowmobiling, but no clear path out. At that point I wasn't looking for recreational trails, I was searching for a trail that would get me home safely.

Darkness was setting in, so visibility was getting worse by the minute. I looked for the right way to get out. I made several small circles. I went back to where I had come from and looked across the valley. Again and again I doubled back, confusing myself even more as I mistook my tracks for those made by others. I looked to the sides, and it was straight up and down.

"There's no way I'm getting out this way," I thought.

I looked to the west and thought there might be an opening. I saw some trees and figured, I can get out this way. It looked like it opened up to Star Valley, although as I looked closer, I saw there were a lot of trees.

By now I had traveled perhaps two miles, but had to turn around and backtrack a half mile and cross the river twice more to get going westbound again.

I made it across the first water hole. I approached the second and could see that the ice wasn't solid or thick. I would need to clear the hole, meaning I'd have to hit it going as fast as I could and at just the right angle. I didn't get as much speed as I needed, and I hit the water and sunk a little—getting wet as I sunk—but was able to keep going, pop the sled off, and hit the bank on the other side.

Once I cleared the river and thought about following it—I knew it would come out in a Star Valley town eventually—I could see that the river dropped about a hundred feet into a deep crevasse; I couldn't get out that way. I had to head through a dense group of trees. Weaving through trees on a sled is called "boondockin'." It's a fun thing to do on a snowmobile, but it's challenging in the best of conditions. It's not something you want to do when you're lost and it's almost dark. There are areas near the base of trees where there's a "false" base, where there's not as much snow; a snowmobile can get sucked down into that false base, which is dangerous because you could hit a tree, damage your sled, or get stuck.

I had a headlight on my sled, but the snow was so high that it was constantly covered. I had to stop every twenty or thirty yards to clear off the light, burning valuable time and what little was left of the daylight. I checked the time on my cell, which still didn't have a signal, but its clock was working.

6:30 P.M.

"Hmm, 6:30, we'd be meeting to head to Jackson," I thought.

Though I could hardly move ten yards without having to try to cross water again, my mind was going a hundred miles an hour. I continued to try to work my way out and thought I could start making some real progress.

"I can still make dinner if I get going," I said to myself.

I came to another river crossing. After being successful on only one crossing—the third crossing of the four I'd consider only a partial success, since I made it across but had gotten wet again—I knew I had to get across this time without going into the water.

I accelerated and was grateful for the smooth ride as I worked my way down the river looking for a way across. I felt pretty certain this route would turn out into the valley.

The strip of barely passable land along the river on which I was riding narrowed again. I had to cross the water, because there was nowhere else to go. The sled simply did not have another steep climb left in it; I had already used the spare belt and had submerged it three times. That sort of waterlogging takes almost as bad a toll on the machine as it does on humans.

I looked around at the breathtaking view. In the fading light, I could see only the outlines of the mountain peaks. These mountains had inspired me for so long. They are a spectacular part of the amazing landscape in this area. But now they had become prison walls for me, their shadowy rolling peaks and hills forcing me to look elsewhere for a way out. They formed guard towers, as it were, to keep me penned in, away from safety, warmth, and my family and friends.

The spot I had to cross was strewn with rocks, but I had to try it. The last bit of sunlight was fading, so this would be my last best chance. I had to be 100 percent committed in order to get across without getting wet or damaging the sled. I knew if I fell in the water again, I could be in real trouble, because the sled would probably be stuck in the rocks. I'd have no way out until someone found me. Since I had not heard any sleds, planes, or other vehicles, I figured no one was looking for me yet. I had to get out on my own.

"There's a few rocks, but, hey, it's just a snowmobile; I can fix it," I thought.

I came around and over the rocks in the shallow water, riding about twenty yards until I came to a boulder. I tried to squeeze around it, but couldn't. I was stuck—couldn't move the sled in any direction. I grabbed everything I could from the sled, left it, and started to climb up a snow bank. I made it only about twenty yards. Each step took so long because the snow was so deep, up to my hips, and getting footing was impossible. So I spent twenty minutes on foot, with no escape route in sight.

"Are you kidding me?" I said to myself. "This is crazy. You have to get back on the snowmobile and you'll get out of here. The only way out of here is the snowmobile."

So I climbed back down, about a five-minute walk back to the sled. I knew I was going to have to challenge myself to get the sled up a steep incline—no matter what direction I took—to get out.

I started up the snowmobile and pulled and pushed it through the rocks. Finally, I hit another set of rocks as I hit the bank of the river and got stuck again.

"Now what do I do?" I asked myself.

I had no other choice at that point but to try to push or pull it through. So I got off and pulled with all I had, but my hand slipped off the snowmobile and I fell backward into the river. I ended up flat on my back amid water and rocks. The water was only two feet deep, but I was soaked. Just to get up, I had to roll over to my stomach in the water, which soaked me all the way through. I put my hands in the river to push myself up.

My entire body was now soaked.

7:15 P.M.

"It's time to get out of the water," I told myself.

Earlier in the evening, when I hit the first and second

water holes on my first crossing of the river, I was glad that I had a second pair of gloves, because the pair I had been wearing had been soaked. I had put on the second pair of gloves, because at the time, I figured I was done crossing the river and wanted to have warm, dry hands as I rode out. Now the second pair was soaked completely through, and the first pair had already frozen solid.

I would have to leave the sled and start walking. I couldn't force the sled through the rocks anymore and didn't want to risk falling into the water again. I tried to sense the right direction to go. The first time I had tried walking out, only a half hour earlier, I had not found a viable path and had had to head back to the snowmobile.

"You have wasted time and energy with these few decisions," I thought. "If you keep this up, it's going to kill you."

I could feel the water freezing on my back and in the arms of my shirt. As I left the snowmobile for the night, I took what I could. All I had left was a brand-new "head sock," which you wear underneath your helmet. I strapped the helmet securely to the back of the snowmobile. The visor had broken on it earlier, and I had taken it off because it was too hard to see through the crack.

I put the head sock in my pocket; it was the last thing I had that was completely dry. It ended up saving my ears and nose from frostbite.

I started walking. After about fifteen yards—which took at least another twenty minutes—I saw a small switchback area in the river, a small clear place with no snow on top of the ice. I was incredibly cold and fatigued from all the effort it took to work with the snowmobile and from walking in deep snow. I was hungry and dehydrated, but all I could feel was the freezing chill running from my head to my toes.

I finally got to the switchback area.

"A nice clear spot. I just need to lie down," I told myself. I did, and even though the area didn't have the huge snowdrifts, it was still icy. As soon as I lay down, I started shivering more violently.

A small voice inside me said, "Get up, move! If you don't, you will freeze to death."

I headed back along the riverbed. Fatigue continued to overtake me.

So I trudged to a group of trees about fifteen yards away, which took about fifteen minutes to get to. There was a lot of snow in this cluster of trees, so I worked to clear out an area of snow and branches and sat down. I realized that my socks and boots were starting to freeze.

8:15 P.M.

I knew it would be a long night. But I didn't know yet just how long it would turn out to be.

"I'm here in this messed-up situation," I said to myself. "How do I survive the night?"

I tried to think clearly. Getting out on my own was no longer an option. Survival was the name of the game.

"Be focused, stay positive," I said. "Get a game plan and stick with it. You can't be passive, but you can't be impatient."

I knew from my wrestling career how to prepare. If I

had put all my hopes into getting rescued in an hour and it didn't happen, I'd be setting myself up for failure.

"It doesn't matter how much time you're out here," I told myself. "Just have a plan. You need to focus and relax."

I had to concentrate my energy and then find a way in my mind and body to relax.

There'd be no sunlight in this area until morning. So, since the sun had been down for almost two hours, I had to be prepared for about twelve hours in the dark.

"Twelve hours, that could be tough," I thought. "There is going to be a series of critical points. Get ready."

My toes were absolutely freezing by now.

"I'm pretty much frozen," I thought. "Stay focused. Be ready for the challenge. You can do it."

The head sock was such a blessing, the only dry garment remaining.

I pushed some snow around to clear a small, protected area under a couple of trees that were close together. All the water from the river soaking my back had frozen. But my feet . . . those were the coldest parts of my body. It was a kind of cold I had never known existed. I was certain I would be facing hypothermia and frostbite in the next hour—but at that point I figured rescuers were on the way and would find me since so much time had already passed—so I tried to thaw out my feet.

I could hardly feel my toes. As I saw all the ice on my boots, I realized getting them off would be no easy task. All the water had frozen, so I literally had blocks of ice for shoes. First I took off my wet gloves and tried to warm my frozen hands by putting them inside my bib overalls. My hands were so cold that they took forever to warm enough to be functional.

Once my hands had feeling again, I worked to take off my left boot. The water had frozen my pant leg to the boot, so I had to work those apart. I got the pant leg up, unfastened the boot, which took several minutes because of the ice, and finally pulled it off. After I got my sock off, I rubbed my left foot. The foot was extremely cold, just frozen. Though I was trying to warm it, the blowing wind and below-zero temperature were making my foot even colder. I started to put the boot back on, but it had already frozen solid again, so I had to work it back on. My hands were freezing again. I knew I had to take the right boot off to warm that foot, but my hands were so cold that I couldn't control them. The water had frozen all my clothes, so even moving my arms and body was difficult; I could hear crackling ice as I bent forward or moved my arms. I made a decision to leave my right boot on. But I would pay for that decision the next day, because that foot was frozen solid.

I tried to wiggle my toes and move my feet, but what little movement I could make was unbelievably painful. I could feel the ice between my toes, the frozen skin on my feet.

My long shirtsleeves were my mittens. I stretched each sleeve out over my hand and then folded the material into my palms. I held on to that material all night, since I couldn't use my soaked, frozen gloves.

When I decided to check the time again, the ends of my sleeves had frozen so solid, I had to blow and blow on them to break the seal and get my hand out. It was completely dark now; the evening was over and night had begun. I checked the time on my cell phone.

8:30 P.M.

"They know that I'm lost now," I thought. "They know I need help. It's just a matter of time until they come."

I thought maybe Danny and the others would come up the backside of the area, avoiding the mountains, tracking the river. I believed that I had made it through the worst part of the ordeal, that it would soon end and I'd be found. I decided to try to relax, but at the same time tried to keep moving while standing in place.

The mental aspect of hypothermia and frostbite is as dangerous as the physical aspects. Your mind becomes delusional as it tries to convince the body that it is actually warm. I fell asleep for brief spells, always dreaming I was in a warm shower. I thought about the jet tub in the house I'd recently bought in Cascade, Colorado. In my dream, those warm jets felt so good.

I snapped awake and found myself shrouded in a blanket of frozen ice, the air freezing as the temperature sank down to the 20-below-zero range. The colder the air got, the harder it became for me to keep moving. But I had to. I now truly realized that I was stranded, soaking wet, in the Wyoming wilderness. The idea of dying was very real at that point. It scared me so much that I forced myself to move around as much as I could. I tried to run in place, even though just picking up each foot was a challenge. I tried to do "mountain climbers," an exercise that I thought would help me fight the bitter cold and keep the blood flowing through my feet, legs, and upper body.

I'd dream that one of the heaters we'd keep outside on the farm was here in front of me, but then I'd wake up, a cold slap in the face from the weather beating my frozen body. Trying to move was getting more and more difficult, more and more painful.

I kept dozing off and waking up, again and again. I made sure I wasn't comfortable, because if I fell into a deep sleep, I'd die. Every time I woke up, the painful, stinging sensations came back. When I moved my toes, I could feel the icicles stabbing the tissue. It wasn't actually my feet that were coldest at that point, but my thighs. I'd try to roll over or at least continually shift, trying to stimulate circulation in my body. That's when I realized how different the sounds of nature are from one angle to just a slightly different angle. On one side of the tree, I could hear the river sounding like only a trickle. When I'd move even a few feet, it would sound like a raging river.

From about 8:30 to midnight, I continued shifting as much as I could. When I tried to move my toes, I could feel the ice in my boot, like razors deeply shredding the skin on my toes.

The movie *Armageddon* came to mind, where those guys chasing the meteor have these huge shards of razor-sharp ice flying toward them; that's what I felt like I had in my boots. The pain was almost unbearable, but what else was I going to do? Besides, I reasoned, the pain and stinging was a good sign; it meant that I was still alive and still fighting. I knew that if the pain mysteriously went away, the end would be near—the end of my life.

As often as possible, I tried to rest in a standing position so that when I fell asleep, I'd wake up as soon as I fell over. My best friend was a tree branch just low enough and just strong enough to take some of my weight when I leaned against it, but if I put all my weight on it, it would give way and I would fall over, waking up quickly.

It had been, I thought, about eight hours or so since I had last checked the time, so it would be maybe a little after 4:30—about two hours until sunlight. My goal was sunlight. Light was heat, and the sun would bring survival. I worked two fingers out from the frozen sleeve and reached up to try to get my cell phone.

I didn't need a thermometer to tell me that it was at least 25 below zero, because the cold was as searing and sharp as it had been all night.

Finally, I worked the zipper on my bibs and tried to find the cell phone. By then, though, I had lost feeling in the two fingers I was using to snag the phone. I blew on them until I got the feeling back. I slowly warmed up a finger and pushed the button on the phone. My heart sank.

MIDNIGHT

"You are in trouble!" I thought to myself.

I had been thinking maybe two hours until sunlight, but it was going to be closer to six hours.

"Okay, this is going to be a tough one, and a long one," I said. "Better get ready for it."

I had been out about eight hours, and I still had nearly six hours left until sunlight, when I thought I'd surely be rescued. I had to pace myself. As an athlete, you have to have a mental clock that gives you an accurate perception of time. You can't expend all your energy in the first thirty seconds of a match, or you will have nothing left and will be vulnerable for the remainder of the match. There was no "quick win" for me this night, so I had to pace myself for maybe another seven hours or so.

It was disheartening to realize that only three hours had passed since I had last checked the time, but complaining and self-pity wouldn't help the situation. I needed every ounce—every fraction of an ounce—of energy.

To survive, I was going to have to be tough. I kept telling myself that I'd be okay, that I'd be tough enough to make it through. Another short nap. Hallucinations. I was home, and it was warm. I awoke to shivers. I'd lean on the branch to sleep standing up.

1:30–2:00 A.M.

I didn't check the time, but I'd learn later that it was between 1:30 and 2:00 in the morning when I heard the snowmobiles used by the searchers.

Since I knew I couldn't walk very far, I tried yelling and screaming, and when I realized I didn't have much voice left and that the fifteen-mile-an-hour wind blowing east to west was blowing at me, dulling the noise toward the rescuers, I started whistling, which I can do very loudly. I didn't walk out to the searchers, because I figured it would take me a good half hour to get there and they'd be in this area only fifteen minutes or so before they moved on. My energy was better spent in trying to make noises and hoping they'd hear me.

As it turned out, the rescuers had gotten stuck in that same stream crossing that I'd been stuck in.

I thought my mind was playing tricks on me. After I heard the snowmobile noise start up—just an idea at first, and then the gunning of the engine as the throttles opened up—and then fade a second time, I figured it was because they were moving on to a different area to look for me. What had really happened was that they had shut the snowmobiles down because one had become stuck, and it took everyone working together to get it out of the water. Lane Walton, one of the best snowmobile riders in Star Valley, had crossed the river and was trying to come up the bank when he buried his snowmobile in the water—the same thing I had done several times that day. Everyone had to stop their sleds to help Lane get his out of the water. They drained the water out of his snowmobile to start it again.

They had to work on it for a while. Had I known they'd be there for at least a half hour, I would've started walking right away. I could've made it that far in a half hour, and I would've been saved.

About an hour after I first heard them, I heard the noises again and realized they hadn't left.

"They're still here!" I thought. "They haven't left."

I realized I had to hurry, but before I could get started, the noises faded away. I knew if I tried to start walking, as wet and frozen as I was, I would never reach them before they left; I would have expended all that energy for nothing. Despite the enormous disappointment of this missed opportunity, I tried to relax and stay positive. Besides, if they were on the move again, maybe they'd loop around and find me. I really believed it was only a matter of time before they'd come around from the other direction. A little while later, looking for encouragement, I went through the routine of thawing the ice, getting my hands out of the "sleeve mittens," and checking the time.

"A lot of time has passed," I thought. "It must be around 5:30 A.M."

2:30 A.M.

Once again, I was heartbroken at seeing the time. Only half an hour had elapsed since my rescuers had turned back. My legs were in so much pain and I was shivering so violently that I made myself stand up. I let my body shiver as much as it wanted to, because that's how the body deals with extreme cold that's the only thing the body can do to warm itself.

There was no moon that night, just light from the stars. What was ironic was that just two nights earlier I had given a speech in Key West, Florida, and had been out late in the evening. The temperature had been 75 degrees, and I had been loving life that night. Just two days later, from that warm Florida evening to this bitter cold Wyoming night, I was soaking wet and the temperature had plunged 100 degrees from that night to this moment.

I thought about the speech and how great it was to meet so many fans, to recount the story of beating the great Alexander Karelin and the skyrocket ride to fame, the appearance on the *Tonight Show*, Oprah, Rosie, and everything else. And I thought this: I'd trade all of that, every accomplishment in my life, for one wooden matchstick.

I could've started a tree on fire—not uncommon in the wilderness, as sportsmen and hikers often pick out a dead tree and burn it for warmth on cold nights. I could've dried off my clothes and warmed up. I'd gladly have given everything I had done in my life for one match.

I shook my whole body. When I shook my arms, the moisture that was closest to my skin, which hadn't frozen at that point, would touch my skin and make me colder. I'd feel more miserable, and start shivering even worse, so I stopped trying to move as much.

By then I had no feeling in my toes and feet. I tried in vain to move them, but nothing was happening, a result of the combination of frostbite and limited circulation in my feet. All I could feel was pain; yet that pain sustained me, and once again I told myself that pain meant I was alive and still fighting.

I embraced the pain and began asking myself, "What are you willing to give up to live? What are you willing to suffer to make it out of here alive?"

3:00 A.M.

The situation could not get any bleaker. The searchers were gone, the coldest part of the night was upon me, and I was so thoroughly frozen that I was losing feeling in various parts of my body. At times, the pain would disappear; I knew what a dangerous situation that was.

I heard a branch snap close by. In the days that followed, searchers would find coyotes feeding on a dead cow. Cows are grazed on the national forest grass during the summer, so this cow had been either forgotten or overlooked and had spent all fall and winter in the area. It had fed itself and survived well into the winter. Eventually, though, the cold and snow caught up to it. And so had the coyotes. They tracked the weakened animal and, in killing it, found sustenance for themselves.

I had been hearing a lot of noises through the night, but I'm pretty sure that snapped branch was caused by some sort of animal.

4:00 A.M.

Time to move, I thought to myself. I should try to walk out again. My mind was telling me a million different things. One idea would make sense one moment, and no sense at all the next moment.

But I physically could not walk out.

Just the energy I used to start had sapped me again, so I lay down. I made sure I was uncomfortable so that I'd wake up again from the pain, a pain that would stay with me for weeks, months, even years in my feet.

My fleece top was completely frozen; I thought that if I could take it off I'd probably be warmer. I tried to move my arms and heard snapping and cracking like sticks breaking; it was the icicles breaking in my shirtsleeves and on my back.

I tried to think through the process of how to do this and what the effect would be, as I had learned to think things through from my teachers and coaches through the years. So I thought, "What's going to happen when I get that fleece off?" The answer is that my undershirts were going to freeze. Would I take those off, too? No way. Even though the fleece was frozen, it was insulating the undershirts. I started shivering again, uncontrollably, as I had been doing most of the night. My focus was lasting only a minute or two before I'd start to nod off and go into some sort of vegetative state, where I was unable to expend much mental energy.

"Just stay focused, and they will come and get you," I tried to convince myself.

4:30 A.M.

I woke up with a start. I had had a dream about my late brother Ronald, Jesus, and God. I had never needed them more, and they came through for me. The vision gave me an affirmation that I would make it through this, that the faith that had nurtured me all my life was with me, that God was giving me every chance to live, and that Jesus, who had made the ultimate sacrifice for us all, was with me. I was giving every ounce of my soul as I fought to stay alive. In the dream, I felt a peace and calm about me as I fell forward and woke up, but I was 100 percent certain that Ronald, Jesus, and God had given me a spiritual blessing—I had the strength of the Lord with me. That was an awesome feeling, one that I desperately needed.

I kept coaching myself, taking lessons from all the mentors I had been fortunate enough to have in my life. Two more hours until the sun comes up, I'd tell myself. Two more hours of darkness, then the sun, and you'll be saved.

"Hang in there," I told myself. "You'd better focus. You have to focus. If you don't concentrate right this minute, you are going to die. Focus!"

I was in a fight for my life. I had to coach myself like I'd been coached all those years. Now I was in a match with the ultimate opponent: death.

"I need to get out of here," I said. "Time to walk out."

I made it fifteen feet. I found another protected tree, but had to dig out a bunch of snow. I was so tired, beyond what I believed to be the ultimate exhaustion, that I couldn't spare the energy. If my body got any more tired, then that would be it. I'd fall down and sleep, and it would be lights out—for good.

I dozed again. And then awoke.

"You need to start walking, because your body is 'settling' and it will start shutting down," I told myself. I started heading toward the middle of a meadow. It took me about five minutes to make it ten yards, and I thought, "What are you doing? What are you thinking?" I knew that people with hypothermia convinced themselves that they were warm or could move. In hunter's education, I had learned that people suffering from hypothermia can no longer make rational decisions.

"This is the coldest part of the night," I said. "Sit down and wait for the sun to come out."

I got back to my spot and tried to shake my arms. But everything was frozen.

* * *

Every now and then, a jet would fly over. I knew it was either a private plane or commercial jet, and I thought, "Man, I wish I could buy a ticket to be on that plane, because I could feel the heat and just relax." My mind was everywhere, all over the place. Though there was no moon, the stars were out by the thousands. I thought of all the heat stars give off. It must be boiling hot within the range of each star's heat.

Several times through the night, but at this moment particularly, I started thinking about the people I cared about, people I loved and who loved me. I knew they would be concerned, that they would be up all night worrying about me. Of course, I wanted them—or someone, anyone—to find me, but I also wanted them to have some peace of mind. I thought about how fortunate I had been to grow up with such a great family, especially such wonderful parents, with a community that rallied around when the family barn burned, that raised money to send my family to the Olympics. I thought about the teachers who had stepped up and helped me get through school, doctors who had patched me up, and people from my church who had helped shape me and care for me. I wanted them to know that even though things looked bleak on this night, I cared and loved them all very deeply, and I appreciated and respected them for who they were and what they did for me. The love of my family and friends is what kept me warm that night. Kept me alive.

I kept thinking that within a mile or two of where I was located there had to be a house, or houses, and I know those people would've welcomed me into their homes and let me sit in front of their fireplace under warm blankets, with the electric or gas heaters on high, blowing warmth to my frozen body. I also knew that if any of these people had known where I was, they would've rescued me. I know I felt their prayers and thoughts that night, because I had so many signs of affirmation when things seemed the most hopeless.

One of my biggest motivations for surviving that night was the thought of my family or friends finding my frozen body. Remember Jack Nicholson's face when he was found frozen to death in the movie *The Shining*? I didn't want anyone to find me like that. I didn't want someone I loved to see the horrid sight of me frozen to death, my eyes and mouth open, the life completely gone out of me. What would something like that do to a person? I didn't want that to be my family's last, enduring image of me. If I had ever truly believed I was going to die that night, I would've found a spot where no one could ever find me, and hoped no one ever came across my frozen corpse.

As the stars began to fade, I remember thinking, "This is it, this is the end." Coming in and out of consciousness, I thought that everything was fading out on me, because, finally, I was losing, and I was dying. I had made it so long, it was almost morning, but now, well, it looked like I was finished. Please, let no one find me frozen, I prayed.

But then something in my mind clicked and brought me back to reality. The sky was starting to lighten—that's why the stars were fading. The sun was starting to come up, bringing with it blessed warmth.

"I've made it through the night!" I cried.

Life was coming back to the wilderness, and I was coming back to life. I decided to stand up.

It was time to walk back to life.

6:30 A.M.

I started walking toward the river, which was only fifteen yards away. It took me fifteen minutes. My legs were shaking so violently that every step was exhausting labor. On each step, I had to lean back and almost sit down on the snow, the shaking was so severe.

I did my best to waddle through the snow. I had to lift my neck up, then rotate my hips, no easy task, and push my leg forward for each step. I had taken in only about six ounces of fluid in the past seventeen hours—that brief sip from the river the night before—and I knew dehydration also could be a killer.

6:45 A.M.

Time for a drink.

I knew I had to get my hands covered back up. The night before, I had taken the less-soaked pair of gloves with me when I left the snowmobile and stashed them in my bib overalls overnight, hoping my core temperature would help the gloves dry out by morning.

Trying to put on the gloves was another effort in futility. I couldn't feel my hands. I had to once again blow on the end of my shirtsleeves to unseal the ice to free my hands. It took almost fifteen minutes of blowing on the sleeves just to get my hands out. My right hand was frozen worse than the left. Still, there's no doubt that pulling the sleeves down and using them as mittens saved my hands from extreme frostbite. I easily could've lost my hands had I not done that.

The gloves were still wet and started to freeze again as soon as they were exposed to the air. I thawed the sleeves, but my frozen hands were almost useless. I spent ten minutes putting the gloves on. I had a broken pinky finger on my left hand, so I never got the left glove completely on.

I was so thirsty, but drinking the river water, at 30 or 40 degrees, would bring down my body temperature even more. I would hit the fatal range if my body temperature dropped much more. I put my hands on some exposed rocks and put my face to the water, taking a little sip.

And now I set about surviving.

Again.

That sip might have staved off dehydration, but it was hardly enough to give me any energy. My lungs burned with each breath, my nose was practically frozen shut, my mouth a collection of ice crystals every time I opened it.

Though dawn had arrived, the sun wouldn't be high enough in the sky to shine on me and give me any warmth until about 9:30.

7:00 A.M.

As I watched the last of the stars fade, I heard a noise and realized it was an airplane. I said to myself, "Hey, look, it's an airplane." As I tried to raise my arms up, I heard the popping of the ice in my shirt.

I looked around. The snowbank lining the river was about seven feet deep. To get over it, I would have to clear a lot of snow, creating steps to walk up the bank. My energy stores were empty. I couldn't clear a single flake, much less enough to get through a seven-foot snowbank. I found a V-shaped rock and sat back, looking at the sky. The day was going to be clear.

I was very close to dipping out of consciousness or nodding off to sleep, I couldn't tell which; I tried to stay awake, if not quite alert. Later I would find out that because my body temperature was in the lower 80 degree range, my body was ready to fall into a coma.

A few clouds drifted, and as they passed, the last of the stars disappeared. The plane had come up over the ridge I had tried to ride the night before.

"Well, it must be a good thing that there's a plane," I told myself.

After seeing the plane—piloted, I'd later learn, by Star Valley native Mark Heiner, who is just an amazing and wonderful person—I regained enough of my wits to think that snowmobiles might be on the way.

"Maybe Danny will be coming soon on his snowmobile," I thought.

As plane passed a second time, my senses came back to me, if only a little, and I waved with both arms.

The pilot dropped a plastic bag into which, I later learned, he had stuffed his coat. I watched it spiral down toward the ground, but it went out of sight on the other side of the big snowbank; I couldn't see what it was, or where it had landed. I knew the general direction, but also knew it would be hard to get there.

The pilot dipped his plane's wings to each side to show he had seen me.

I thought about where the thing he threw might have landed. I figured it had to be something to help me and it would be dry. So I decided to get up out of the rocks I had been sitting on and walk in that direction. I pulled down snow until I was able to climb on top of a drift. I didn't see the bag. I kept digging and digging; I wasn't going to quit until I found that bag, but after ten minutes of effort I still hadn't made any progress.

I finally righted myself and dropped on all fours so that the snow could bear my weight—the snow was at least waist deep—and made it a few feet to my left. Then my mind started playing tricks on me. Maybe he had thrown it to the right. I walked left. Then came back to the right. I went back past the place where I had started and went ten feet to the right and then back again. Nothing.

"Whatever it is, it's too far away," I said to myself. "I have to stop."

Just as quickly as they had been sparked, my mental faculties faded again. I slumped forward, my head resting on my chest.

If the pilot had seen me then, he would have thought I was dead. I fell asleep as the tiredness overtook me. I slept for perhaps ten minutes and then woke again.

I had drawn a little bit of energy from the excitement of seeing the plane and the thrown package, but that energy had disappeared completely now. I could barely move my legs, so I sat down for fifteen to twenty minutes. I lowered my head again as the plane continued to circle above me. He had flown out of the canyon to inform the search party that he had found me. Now he was circling above me, acting as a homing beacon for the searchers. Just as importantly, he was keeping me company.

I was losing rational thought. Even though the plane was circling overhead, and even though I thought I saw the pilot drop something near me, I kept wondering if he had really seen me. Was my mind playing tricks on me again? Maybe he was circling because he hadn't seen me, and he was still looking.

"Did you guys see me?" I thought. "Are you coming back for me? Do you know I'm here?"

I put my hands up over my head and waved my arms.

"You know I'm here," I said, "please come and save me."

After the rush of first seeing the plane, I was disheartened to neither hear snowmobiles nor see any other signs of rescue.

"You've made it through the night," I said to myself, "don't lose it now. Be patient. They'll be here."

For more than two hours, I sat there wondering if I was really hearing a plane. Then the plane engines faded. Soon, though, I heard another noise and saw a helicopter.

"Uh-oh, now everyone else knows I was stranded out here overnight," I thought irrationally. Everyone knows that once the LifeFlight helicopter has been called, something bad has happened. I didn't want everyone thinking I was a knucklehead. I remember several members of the Unser family had been stranded in Colorado or New

Mexico a few years earlier and had gotten in trouble for what they were doing on national forest land.

"I hope this isn't a big deal or anything," I thought.

The helicopter circled, dropped in, but then rose into the air again, moved to a flatter area, and landed.

"Good," I thought, "they really are here."

I tried to walk, but couldn't. I needed to stay on my hands and stomach so my weight would be better distributed on the snow. It wouldn't matter if I got colder at that point, because I was going to be saved. I crawled on my belly, pushing as much as I could with my legs, dragging myself forward on my forearms.

I couldn't see a thing because of the blowing snow, but I could tell roughly where the helicopter had landed. I felt the most happiness I had ever felt in my life. As incredible as I felt when I beat Karelin and won the gold medal, it was nothing to the euphoria I felt now. This time I had won the most important match of all—for my life.

Finally, it came into sight. A woman inside the helicopter asked, "Can you get in?"

"I think so," I replied.

A man jumped out of the helicopter and helped me put one leg up. The woman pulled me from inside while the man put his shoulder to my backside and pushed. Finally, I was in. I flopped down on the floor, unable to move, all my energy or adrenaline spent with that effort. But I had been found, alive. No one would find me frozen to death.

"You have to turn this way and sit down," the woman said, a nurse.

I struggled and struggled. The woman put a blanket on me, and then a safety headgear.

"We're ready!" the man called out to the pilot.

I tried to watch out the window as we lifted up. I wanted to see where I had been, see how close I had been to getting out. But I was too exhausted and disoriented to see anything.

It was a quick flight to Star Valley's hospital, bumping up over the top of the mountain and into the valley. Lee Gardner, a relative who is the sheriff of Lincoln County, was waiting when we landed.

"Hi, how you doing?" I asked him. He looked stunned. I still didn't realize exactly what I had been through.

They brought a wheelchair and took me into the hospital. As soon as we got in, someone said, "We have to get your stuff off. Let's get the boots first." But they were frozen to my pants.

I remember everyone's faces, all the concern, so I kept smiling at them to let them know it wasn't that big a deal, that I was going to be all right. Yes, I was uncomfortable and frozen. But I knew I was going to live.

"We have to get your clothes off," someone said.

I tried to stand up, but all those trips into the river had left several inches of ice on my boots. When I tried to stand, it was like being on a hockey rink, a six-inch chunk of ice on my boots.

"Stay down, we'll take them off you," I was told.

They cut down the front of the left boot and worked to get it off. It took two or three people holding me in the wheelchair and two more pulling the boot. Finally, it came off. Once my sock was removed, I got a look at my foot. I wasn't able to move or even feel my toes, and they were various shades of silver and gray in color. The right boot was more stubborn—that was the one I couldn't get off the night before.

"I can use my left foot to push it off," I said.

"No!" came a chorus in reply as everyone freaked out.

"You could break your toes off because of the frozen tissue," someone told me.

"Get the cast saw," a doctor ordered.

They got the cast saw and worked for several minutes, finally getting it loose and then pulling it off. The first toes I saw were completely white.

"Oh, good, they're still white," I said, not knowing if that was a good or bad thing.

They stripped me of my frozen clothes, ice and snow falling everywhere. My body temperature had been in the mid-80's when I was picked up. In the half hour I had been at the hospital in Star Valley, it went up to 88 degrees—registered via a rectal thermometer, as if the past seventeen hours hadn't been bad enough. The doctor examined my body.

"This doesn't look good," a doctor said. "There's nothing we can do here. We're going to have to take you to Idaho Falls."

That decision probably saved my life and certainly saved my feet. I was later told that had they warmed my feet before my body warmed up, the result could have been disastrous. If the extremities are warmed before the body, the blood will rush to the warm area first, and it could prove fatal, causing a heart attack.

I also talked to Danny Schwab, who was torn apart from the incident. I can't believe the courage and sacrifice all of the search and rescue people made for me. Danny; Lane

Walton and his fifteen-year-old son, Casey; my brothers Rollin and Russell; another relative, Randy Gardner; Alan Jensen; Dusty Skinner; and the others who went out in the darkness, fell in the river, and kept looking for me—I'll always be grateful for their efforts. Danny and Trent went out again in the middle of the night to find another route to reach me. Mark Heiner, the pilot, not only spotted me, but also gave me hope at a time when I needed it the most. All of those men, and all the others who were part of the search that night—and there are dozens—showed incredible strength and character to give everything they had to try to save my life. I will never be able to thank them enough.

At Star Valley Hospital they switched me onto another gurney and then loaded me onto the helicopter to head to Idaho Falls, which had a bigger hospital and more resources.

"Get comfortable," someone said.

I was still shivering as they loaded me back onto the cold helicopter. Nineteen hours of shivering and counting. In the helicopter, I started to develop cramps because of the buildup of lactic acid in my body. I kept trying to turn to my side in the helicopter to relieve the cramping and take some pressure off my back and legs.

It was very cold on the helicopter. When I got to Idaho Falls, my body temperature was still 88 degrees. No matter how many blankets they put on me, I was still freezing. Finally, they pulled out a blanket that looked like a mattress and draped it around me—it blew warm air. It was so amazing to feel warmth again. I could've kept that air-blowing blanket on for a month. Though they had all kinds of wonderful resources and a great wound-care unit at Eastern Idaho Regional, what I was most thankful for right then was that warm-air blanket.

I could tell from faces of the doctors and nurses at Eastern Idaho Regional that my feet were in real trouble. They'd look, and squint, making a painful expression with their mouths. No one said anything at first, but they didn't have to. Their faces said it all.

Doctor Timothy Thurman came into my room.

"How is it?" I asked.

"It doesn't look good," Thurman said.

"What does that mean?" I asked.

"It just doesn't look good," he repeated.

"Yes, but what *exactly* does that mean?" I pleaded.

Thurman admitted that he thought I would lose all of my toes. In addition, the front of my feet also would have to be amputated, meaning I'd lose the front third of each foot. That would end my wrestling career, and for the rest of my life walking would be difficult, though not impossible.

But frostbite is unlike anything else that doctors see. They say that "frostbite is something that happens in the winter but is treated in the summer," because only time will tell how severe the damage is. There are no specific treatments for frostbite as there are for other diseases. There is not a surgery to repair damage, or a pill to help regenerate tissue and capillaries. Time is all that works for, and against, a patient. Either the body heals itself and regenerates the needed tissue and blood flow, or it doesn't. But that first day in the hospital, the big key was making sure I was going to live. When someone's body temperature is as low as mine was, the big risk is a "cardiac event"—a heart attack. So they warmed my body first before turning their attention to my feet.

Finally, my body temp reached 97, and the doctors decided to defrost my feet. They put my feet in 104-degree water. After fifteen minutes they took my feet out, but my toes got cold again because they were still frozen. They had to bring in more and hotter water because my frozen feet had cooled the hot water so dramatically. They went through the same fifteen-minute routine, putting my feet in the hot water, then taking them out. After the third time, my toes and the front part of my feet started to blister.

Doctor Thurman explained to me that frostbite is similar to burns in some ways, accounting for the blisters happening before our eyes.

The skin started to fall off. Finally, after the fourth time, my toes were starting to warm. They took me up to the intensive care/wound-care unit and wrapped my feet.

I remember in wound care, the doctor touched my toes and asked me if I could feel it. He did this over and over again. "Can you feel me touching your toes?" I kept answering, "Yes. Yes. Yes." But I had no feeling whatsoever, and couldn't feel any of his touches. I *believed* I could feel it, but the truth is, I simply couldn't. I thought that if I claimed I could feel their touches, they might hold off on amputating my toes or the front third of each foot.

I wanted to keep these things. I needed them.

After being plucked from the mountains, my road back to the Olympics had officially started.

★ ★ ★

Danny Schwab later recalled how the evening unfolded for himself and the other rescuers: "When I left Rulon and Trent, we talked about meeting at six that evening to leave for Jackson for dinner," Danny said. "I told Rulon to call me at four to confirm that I made it out okay and that he would be on his way. So at 4:00 P.M. he called me from the top of the mountain and said he was on top of the world and couldn't believe how beautiful the view was. I knew time was running short for him to make it back in time, so I said, 'Well, hurry it up because we're going to be late for dinner if you don't get back.'

"After we got off the phone, it turns out, was when Rulon's problems began. When 6:00 rolled around, I was concerned. First of all, Rulon is late for everything—except dinner, he's never late for dinner.

"When Trent showed up at my house, he had this horrified look on his face, and I thought, 'Oh no, there's been an avalanche.' But it wasn't an avalanche.

" 'Rulon's stuck in a ravine and he can't get out,' Trent said. Trent could hear Rulon's snowmobile running up the hill, as it turned out, in an attempt to get up the mountain and out. Trent said he could see Rulon's headlight from time to time as Rulon made run after run to try to get out. 'This is something we can handle,' I figured at that point. 'The more I talked to Trent, the less things started to add up as far as where Rulon had dropped off the mountain, where he had headed down the ravine. His mention of the headlight disappearing was also a concern, but I realized Rulon was probably going to try to find another way to get out. 'Did Rulon ever get his coat?' I asked Trent. When Trent said Rulon was still just wearing the fleece, I grew more concerned. I made the decision to call Search and Rescue, even though it would upset Rulon, because he'd have probably thought at that point that he still wasn't in any real trouble. I told Search and Rescue that Lane Walton and I were headed up to the area where Rulon had last been seen. Rulon was probably seven to eight miles south of Smoot at that point, as the crow flies."

"By 7:00 P.M. I had already called Lane, who is a very experienced rider. 'Something has happened to Rulon, we have to hurry and get up into the mountains.' Lane knows the area very well. I have a cabin up there and also know it well, which is why I took Rulon and Trent up there with me.

"The Search and Rescue guys, led by Dusty Skinner, obviously were worried and wanted to find Rulon, but not many of those guys were as experienced riders as me, Lane, and Lane's son, Casey, who is an absolutely amazing snowmobile rider, maybe even better than his dad. We decided not to wait for Search and Rescue—they knew what was going on, and I had told them as much as I knew at that point—and I headed out with Lane and Casey.

"We got to a place called 'The Chute,' almost a half-mile slope where it's almost vertical—nearly straight up, in parts, very dangerous—and I knew a lot of the Search and Rescue guys, even with the best of intentions, couldn't make it. So Casey and Lane went ahead. I have a souped-up snowmobile, so I had Lane take that, because it's very powerful and he'd need all that and more to get through the area, and I waited for the Search and Rescue guys, to help them make it up the Chute since I could do it. But that ended up not working out. Six or seven of the guys still hadn't made it up at that point—because the guys were rolling their sleds trying to make it in—it was just rough terrain. Lane and Casey, who were out searching, came back at that point—on one snowmobile together, because they had gone into the water on mine, the exact same thing that had happened to Rulon.

" 'Danny, Rulon is in trouble,' Lane said. 'And your machine is in three feet of water.' I looked at him. 'What? There's no water up there, we're up on the mountain.'

"At the bottom of the ravine, it narrows to maybe three or four feet wide, at most. Rulon followed that and came to a fork in the canyon. Unbeknownst to all of us, there is a spring that comes out of the ground there, causing a pool about twelve to fourteen feet in diameter—in almost a perfect circle. It had been covered with snow and a thin layer of ice before Rulon went across it, and it just collapsed under his weight. That's where Rulon had to lift the snowmobile six feet, straight up, to get out of the pool of water. 'You can see where Rulon went in the water,' Lane explained, 'and how he pulled the machine out.'

"We took off to get my sled together. It took six of us—Rollin, Lane, Casey, Keith Hart, Dusty, and myself—to get my snowmobile out of the water, so how Rulon pulled his five hundred-pound snowmobile that was soaking wet from the water, all alone, I will never know.

"At that point, Lane and Casey took off together. We had pulled my sled out of the water for Lane to continue on, and Casey, a fifteen-year-old kid and amazing rider, just skipped his sled right across the water.

"The rest of us had to get across that twelve-to-fourteen-foot pool of water too, so we made a snow bridge and stomped it down. In no time, it froze into a bridge of solid ice, so we could get across the water, since the other guys, like Rulon, had fallen in earlier.

"So Casey and Lane picked up Rulon's tracks briefly after about a half mile, though the tracks ended with a drop off into the head of the Salt River Canyon. Casey and Lane came back, told us what was going on, so we all walked to check it out.

"We could see trees at the bottom, and figured Rulon had had an accident, so we were hoping he was okay, because we figured we'd find him down there. Then we saw his tracks, where he had dragged his legs to slow his speed, and had avoided these trees, including a big Douglas fir in the path that had a three-foot trunk.

" 'Good Lord,' Lane said, 'Rulon headed down the canyon.'

"At this point night had fallen—a clear and bitterly cold night, but no moon. The silence was pure and complete. We listened for Rulon's snowmobile engine, and then would yell his name. We were hoping our voices would carry to him, because noise travels so well in that canyon, surrounded by mountains. But as we yelled, we'd hear the echoes bounce around loudly, and then nothing, complete silence, as our voices disappeared in the night.

"Between 10:30 and 11:00 P.M., Search and Rescue contacted Alan Jensen, who lives in Smoot and snowmobiles the area more often than us and knows the area better. It took some time to contact him and get him to where we were at the base camp we had established on the southwest corner at the base of Wagner Mountain. We waited around our campfire, and Alan, who would be the guide, was there in about an hour, close to midnight.

"Most of the Search and Rescue guys—a group of volunteers from the community—were in unfamiliar territory, and since I knew the area better and had been part of the search that evening from the start, Dusty Skinner, who was coordinating the search and rescue—he was clearly in charge that night—had me stay with them. If Alan got in trouble, I'd be the only one who really knew where to find him and how to get to him. Dusty left at that point to go to Smith Fork to snowshoe back up the river from that direction with at least two others.

"So Alan Jensen, Lane Walton, Casey Walton, Rollin Gardner, and Randy Gardner headed back in after Rulon on the new route Alan had decided upon.

"That group of five crossed the big meadow, followed the river where it narrowed, and came upon another area that was nearly impassable, but they could tell this had been Rulon's route. Had Rulon stopped at any of these places, we'd have found him much earlier, because we hit all of the places he had hit, I would guess, within an hour or two of him being there. But he was in survival mode at that point, soaking wet, and he thought his only option was to never stop pushing. Knowing Rulon, he kept on, because he would not give up, would not give in, not allow himself to be defeated.

"The radios were fading as the batteries froze. 'Rulon keeps crossing Salt River,' we were told by the searchers.

" 'Rulon is panicking,' Lane said over the radio. 'I can tell by the way he's riding, because he keeps crossing open water on the river.' The searchers would try to cross and get stuck or submerge their snowmobiles as they tried to follow Rulon's tracks. Finally, they were stuck so badly that they had to shut down the machines, get them out of the water, and dry out the spark plugs to get them started again. This would've been between 1:30 and 2:00 A.M., when they were only 150 to 200 yards from Rulon.

" 'Tell Danny that you guys will find Rulon right there,' Lane radioed, 'in the meadow, because Rulon just could not have gone any farther.' They needed about ninety minutes to get the snowmobiles out of the river and running again. They had to get out of there, because they were wet and freezing.

" 'All five of our guys are wet,' Lane radioed in the last transmission before the radios quit. 'If we don't stop, we're going to have five more guys who could die out here.' They had to come back to base camp, or they would die, soaking wet and freezing. Since Lane had given me good directions to where, as it turned out, Rulon was, within 150 yards, I knew I needed to go into the area from the south to Salt River and follow it up to the meadow. With all the great information they provided, I knew I had to avoid the water as much as I could, but I also knew just about exactly where Rulon had to be. 'I'm going to leave Base Camp, Trent and I, and come in from the other way and get to him,' I said. The other Search and Rescue guys, it was decided, needed to stay at the base camp and keep the fire going, because the five coming out could be in very bad shape, freezing and soaked. I drove to the Smith Fork parking lot with Trent, getting there a little after 5:00 A.M., and was getting ready at 5:30 to snowmobile in when the Search and Rescue guys who were at Base Camp showed up at Smith Fork. So Lane and the other four had come out to find no fire, no one waiting for them. I understand the searchers all just wanted to help, just wanted to find Rulon, but I was also worried for the other five coming out, knowing they were wet and frozen and exhausted after pulling sleds from the water. Lane called when he got to base camp.

"I thought you guys had a fire going," an upset Lane said. I explained what had happened, and Lane and Casey and the others had to rush home to warm up, hypothermia setting in and frostbite a real danger.

"It was time for me and Trent to go in after Rulon.

"I just hoped it wouldn't be too late. Trent and I, with a fresh radio given to us by Sheriff's Deputy Wade Harmon, started our route, but ended up on a real high knoll overlooking the Salt River drainage, and were in another area impossible to reach Rulon from, because of the steep slope and timber. I was frustrated, and heart-broken, because I knew I was probably a half mile at the most from him. I could not believe the cold that night—and Trent and I were dressed for it—because even for the Star Valley . . . my word, it was cold.

"I knew he was soaking wet, it's 25 below, and it hits me at that point: Rulon's dead. I walked a ways discreetly away, and dropped to my knees, and prayed, pleaded, for Rulon's life. Though I was out of sight, Trent knew what I was doing, and he saw the tears frozen on my cheeks when I got back to him. I knew Rulon was dead. This amazing young man who had accomplished so much, had exceeded so many expectations. I wish I had prepared him more for something like this. I had taught him to ride, and he had always followed me. I had taken him into this area to show him extreme snowmobiling. I had yet to teach him how to start a fire using the sled. And I had taken the survival kit with me when I left that afternoon. We were fighting the elements, and we were dressed for it. And we weren't soaking wet, as we knew Rulon was, because they'd seen where his sled had gone into the river—several times.

"My fingers and toes were numb at that point. 'I know we've lost him,' I said to Trent.

"At that point Mark Heiner, my cousin, who is a test pilot for Aviat Aircraft, was going to start flying over the area at first light. As the sunlight opened the sky, I heard an airplane and knew it was Mark.

"We started communicating with Mark on the radio through Search and Rescue. 'I have spotted Rulon!' Mark called out over the radio. 'He is moving—he waved his arm. Rulon is alive!'

"At that point I just said, 'Get him out of there!'

"LifeFlight in Las Vegas was sending its helicopter to get him. But my tears of joy turned to tears of anger when I heard on the radio that the helicopter had decided not to come. 'He's too heavy,' they said. 'They turned back.'

"Mark felt totally helpless at that point. He dropped his coat to him, but Rulon was showing no signs of movement since the initial wave. 'Rulon has totally stopped moving,' Mark called over the radio. 'Please, get Life-Flight here, quick!'

"Tears ran down my face. We had found him, and now we were going to lose him. Our snowmobiles couldn't get even ten yards closer to him from where we were. Then over the radio someone said, 'The Olympic Committee or someone has got a LifeFlight from Utah.' It's been more than a half hour since Rulon was found, and because Mark had seen no further movement from Rulon, Mark believes we have lost him, that Rulon has died because his body could not fight anymore, because we could not get to him, because the chopper from Las Vegas bailed on us, because everything has gone so tragically wrong.

"Another hour or so goes by, and there is no chopper in sight from Salt Lake City. Just what in the world is going on? I watched the southwest sky, waiting to see it or hear the helicopter engine, and there is nothing. No chopper, no sounds, nothing. And my friend is dead, or dying, a half mile vertically below me.

"All of a sudden—about two to two and a half hours after Rulon had first been spotted by Mark—literally out of nowhere I heard a loud noise. I jerk my head and look north, because right over the hill comes the LifeFlight chopper from Eastern Idaho Regional Medical Center in Idaho Falls. Eastern Idaho's chopper swoops in and, after an initial pass to find an area, lands, and less than four minutes after I first saw the chopper, they radio that they have Rulon on board, and are headed for the hospital in Star Valley. Four minutes. That's all it took. We waited more than two hours for a chopper. And then it was just 240 seconds to get him once it crested the mountains. If Eastern Idaho hadn't stepped up, Rulon doesn't live. It's that simple.

"When I saw Rulon just a short while later at the hospital, I must've had some odd look on my face, because the second our eyes met, Rulon burst out laughing. It seemed so incongruent with the situation, the circumstances, everything going on around us, everything that had happened the past twenty hours. Finally we were able to talk for a few minutes, with Sheriff Lee Gardner—

another relative of Rulon's—and Steve Perry in the room. Rulon explained, just as we thought, that he was following the Salt River, thinking it would take him out, not knowing it would change direction, not knowing there'd be so many impassable areas of rocks and cliffs and ravines.

"I smiled back at him, so glad he was alive. But I turned solemn when I saw his feet: those were frozen, white, solid blocks—they looked like if you hit them with a hammer, they would shatter. The doctors and nurses kept taking his core temperature, which was in the low 80's when he was first found but was up to the mid-80's as he warmed a little. I knew he was going to lose both of his feet at that point—everyone in the emergency room could see that—no one wanted to say it, but it was written on everyone's face."

The pilot who found me, Mark Heiner, sent me this heartfelt letter after I was rescued and had begun my rehabilitation.

Oct. 5, 2003

Dear Rulon,

I hope this letter finds all well with you. I have been thinking about writing this letter for a long time. It seems hard to get down on paper some thoughts and feelings with regard to the night and day you spent in the mountains and my part in helping you. I have asked your brothers and others to give me a call when you are here in the valley so we could sit down and have a little time to talk about what happened. Between your time and mine sitting down together has not happened and so I have decided to write this letter. I have a lot of feelings and thoughts about that morning I feel you would want to know. So, after a long time, here goes.

I received a phone call for the search and rescue at 2:30 A.M. on that morning telling me a celebrity person was long overdue and feared lost in the head of Salt River. They asked me if I could fly and help find this person. I told them I would not fly in the dark in that country but I would be glad to be in the air at first light looking. They said that would be great.

I got out of bed and went and looked at the temperature outside and became concerned. The temperature at my house was 10 degrees below zero at 2:30 in the morning. That would drop down to about 20 degrees below zero just after the sun would be up. How would I get an airplane started in this cold? The only choice I had was to get an airplane that was in a warm building which meant it had to be a Husky from Aviat Aircraft where I work as the test pilot. The next concern I had was whether there was one at work that I could fly. I tried to remember if there was one ready to fly. I just couldn't remember.

I decided to go back to bed and sleep for a little while which of course didn't work. My mind kept thinking about the person lost, alone in the mountains in this cold.

I finally gave up on the sleep and got up and got ready for the day. I knew it would be cold flying so I dressed for the cold. After I got ready I drove to the Search and Rescue building to get more information on where and who I would be looking for.

As I visited with the Search and Rescue personnel they were hesitant to give me your name. Finally one of the personnel told me what you were wearing and who I would be looking for. (I have found it helps me a lot if I know what color of clothes and the size of person I would be looking for.) I was told you did not have a coat and instantly became concerned. I said a silent prayer that you had a fire started and that you would be alive for me to find. I also asked in the prayer for help and direction in helping to find you.

We (the Search and Rescue and I) visited and decided on the radio procedures I would use to stay in contact. We also decided I would use my cell phone if I could not reach them on the radio. They asked me to look for you in the head of Salt River Canyon just under Wagner Lake. I had a thought placed in my mind at that moment that that was not the place to look. I kept that thought to myself and left for the airport.

I could not shake the thought or prompting, while I was getting the airplane ready to fly, that I needed to look in a different place, but where? Again I asked for help in the search in a silent prayer. I was still uncertain where to look.

I gathered together my survival gear and placed it in the back seat and pushed the airplane outside. It really seemed cold. The temperature was showing 18 degrees below zero when I started the airplane. It was still dark but I had decided to get going as soon as possible. I took off at about 6:35 A.M. and started south. As I flew over the mouth of Cottonwood Canyon I felt the impression not to look up the canyon but to look down from the meadows. With this impression I headed for the meadow in the middle of the upper Salt River Canyon.

I flew direct to the meadow and saw your snowmobile tracks there and turned down canyon. I had only made the turn and started down the canyon and saw no more tracks. I was flying down in the canyon so it would require getting to one side of the canyon to turn around and go back up and retrace your tracks. I moved to the north wall and started a turn to the south. About halfway though the turn I saw your foot tracks in the snow and followed them to a tree and out into the river. You were standing in the middle of the river when I first saw you. You were waving one arm over your head. I flew over you at about 100 feet to get a good look. What I saw really scared me. You were covered with what appeared to be ice and you were standing in the water not on the bank.

I flew up the canyon to make the turn and was trying to decide what to do. I knew you needed a coat and a way to get warm. I took off my heavy coat and put it into a plastic bag so I could drop it somewhere close to you. I flew back over you and dropped the coat as close as I could without hitting you (not my best drop). I watched you for a couple minutes. You took about six steps toward the coat and stopped and sat down in the snow. I buzzed by a couple times and you didn't wave or even move.

I have been cold and have had frostbite a couple times in the past. What I saw you do made me very concerned for you. I climbed back out of the canyon and tried to get help to you. While I was flying over you I had taken the location on a GPS so I could direct help to you. I could not get any reply to my radio calls so I took my cell phone and called the Search and Rescue. I told them where you were and gave them the GPS location. They told me they would have a chopper there in a short time. They asked if I were returning to Afton. I thought about it for just a couple seconds and said NO. I thought you needed to have me there until help arrived. I told them I would stay until the chopper arrived to direct them to you.

I flew back into the canyon and started circling overhead. I found it was a little warmer if I flew about 1,000 ft. above the canyon floor. The temperature there was about 8–10 degrees below zero. Because I was flying so slowly it was hard to keep warm even with the heater on in the airplane. I really felt how much you needed help. I watched you and it became very evident you were in the advanced stages of exposure. Your movement (when you moved) was extremely slow. You were wandering in no direct path. You would sit down in the snow and not move for the longest time. After you had sat in one location for about 15 minutes I would drop down and buzz you as low as I could to keep you from lying down. (You did lay down a couple times). I wanted to keep you awake.

After about 45 minutes I climbed back out of the canyon and called the Search and Rescue again to see what was taking so long. They said the chopper could not come from Salt Lake City and they were trying to get one from Idaho Falls. I asked to speak with Bonnie (Hunsaker, a Search and Rescue volunteer who was coordinating radio contact). After she came on the phone, I told her you were in a very bad way and I was very concerned you were dying and if they didn't get a chopper in very soon they would be removing a body. I think it really scared them when I told them what I was seeing.

I returned to the canyon to check on you and you were lying down again. I did the "buzz" on you again to get you back up. In my heart I was having the hardest time I have ever had in my life. I was watching someone die and there was not a thing, it seemed, I could do to help you. I thought about putting the airplane down in the snow just below where you were but that didn't seem like a good idea either. The only idea I could come up with was to pray. It seemed the only help I could give you. I felt the impression your life had a purpose and it was not your time.

Just after that moment a call came over the airplane radio from LifeFlight from Idaho Falls asking for directions to you. I was low in the canyon when they called so I instructed them to fly down the canyon and then fly up canyon until I called your position. They flew up the canyon until I called your position. They acknowledged they had you in sight. I stayed until they had landed. I asked if they had time to recover my coat but that you were the priority. I also explained your condition to them as I saw it. They thanked me and I informed them I was returning to Afton.

I landed back at Afton at 9:10 A.M. I was about as cold as I wanted to be. It took about an hour and one half to get my temperature back up so I really felt for you.

It has been over a year and one half since that day but it still seems as if it just happened. The feeling still is strong and still brings tears when I remember how you looked and my inability to help you. You have often been in my prayers and thoughts over this time.

Thanks for your time and letting me explain the feeling I have had. I have needed to express these thoughts and feelings to you for quite some time.

Thanks.
Sincerely,
Mark Heiner

Nineteen

ANOTHER RUN AT THE OLYMPICS

ONCE IT WAS clear that I was going to live, the doctors focused on my feet. The hospital turned into a circus. Forty-six women showed up wanting to see me, all claiming to be my wife—I know, I know, go figure that one out. But the person in charge of keeping out non–family members actually counted. We were in a strong Latter Day Saints community, where I was as well known as I'd be anywhere. Most of these people had followed my story from the Olympics and after. My guess is that these women just wanted to let me know they were on my side, pulling for me. The outpouring of support was overwhelming.

The media was giving the story a lot of play. I was in no condition to deal with media requests, leaving my family to answer for me. Stories circulated and misinformation was rampant. The only known truths were that I was lucky to be alive, and that I'd be fortunate to keep either or both of my feet—frontal amputations seemed imminent. I'd be lucky to walk again. Wrestling, I was told, wasn't even in the picture. I was told if I could just get back to walking functionally, it'd be miraculous.

The feet looked horrible, pink and flaking what little skin was left. I was taken down to Pocatello, just a short drive down Interstate 15, for treatment in a hyperbaric chamber, which takes you "below sea level" to stimulate healing by increasing the oxygen in your blood.

The hyperbaric treatment came the day after the first surgery on my feet. Doctors inserted pins into my toes to keep them straight. The lost and damaged skin was a concern, but even more so were the damaged ligaments and joints.

My family had been there supporting me right after I was rescued and taken to Eastern Idaho Regional Medical Center in Idaho Falls. But as days and then a week went by, I realized that there were parts of this I had to go through myself. My family and friends were great, don't get me wrong, but part of recovering would involve gathering my thoughts, getting my focus, and dealing with everything in front of me. I couldn't talk that out with people, it had to come from within me. I thanked my family, then asked them to leave, and they respected me enough to give me that space I needed.

In wound care, the techs took off all the dead tissue—with sandpaper—that was still coming off, and changed the dressings. At first it was twice a day, then once a day, and then a couple of times a week—more often, though, if I just had undergone a surgery.

On my third treatment, I went alone to the hyperbaric chamber in Pocatello.

I got around via wheelchair at that point, but I decided

to drive myself, even though my doctor obviously wouldn't have wanted me to. I'd wheel myself out to my truck, throw the wheelchair in the back of it, and then climb into the truck, get on the highway, and set the cruise control so I could elevate my really bad leg—the right one—as I drove, to keep the circulation up. I'd get to the treatment center housing the hyperbaric chamber, get the wheelchair out of the truck bed, and wheel myself in.

I knew the treatment—which included breathing pure oxygen in the chamber—was intended to stimulate healing by getting more oxygen into the affected area, but also into my body in general, again to help the healing. I could feel the pressure on my body in the chamber.

The professionals treating me were very knowledgeable and helpful, explaining to me what needed to be done, because I had a lot of questions and wanted to know exactly what was going on at every step of the way. They also treated me like a person rather than a patient, and I made some lasting friendships while they treated me. I had no idea how long the chamber visits would go on before I'd start to experience some healing, but I knew from Dr. Thurman that the hyperbaric had worked for a lot of other people suffering from diabetes and other illnesses that potentially could cause them to lose a limb. It's a method of treatment that a lot of people think is bogus, because they don't know about it, because it's new and unfamiliar. But I'm testimony that it can work wonders, and in fact can speed healing at a remarkable rate in some cases.

After the third hyperbaric treatment concluded, the technicians and nurses re-did my dressings, and I got into my truck to drive myself back to my Idaho Falls hotel room. Shortly into the trip, I felt a splashing around my feet and thought I had knocked over a water bottle on the seat next to me. But the bottle was there, the lid-closed tightly. Finally I looked down and saw a good half-liter of blood splashing around on the floormats. I couldn't grasp the incredible amount of blood gushing through the bandages—I didn't know I had that much circulation in my feet at that point. I called up the hospital and asked one of the wound-care techs if I could come back in. He said he didn't think so, that bleeding could be expected. I guess I couldn't convey the amount of blood, because he said just to "come in for your regular visit," which was still a day or two away. Finally, I called Dr. Thurman.

"My feet are bleeding," I told him. "I have to see someone."

"Come in the second you get back to town," he said. "I'll be waiting for you."

Although I had panicked at all the blood, Dr. Thurman assured me this was a "good sign."

"I'm very impressed with the blood flow," he said.

I went to those treatments for about three weeks, and my body was healing up miraculously well in that regard, though that would get me to the point where we'd have to address the lack of skin on my toes, the damaged ligaments and joints, and everything that came along with that.

I met some amazing people on those visits, mostly older people being treated for various illnesses or conditions that hyperbaric treatment could help. Those people were wonderful to me. They told their relatives they were going through treatments with Rulon Gardner and asked me to sign autographs. When they told me I had inspired them, first by winning the gold medal and then by surviving the night in the snow, I was humbled, because these folks were, in most cases, fighting for their own lives, showing remarkable courage. The saying among hyperbaric patients was "Life or Limb," as many were getting treatments to stave off an amputation of their own.

I carry their words, their smiles, and their kind thoughts with me wherever I go. They were not quitters, they were fighters—how could that not inspire me?

I had four surgeries in the following four months—and another surgery to graft skin onto several problem toes would come after the 2004 Olympics. Most were skin graft or pin related. The bottoms of my toes had pigskin grafted to them, while Dr. Thurman shaved skin off my upper thigh to put on the tops of the toes. The healing process really just was getting under way in April 2002, but I still had business to tend to, which involved speeches and appearances that had been set up before the stranding in the Wyoming wilderness. I did many of those speeches from my wheelchair.

One of those appearances was part of a trade-out deal in which my brother Rollin, who had come back to Afton to run the family farm, received a new milking parlor in the barn in exchange for a few speeches. One of the five appearances in that trade-out was in Cancun, Mexico. This was two weeks after a skin graft surgery.

On the big toes, the tissue initially had to be trimmed all the way to the ligament and bone. In Cancun, even though I was doing the speech from a wheelchair, I had to walk at times to get around. The toll was high on that trip; the skin from the graft wasn't healing. I sat looking at the bone and ligament on my right toe and wondered if this would be, once again, a situation where my career would be in jeopardy—or if I would even be keeping the big toe.

So when I came home I had another surgery, this one for the skin graft for my right big toe, again.

As my toes healed and tissue came back either slowly or by skin graft, I worked more with the rehabilitation people, trying to carefully establish a range of motion, getting the ligaments to heal and the joints to start functioning again—something that would not occur to any noticeable degree until the pins were out.

The physical therapy part of it was a challenge. On the one hand, I had to challenge myself every day; on the other, the therapists had to make sure I didn't break off my toes at the joint or tear the ligaments by doing too much too soon. I went into each session knowing that I needed to push myself to help the healing, but also aware that a broken bone or torn ligament at this point meant I'd probably have to have that toe, or toes, amputated. And if it were a big toe—I'd hear these words from the doctor—"Your wrestling career is over."

Once again I have to say how amazing everyone in Idaho was—the doctors, nurses, wound-care technicians. They were incredibly good to me, and great at their jobs. What a blessing to have that kind of medical care available so close to where I had been stranded. The community in Idaho Falls was very kind and really opened its collective arms to me. Whether I was out eating or shopping, people would stop and offer a kind thought and support. I was amazed that they had followed my story so closely and were pulling for me to get better. Many told me about how they had prayed for me. Total strangers, yet it was as if we'd long known each other. I left there with a warm heart because of the special people of eastern Idaho, and I'll always be grateful for their compassion and support.

I only had to have one toe amputated, the middle right one, as I readied to return to wrestling. It was too damaged and unresponsive to all the treatment, so Dr. Thurman had to remove it. It's in a jar of formaldehyde in my refrigerator, a reminder of what happened to me that night, and in part what I lost and had to overcome.

I kept returning to Dr. Thurman, but every step forward seemed to be followed by a small step back. Sometimes there would be notable progress; other times there would be no real tissue growth or healing.

I was doing my best to keep from having anything else amputated. Those were the days that scared me; if my feet wouldn't regrow skin and accept the skin grafts, I wouldn't walk again, much less wrestle.

But then progress started happening at a faster rate. I had more movement in my feet. Walking, while by no means easy, was getting manageable as long as I didn't try to do much more than drag my feet, keeping them as flat as possible on each step.

"If you believe in miracles—and I do," Dr. Thurman told a writer about six weeks after the accident as he watched me walking around a hospital room, "then Rulon's story is miraculous."

So was Dr. Thurman's work.

Though there were constant setbacks, there was never a question of "if" I would wrestle again. The only question in my mind was "when."

My weight went up over my usual competitive size to over 300 pounds. This was a more significant issue than usual, because with the addition of women's wrestling to the Olympic program, weight classes were being cut in the men's discipline. The sport's governing body was not allowed by the International Olympic Committee to add a whole new division without cutting a corresponding number of weight classes in the men's wrestling programs—at this point in the Olympics, sports are always trying to get "into the Games" and be recognized as Olympic sports, but the IOC wants to keep the Games the same size, basically. So that meant the heavyweights had to get lighter. My division was trimmed from 286 pounds to 264. I had struggled at times to come in at 286, so making weight at 264 would be another challenge.

Once again—or I probably should say "as always"—I got ahead of myself in the rehabilitation and didn't take it as slow as the doctors wanted. I was home riding around on a four-wheeler. Since I was nowhere close to being able to put on shoes or boots, I was riding around in my flip-flops. I hit a piece of pipe or something, and it knocked me off balance. My foot—the left one, my "good" one—slipped out of the left flip-flop and I drove the four-wheeler right over it. The vehicle ran up the back of my calf, too, leaving several huge abrasions and bruises.

My brother Russell, who seems to be the family's 911 dispatcher at times, helped me. Dr. Thurman was on his honeymoon up in Jackson, a few hours north of Star Valley. So Russell called his cell phone. Thurman's concern was understandable, that the pin in my left toe had bent or broken. I had only two pins left at that point, one in each big toe—the most important toe on each foot, so I needed to keep them. On top of that, the accident had torn off part of the skin graft and damaged some of my tissue. There was blood everywhere.

Dr. Thurman instructed Russell to get something to pull the pin out of my big left toe to make sure the pin wasn't broken or bent. Russell went to his shop and pulled out some vise-grip pliers.

After wiggling it back and forth to loosen it as much as possible, he pulled the pin out and told Dr. Thurman, over the phone, that the pin was straight and not broken.

"Well," Dr. Thurman said, "put the son of a gun back in."

Russell said out loud in a tone of surprise, "Put it back *in?*"

I was screaming, "No way!" I told Russell we could take care of this at the hospital after Dr. Thurman's honeymoon.

"Let Rulon think about the pain for a minute there, so this doesn't happen again," Thurman told Russell, "but then, yes, it has to go back in, right away."

Russell put that thing back in. Even with all the nerve damage, I felt enough pain to send me to the moon. He put some ointment on it and wrapped the skin grafts as tight as he could. Dr. Thurman also told him to apply some adhesive medical "skin" and to bandage me back up.

I stayed off four-wheelers for a while after that.

Though my feet stood in the way of my coming back to make the 2004 Olympic Team—or to even wrestle again, or to even lead a normal lifestyle—I knew I had to wrestle again. Wrestling was the key to my living a "normal life."

Even when I was in a hospital bed being told I'd probably lose all, or both, or parts of my feet, my love for wrestling kept me going. I wasn't thinking about defending my gold medal or even about making the Olympic Team, I just wanted to get back on the mat. If I could get back into training and get onto the mat, I'd know that I was making progress. So the focus was always getting back to being myself. Wrestling would help my feet completely heal, and once that happened, I could enjoy the rest of my life. Wrestling was my motivation to get completely healthy.

As I started wrestling again, the fire was fanned within my heart, and I wanted more than ever to make the Olympic Team. I wanted to finish what I had started in 1996, when I failed to make the team because I missed the weigh-ins.

But as has been the case for most of my life, this wouldn't be easy.

When I first got back to the Colorado Springs Olympic Training Center in late August 2002 to start training— after my right middle toe had been amputated—my feet were still bandaged. Blood would soak through just from walking. I could wear no shoes, only flip-flops.

I knew that the physical therapy at the Olympic Training Center could produce a setback at any moment if I overdid it, or, literally, if I took just one wrong step. Still, I pushed forward, working extensively on a rope ladder, going up forward, backward, stepping inside, outside, sometimes climbing laterally, to get my feet functioning properly again—well, as best as they ever could, because never again would they be the same.

I remember walking into the weight room at the

training center, and everyone wanted to see my feet. I carefully unwrapped the bandages and saw people grimace and wince—it was that gruesome to look at. Many of the wrestlers—and this is a pretty tough group—had to look away, because the simple gore of it was more than they ever expected.

Then the whispers started, some loud enough for me to hear, some repeated to me by other people. No one was ever anything but complimentary that I had survived the night and was trying to come back, but the look in the eyes of the majority of people spoke a familiar message: the Wyoming farm boy is done. Several people who had believed in me in 2000 were simply writing me off: "No way he's getting on the mat with those hunks of meat as feet" or "Well, it was a good run, but he'll be lucky to walk again."

I knew I inspired some people at the training center. People would look at my "raw hamburger" feet and think, "What will it take for this guy to cash it in, to realize he can't make it this time?" I hope I helped every one of them put their own obstacles in perspective. I hope my determination made every one of them want to train harder.

Finally, in September 2002, I was back on the wrestling mat, though with oversized shoes, because my swollen, still-damaged feet wouldn't fit into my regular-sized shoes.

The worst problem I faced on the wrestling mat was that I could not push off with my feet. I had no range of motion, which was a limiting factor. My balance and mobility were strained by the condition of the tissue.

Every day at practice, the pain in my feet was excruciating. I tried not to think about it, letting the adrenaline rush I got while practicing push me through the pain threshold. But after practice, I'd see the bandages soaked with blood and feel ten different kinds of pain emanating from my feet. Stretching my toes was still very hard, mainly because the joints hadn't fully healed and the ligaments were still far from being in the condition they had been in before.

Feet just can't be "forced" to get better. I constantly worried that I'd tear a joint or ligament. If that happened, I'd be sidelined indefinitely, missing valuable training time, which I didn't have to spare. If the joints or ligaments were damaged badly enough, then I'd have to have surgery and could face more amputations.

When I started wrestling again, I slowly got into playing basketball with the other wrestlers, something I enjoyed immensely. It's a good conditioning activity and helps us work on agility. The first time I played, I went up to tip in a rebound. I had shifted my weight and balance. I was able to change direction, something I knew would be a challenge for the joints and ligaments in my toes and feet. So that was a good sign.

I pushed myself as much as I thought I could. I had faith that it all would work out in the end. Getting my coordination back was hard, and the power I used to push off on the mat never quite came back to the level it was before the injury.

The first match I wrestled was with someone who was a friend and would become like a brother to me, Dremiel Byers, whom I had beaten to make the World Championship team in 2001. He was the one going to Worlds this time—where he would win the title—and I was training with him. Dremiel is twice the athlete I am. But when I beat him in "the clinch" the first time we wrestled at practice, I realized that though they were still far down the road, my goals were within my grasp, because I had just beaten the man who in the following week would win the 2002 World Championship.

I continued to rehab the feet and train on the mat, working with renewed vigor in the weight room. I was at a point where I needed every edge I could get, and anything I could do to get physically stronger would help. At the same time, though, I had to keep my weight lower than I ever had before with the new, lower weight class. The 2003 U.S. Nationals were my chance to show I was still a force to be reckoned with. However, I didn't get to face Byers in the final, because I got sloppy and lost to Corey Farkas in the semifinals. Farkas was ecstatic knocking me off. I wasn't 100 percent by any means, but it was his time in the spotlight, and he enjoyed it, until Byers took him down in the final.

I still had a chance to make the 2003 World Championship team, but I'd have to beat Farkas and then Dremiel.

Dremiel Byers and I have a mutual respect. I'm not better than Dremiel, and he's not better than me. He's a gladiator. As the defending world champion in 2003, he had followed with another U.S. Nationals title in 2003. But to get the spot on the 2003 U.S. World team, he still had to win our World Team Trials. Before our match, we told each other that no matter what, we would each be there for the other.

Dremiel has a muscular, chiseled physique and is very

quick. As a soldier in the U.S. Army, he always represents America very proudly. And on the mat, his relentlessness and determination has made him into a champion. Even though we had a rivalry—only one spot exists for the two of us—we always pushed each other to be better wrestlers. So when one of us beat the other, it was up to the one who didn't win to do all he could to help bring home the gold.

I wanted him to win the 2002 World Championships with all my heart. I told him what I had learned, who to watch out for, anything I could think of that would increase his chances. Of course, Dremiel had a great coaching staff from USA Wrestling who prepared him, reviewed tapes, and planned strategies.

The format for the 2003 World Trials was a familiar one: the winner from Nationals gets a bye until the final, where he wrestles only the guy who makes it through the tournament World Team Trials bracket. I beat Farkas 3–1 and had Byers in the final. Byers was in great shape and at the top of his game. It was a best two-out-of-three format. I won two matches and claimed the United States' spot in my division for the World Championships. The match with Byers was the biggest statement of my comeback to that point.

Dremiel took the loss like the graceful champion he is and started practice-training with me again the next day. He wanted me to win the Worlds in 2003.

That was an important step in my comeback, to be able to get back into the biggest tournament of a non-Olympic year and measure myself against the other best wrestlers in the world. To make it even better, I had Dremiel to help me prepare.

When Dremiel won the 2002 U.S. Nationals and World Team Trials to represent our country at the 2002 Worlds, I was very proud of him. Dremiel is one of the more remarkable people I've ever met in my life. We are from very different backgrounds: he is from North Carolina, I'm from the rural West. I respect what he's done with his life: he's in the U.S. Army, as is his wife. he competes in the army's World Class Athlete Program.

Although I didn't perform as I well as I had hoped at the 2003 World Championships, I was able to measure myself against the best wrestlers in the world. I wasn't anywhere near 100 percent in terms of my feet, but my conditioning was good and my feet were making progress. Russian Khassan Baroev won the 2003 World title, beating a very familiar face, Hungary's Mihaly Deak-Bardos, for the gold. Bulgaria's Sergei Moreyko claimed sixth place, and even the guy who I had easily defeated in Sydney, Armenia's Haykaz Ghalstyan, finished in front of me, in ninth place. A tenth-place finish wasn't what I was hoping for, though at the same time it gave me feedback on what I needed to improve.

So that's what I did. I had to get stronger again—not just as strong as I was in 2000 or 2001, but even stronger, to compensate for my feet. So I hit the weight room hard at the Olympic Training Center. My squat went to a personal high of five hundred pounds and I bench-pressed four hundred pounds. I had never been as committed to the weight room as I was then. Knowing that I had to gain every possible ounce of strength I could, I worked closely with the center's strength and conditioning staff. They designed an intense program that pushed me to develop levels of strength I never knew I had.

* * *

Although practice was intense and grueling in college, it was taken to another level in Colorado Springs at the Olympic Training Center. There, the entire focus was on wrestling at the highest level in the country—and the world.

Though the workout schedule would vary as we neared competitions, our primary schedule involved two different programs, one on Monday-Wednesday-Friday and another for Tuesday-Thursday-Saturday.

In the Monday-Wednesday-Friday workouts, practice would start at the Olympic Training Center at 9:00 A.M. On those mornings, I'd ride a bike or jog for warmup. Then it was about seventy-five minutes of intense weight training under the supervision of the training center strength and conditioning staff. We did a lot of basic strength exercises like bench presses and squats, but the program had a lot of other lifts specific to our sport as well—work with dumbbells, medicine balls, and other equipment. After I was done with weights, I'd go eat a late breakfast or early lunch at the training center cafeteria and then head home to my house in Cascade, located at the base of Pike's Peak, up the hill west of Colorado Springs. I'd return for a 4:30 wrestling practice. Again, we'd warm up with some running and do some tumbling exercises and coordination drills.

We would then work on drills geared to improve our wrestling technique. After working on drills, we'd apply what we had just learned in practice, to train our muscles to "memorize" the movement and get strength to make the movements as effective as possible. Then, at about 5:30, we'd start wrestling. Usually we'd start with "micromatches," where you'd wrestle for two minutes as hard as you can, and then do a minute on top and bottom on the mat with your opponent—thirty seconds on top, thirty seconds on bottom. After that, we'd do what's called "grind matches." These were intense matches that would go sometimes for an hour to two hours, where the idea is literally to grind your opponent down to nothing. I remember my last match before leaving for Athens. Dremiel and I wrestled for two hours. Weighing myself afterward, I had lost ten pounds from that afternoon practice. It was that intense, and that draining.

On Tuesday and Thursday, we simply swapped the weight training for another practice in the wrestling room, where we worked on drills, technique, and matches among team members.

To end the evening practices, we'd do some running around the outside of the three mats in the wrestling room. Coach Fraser would blow his whistle, and we'd go from jogging to sprint and then back again. We knew from international competitions that we had to have every advantage we could, and cardiovascular fitness—training at roughly a mile above sea level—was something else in our corner when the big matches started. After the running, I made myself do one more exercise—I always wanted to go that extra mile, to full exhaustion. The strength and conditioning room next to the wrestling room had a machine that looked like a "bike for the upper body." You sat down and put your hands on the pedals, and pushed it around and around, with variable resistance. I'd do that forward for ninety seconds, and then reverse the motion and do it backward for another ninety seconds. After I caught my breath, I'd do it forty-five seconds each way. The last set I'd do as hard as I could.

Our coaches also tried to keep our training fun. Sometimes we'd play basketball or other team sports. We'd also go up to the Barr Trail and "Incline," both located near the base of Pike's Peak, and jog or run up the high-altitude dirt trails. I also took time to go wakeboarding for workouts, something I really enjoy, and it's a good workout.

Coach Fraser is the head coach of the U.S. National Greco team, so he designed and oversaw a lot of our workouts. But the U.S. Olympic Training Center Resident Team, which included wrestlers, like me, who lived and trained year-round in Colorado Springs, was fortunate to have several other great coaches who taught us a lot about the sport and offered various perspectives and great expertise. Earlier I briefly mentioned Anatoly Petrosyan, who came to America from the former Soviet Union and trained Matt Ghaffari before training me and other American Greco wrestlers. Anatoly has helped the U.S. Greco program immensely, because the Soviet-bloc countries had such a long, successful history in the sport, and he brought lessons he had learned there to our program. A tireless worker who got on the mat and wrestled as though he himself was a competitor, Anatoly, the Greco-Roman champion in the formerly Soviet state of Azerbaijan, joined the U.S. program in 1994 after coming to America in 1991—where he first coached with the Sunkist Kids program—and is a proud naturalized American. Anatoly was a key figure in the development of our Greco program. Momir Petkovic, who came to the United States in 1986, was an assistant coach for the 2000 U.S. Olympic Greco

Team. Momir joined the resident program as an assistant coach in 2002. Momir was the 1976 Olympic gold medalist in Greco in the 180.5-pound weight class, representing Yugoslavia, so he also had the international—particularly European—experience that we needed to get our program to the highest possible level. I think both of these men, Anatoly and Momir, are great examples of people who came to this country and made it better. We didn't become the best by luck in the United States—we had to learn from the best. And there are many people who come to this country from whom we can learn a whole lot. This case is testimony to that belief.

I was really looking forward to 2004. My feet, while far from what they had been in the past, were not going to stop me from my best effort. I was no longer the favorite, but I was still considered by other wrestlers to be the one they had to beat to make the Olympic Team.

Less than two weeks before the 2004 U.S. Nationals, on Tuesday, March 30, I was headed to practice on my motorcycle when a 1991 Mazda pulled out in front of me. I knew I was going to hit it, no matter how hard I braked or swerved. I also know who wins when a motorcycle and car collide.

It happened so fast.

I had little time to react, to think. I was going to hit the side of the car doing about thirty miles an hour. I knew it was going to be a hard impact, and I didn't want to get hurt, much less killed. So I made a split-second decision to stand up on the bike and propel myself over the car upon impact. I flipped over the handlebars and the car and saw the ground coming up to meet me. I ducked, put my head completely down, rolled through it, and landed on my heels, scraping my back, shoulders, and arms.

I took Tuesday and Wednesday off from practice and got laser treatment on the damaged skin. The skin on my left forearm was badly scraped.

Four days later, just a week before U.S. Nationals, I went to the Friday practice, but my training partner—Corey Farkas—wasn't there. I had had a good practice the day before, and I believe I had frustrated him so much that he decided not to come train me with me. I needed to work out, so I decided to play some basketball. I was going after a loose ball. When I lunged for the ball, I headed straight for the bleachers off the side of the court. In trying to stop before I hit them, I put my right arm out in front of me. I dislocated my wrist, but kept playing—our team won the game, I remember that much.

I went to the hospital, and doctors said surgery would be needed to allow the wrist to fully heal. I didn't have time for that. U.S. Nationals were less than a week away; there was too much on the line to take time for surgery. Even though I finally was ranked number one in my weight class—based on winning World Team Trials—in the United States again, I still needed mat time before the big show.

The trainers taped my wrist, and since it wasn't going to get any better for the foreseeable future, I would just have to deal with it. Doctors planned to put in pins to stabilize it, but that would have to wait until after U.S. Nationals. I really wanted, and probably needed, that top seed that was given to the winner of Nationals, because that would allow me to wrestle against only one person at the U.S. Olympic Trials, which would be the next month, May 21–22, in Indianapolis.

For the first time in two years, I was able to forget about my feet—because my wrist was absolutely throbbing. It was almost impossible to get a good hold. Since Greco-Roman allows no leg moves, using the hands to clinch, hold on, or throw was critical. It would be a challenge with only one good hand. My first win at Nationals was over Paul Devlin, a big, physical wrestler who has a good throw. I wrestled my way through my bracket and beat Farkas again. I dislocated my wrist seven times again in the tournament, several times against Farkas, but still beat him.

I made it to the final, where I met Dremiel Byers yet again. When I went ahead 1–0, I got complacent. I relaxed for a second and decided to wait it out to overtime and try to win the match there. You can't do that against Dremiel Byers; he forces you to bring your best game to every match. I didn't have it, and he stuck it to me with a 3–1 win. Byers would be the top seed at the Olympic Trials. To get a shot at him, I'd have to wrestle through the bracket. Then I'd have to beat him two out of three matches to make the 2004 Olympic Team.

The first thing I did after Nationals was arrange to have wrist surgery to insert the pins. The doctors explained that the process would take twelve weeks to heal completely, though I might see progress after six to eight weeks if I didn't use the wrist. I didn't want the surgery, but one-arm wrestling wasn't cutting it.

"If you don't stabilize the joints and ligaments, you won't be wrestling at all," the doctor said.

So one week after Nationals, I had surgery to insert three pins into my wrist.

"I understand you want to make the Olympic Team," one of the doctors told me as he explained the pins, "but if you reinjure your wrist and pull the pins out, I wish you the best of luck, because this wrist might not heal if you keep messing with it."

I had only a local anesthetic for the surgery, so I was awake the whole time. It was kind of neat to see what was going on and hear what the doctor was saying.

"You probably won't be able to wrestle at Trials," the doctor told me. "Your wrist . . . will probably prevent that." But I refused to believe that this injury would stop me.

No one from the Olympic Training Center Sports Medicine staff—a member had gone with me for the surgery—was there when the surgery was over. When I called them after the surgery, everyone on the staff was busy. I'm not one to wait around, so I just hopped in my truck and drove home, putting the vehicle in "Drive" with my left hand and holding my right hand up in the air.

I went to see the doctor again a week later. He knew Olympic Trials were coming up. I could move my fingers some, and I told him I had to get back into training. He said I could train but to be careful with the wrist. I tried to wrestle in practice, but I couldn't bend my hand.

I was in the hospital twice for IV treatments for infections that had developed in my wrist. One of the infections was caused by the pins moving out of place. The pins had broken through the skin a couple of times;

imagine being able to detach your hand from your wrist, and slide it back—that's what my hand and wrist looked like. The bones in my wrist weren't stabilized, so I couldn't hold my hand in place.

Two and a half weeks before Olympic Trials and I still couldn't wrestle. I thought, What can I do? I did all the weightlifting I could without using my wrist. I was up to 513 pounds for three sets of squats. I had never lifted that much weight before.

When my right ring finger wouldn't straighten out, I went to see the doctor. The ligament had been "pinched," causing the finger to hang down. The doctor took the responsible pin out. I ended up with another infection, which required another doctor visit and more medicine.

It was one week before Trials, and I had to ask the doctor on that visit for relief on another pin that was bothering me.

"Please pull the ring-finger pin out, because it's killing me," I pleaded with the doctor. He pulled it out, but insisted the one in my pinky finger had to stay. It was the most unstable finger in my hand.

I kept training with my new training partner, Khoren Papayan. I was wrestling using only my left hand. A couple of days before Olympic Trials, Corey Farkas came by to see me.

"I want to get your cell number so we can stay in touch after Trials," he said.

Corey and I, like a lot of athletes who train together, have had a rivalry and an up-and-down relationship. And I took his asking me for my number as a proclamation that he was sure I wasn't going to win at Trials. It made me mad.

Under my breath I said, "You've got another thing coming."

I was okay if this was going to end, but having someone else point it out to me, if that's what he was doing, didn't sit well with me. I had put four years of my life into this, and I wasn't going to go out with a whimper. Yes, I had made mistakes, playing hoops, going for the ball and dislocating my wrist. The motorcycle accident, though less preventable, was another obstacle on this last leg of the journey. So I was injured. So what? When had I *not* been hurt before a big moment in my life? This was my chance to make a statement, that I wasn't walking off into the sunset before the Olympics. Not yet. And not on anyone else's terms.

The hard part this time was that either before or after the Olympics, my journey would soon be over. I'd been wrestling since I was five years old. I didn't want to even think about this rollercoaster coming to an end at the Olympic Trials. Yes, the 2000 Olympics in Sydney was the mountain, the peak of the mountain, and 2001 was another celebration. Maybe I wouldn't have a 2004 medal, but the thought of ending my road at such a low point before the Games wasn't something I would do. Not without a fight.

Even *I* realized that the odds against my making the Olympic Team were very long. A healthy, well-rested Byers would be awaiting the winner of the bracket, and there were a lot of hungry wrestlers who wanted to earn that shot at Byers. I don't think anyone was overlooking me, but during practice they could see for themselves how my wrist injury affected my wrestling.

I thought, "Well, I should really give some serious thought as to what I'm going to do with the rest of my life." But then I thought about how I had been written off in 2000, written off again in 2001. I thought that if I didn't go out with my best effort, then this whole comeback had been for nothing.

I had to remember who I was, where I'd come from, and what had gotten me to this point in the first place. How many athletes get the chance to make one Olympic Team, much less two? There was a war going on in Iraq, as well as in Afghanistan. Who was I to throw a pity party for myself? After the 2000 Olympic win, I had been invited to, and gone on, several USO tours to the Persian Gulf, visiting several navy ships in the Persian Gulf and troops in Bahrain in 2001 and again in 2002. I also visited troops in Japan and Korea in 2002 after my stranding in Wyoming. I thought about the challenges those soldiers faced every day—life-and-death challenges. Compared to that, my dislocated wrist was nothing. I chided myself for having the nerve to feel sorry for myself.

My dream might end at the 2004 Olympic Trials, but I would do the best I could to make it to the final and give Dremiel a run for his money. If that wasn't good enough to make the team, it was the best I could do and I would still walk away a winner.

On the eve of Olympic Trials in Indianapolis, I found a sudden peace within myself. My attitude was, "I hope you all are ready, because I'm coming for it."

This is what I had been training for. This is what had inspired me to rehab my feet and walk again. This is where I was supposed to be.

When a wrestler retires, he leaves his shoes in the center of the mat. At the 2004 Olympic Trials, I started to realize that this could be it for me, and that if I lost, I'd probably be leaving my shoes in the middle of the mat. At this point, at age thirty-two—and I'd turn thirty-three before the Games—my body was winding down for what we have to put it through to be elite athletes, and with the uncertainty surrounding my feet, the end of my days as a wrestler were coming soon. I know it's an emotional scene, but I hadn't really grasped the entirety of it until Trials, when Kevin Bracken, an accomplished teammate and Olympian, lost his match. Also thirty-two years old at the time, Kevin, whom I deeply respect and admire, wouldn't be on the 2004 Olympic Team that went to Athens. He's a lighter wrestler, so I had some time until I wrestled Dremiel Byers in the final of the heavyweight class. When Kevin lost, he left his shoes on the mat, and we all felt some of the emotion that had just taken him over as he left the sport in which he had accomplished so much through the years. He had dedicated his life to the sport, and this moment was the end for him. I knew then that I had to find more in me, that instead of thinking about what I'd do if I lost, I had to keep driving my hardest and find a way to prove everyone wrong and make the team again. Kevin was a terrific inspiration to me that day, seeing him walk away with class.

But I wasn't ready to leave just yet. I wasn't going to let my career end.

Of course, as the reigning U.S. National Champion and the 2002 World Champion, Dremiel was the favorite. I had to wrestle through the bracket once again to get a shot at him. I had to face Corey Farkas again.

Corey had beaten me the previous year, but this year was different—I pinned Corey at 5:25 of our semifinal match. I moved into the final against Dremiel.

Dremiel seemed to be at the top of his game. But I was running on pure adrenaline. I knew that I had defied the odds, once again to get into the final and I wasn't going to let it slip away. My wrist was taped up well, and I just tried to forget about it.

Against the best wrestler I know, I won the Olympic Team berth, beating Dremiel two of the three matches, in overtime. I had made the 2004 U.S. Olympic Team.

Even though I had beaten him for the Olympic Team spot, Dremiel once again stepped up to the plate. I'm so proud to be this man's teammate and friend. I called him the next morning and said, "I need you to help me with this." Dremiel was the perfect teammate, perfect soldier, perfect professional when he responded, "I will do whatever I can to help you win a medal. I will be there for you." I decided to split any medal money—both the U.S. Olympic Committee and USA Wrestling pay set amounts for Olympic medals—I won at the 2004 Olympics in Athens with him. I would not have made the team without Dremiel's support.

"Loyalty behind the flag," Byers explained to a reporter. "They can't beat us both."

Having him as a training partner and as a resource for opponents' strengths and weaknesses was invaluable to me. We'd wrestle and talk about different opponents, and he'd say, "No, against this guy, you can't do it this way— you have to do it this other way," and he'd take me through the move. We worked on my own weaknesses.

Although we had worked together for many years, this was the first time we had opened up completely and shared everything. I admire Dremiel Byers to no end.

At one of the 2004 pre-Olympic tournaments in Poland—similar to the one where Yuri Patrikeev had pinned me just before the 2000 Olympics—I faced Yuri again. Yuri had beaten Deak-Bardos for gold at the 2002 European Championship, and was the favorite because he had turned into "Karelin Junior," beating up everyone he faced and throwing with the same authority Karelin had demonstrated.

His ferocity and strength were overwhelming, and he was clearly the heir to Karelin's throne as the top Russian. But at that meet in Poland, I beat Yuri 2–0 by shutting him down and keeping him from doing the things he had done so well against the other guys. He didn't throw me as he had before the 2000 Games, and he didn't build a 3–0 lead like he had with just thirty seconds left in our quarterfinal match at the 2001 World Championships. I wouldn't let him score on me. That match was important to my comeback, because I knew that even though my feet were still a problem, I was back to where I needed to be in order to be competitive at the Olympics, an important factor since I had finished only tenth at the 2003 World Championships.

As Yuri walked off the mat after the match, he appeared devastated. I looked over to where he sat down, and he was crying. His coaches and the tough-looking crowd that travels with the Russian team didn't look too happy either. The Russians don't have the same system we have, where we wrestle off for World and Olympic teams. They pick the guy they want—don't get me wrong, whoever is the Russian representative is tough and one of the best in the world—based on their own evaluation, not head-to-head competition. I guarantee you that the match in Poland before the 2004 Games is one of the reasons Yuri was not picked to make the 2004 Russian Olympic Team, not after losing to me, not after the devastation I saw on his face after that match. Perhaps making the team was contingent on his beating me—I don't really know. But I know that loss probably sealed his fate and kept him out of the 2004 Olympic Games in Athens. The sadness that was swallowing Yuri had narrowly missed enveloping me at the U.S. Olympic Trials.

Twenty

ATHENS, 2004

PART OF THE excitement of being in Athens was seeing the city's rich history. One of the trips I was looking forward to the most was seeing the Acropolis. A group of protesters had put up a banner, probably a hundred feet long and fifty feet high, in advance of Secretary of State Colin Powell's visit, "Powell: Kill or go home." You could see that thing from a long way away. I had on my red, white, and blue team warmup. I was rather upset that the protesters had created a negative situation at the Olympics, where countries have an opportunity to unite or at least communicate in peace. And the protesters had the freedom to say what they wanted, but I didn't appreciate seeing my countryman disparaged like that. So I wanted a chance to exercise my freedom. That's one of the precious ironies about freedom: these protesters expected, and were entitled, to express their point of view in Greece, a free country. But freedom allows "the other" side to make their voices heard as well. We obviously were not wanted in the country by these particular people.

I noticed several of the protesters proudly sporting communist symbols on their shirts. "All right, where's the American flag?" I asked. I wanted to put the flag up there and let everyone know that there were some proud Americans present whose point of view was different from theirs. I wanted the flag to be seen, because to me the flag is a symbol of the ideals that make the United States a great nation and a protector of the kind of freedom of expression these protesters were being allowed to demonstrate. My family was with me, and my brother Reynold pulled a flag out of his bag. The wind was blowing as I unfurled the flag at the Acropolis. I had goosebumps to be representing my country at such a historic monument. About thirty of the protesters gathered nearby. Several were yelling at us and whistling derisively.

A Greek police officer approached me.

"You must put your flag away," she said. "You can't have that out."

"Okay, but then you have to make them take the banner down," I answered.

"Please, don't represent yourself this way," she said.

"I'm not here to fight," I said. "But I am here representing my country. We just want to see the sights and learn about your history."

She started to reach for my flag.

"You will not touch my flag," I said. She and another officer backed down, but kept insisting we put the flag away.

"Those people," I said, pointing toward the protesters,

"can say what they want, but why can't we express our point of view?"

I wanted the people to know I was an American, and I wanted to defend our leaders since these protestors were attacking Secretary Powell.

The incident ended, but I was proud, because it was important for us, as Americans, to make the point that we still are proud of our country and that we won't be kicked around publicly without expressing our support for the troops and the American flag.

I never felt unsafe in Athens. It's important to note all the impressive security our government had for us there. People we'd never have guessed to be protecting us at times, including Army Special Forces, Navy Seals, Secret Service, and many other brave civilians. It was amazing to see these people willing to risk their own lives to allow us to represent America by competing in the 2004 Olympic Games. Just to strike up a conversation or get a smile returned by them meant a lot to me.

I was wrestling for them, too.

For all Americans.

Whereas many of my 2000 U.S. Olympic teammates from other sports didn't know much about me at the Opening Ceremonies, in Athens, most at least, knew about the Karelin match and my overnight stranding in the Wyoming wilderness. I was able to do some TV appearances, and USA Wrestling had me help promote the sport and our team. Once again, I was excited to see some of my sports heroes, such as San Antonio Spurs star Tim Duncan, who is a person I truly admire for his humility, his class, and his composure. What a sincere person he is. The real deal, for all the right reasons.

"Rulon, the wrestling guy!" Tim said, shaking my hand. "Coach [Greg] Popovich showed us your match against the Russian before our NBA Finals game—that was awesome!"

Tim handed his camera to someone.

"Here, get a picture of us, please," he said. Tim was so great, and he took time to pose with another U.S. wrestler, Kerry McCoy, for a picture. Roy Williams, one of the basketball coaches, was also nice. But as had happened in 2000, many of the other Dream Team basketball players exhibited less-than-warm attitudes. I was excited to see Carlos Boozer, who had signed a free-agent contract with my home-team Utah Jazz in the off-season.

"Hi!" I said, "I live in Utah now, so I'll see you back home."

Boozer blew me off. So did several of the other players. I remember trying to talk to Amare Stoudamire, who acted like I wasn't even there. I don't want to come across as bashing the basketball team, because those guys got a lot of grief in Athens and I'm sure they have pressures on them that I can't understand. But aside from a couple of special people, they didn't come across as being excited to represent America. That's just my view.

Tim Duncan makes millions of dollars, but is still friendly and real as a person. I hope everyone who watches Tim on TV learns from him how a true superstar should carry himself.

★   ★   ★

Athens was my last competition. I knew that. Back before the 1996 Olympic Trials, I had set a goal of wrestling in two Olympics. Since I missed the weigh-in and had the staph infection in 1996, the end of that goal was extended four years to 2004. I had done what I set out to do in qualifying for two Olympic Games. At my age, thirty-three, my body wouldn't be able to go through another four years, when for 2008 I'd be in my late thirties. So Athens was it for me.

Athens was quite a different experience from Sydney, because by that time I had been through so much. I entered Sydney an unknown, could walk the streets without ever being recognized, which all changed after I beat Karelin for the gold. But simply getting to Athens was amazing for me, to let it sink in that I had rehabbed my feet the best I could, that I had overcome the dislocated wrist and beaten a world champion to make the U.S. Olympic Team.

The thing is, I still remember feeling like some people were looking down on me. All of these years and accomplishments later, I still felt inferior on several levels. But that was all right with me, and I embraced the challenge. I had stared down challenge after challenge my whole life, and this would be another time I had to rise to the occasion, dig deep, and see what I was made of as I wrestled my last tournament.

So, although I had been well known for a while, I felt like I was back to being an unknown: people knew only that I had been lost in Wyoming and had suffered frostbite and had some problems with my feet. I had placed only tenth at the 2003 World Championships, so no one in the wrestling community knew if I had gotten back to even close to what I had been in 2000, even though I had beaten Dremiel Byers to make the team. And because I still had ten toes and no residual pain from a dislocated wrist in Sydney, there were some people in Athens who discarded me as a medal contender. That and the fact that the heavyweight Greco-Roman class was so much better, top to bottom, than in Sydney led people to forget about me a bit. Entering Sydney, it had been a foregone conclusion that Karelin would win, whereas this time the gold was there for anyone's taking, the presence of the defending Olympic gold medalist—little ol' me—notwithstanding. There were ten great wrestlers, by far the deepest pool of talent that I had seen in eight years of international competition. Though there were several outstanding experienced wrestlers, there were also some younger wrestlers who could knock off anyone on any given day.

I think I was actually more prepared for Athens in some ways than I was for Sydney. First of all, I had much more experience. Second, and more important, I had been through this arduous, testing path just to get back on the mat and make the team, and the route had been filled with some obvious, and many unseen, obstacles along the way. And last, I had prepared mentally for every single match to be a ferocious battle.

My first few matches in Athens went well. For such a tough field, I had a very good draw. The quarterfinal match was against a familiar wrestler, Bulgarian Sergei Moreyko, whom I had beaten at the 2001 World Championships. He has been one of the best in the world, year in and year out. This was possibly his last chance at an Olympic medal, and if he beat me, the defending Olympic gold medalist, he'd make it to the semifinals, where he'd assure himself of a medal with a win. I scored a point out of the clinch, bloodying him accidentally—those things happen on the mat at times. The crowd didn't like that; they thought I had cheap-shotted him, booing my family for cheering as that point was put up on the scoreboard. I realized at that moment that a lot of people wanted to see the American lose. But I held Moreyko off in overtime and advanced to the semifinals—the round of four.

The semifinal match was against an up-and-coming wrestler, Kazakhstan's Georgi Tsurtsumia, who had trained at the Olympic Training Center in Colorado Springs. I had beaten him in our previous match at the Dave Schultz Tournament in Colorado Springs a year earlier. He's another wrestler from a former Soviet Union state. The match was tight. He's a big, strong wrestler and had made a logical progression up the rankings over the past two years. He was considered to have an outside shot at a medal in Athens.

We were tied at 1–1 and had to go to the clinch, just like I did with Karelin in 2000. So I went for the same move that had worked for me before. How ironic that I would see an opening for this move again. I went "around him" and knew that I had him, but Georgi simply off-balanced me.

He took advantage of a situation that I hadn't prepared for—I didn't know he had the same off-balance move that Dremiel had. If a wrestler gets aggressive and off balance, you take advantage of his lack of agility and knock him on his back. Dremiel had used this move against me several times, but I didn't see it coming from Tsurtsumia.

So with that move, he gained three points, and my gold medal repeat bid ended with the 4–1 loss.

But that's life.

I didn't look at what I lost, I looked at what I still had. I glanced over at Coach Fraser and he mouthed, "Sorry." I knew this hurt him, because the road back had been so incredible, so amazing for him and for me. Coach Fraser knew success and defeat, and even to reach *this* stage again was unreal, though it was just as shocking to have it all end so suddenly, so unexpectedly, especially when it looked like I was making a move to notch the win and a berth in the gold medal match—which would've once again been against a Russian.

I wish I would've gotten that win, but I didn't. Someone asked me after the semifinal match: if I had still had all the feeling in my feet, would I have been able to react a split second sooner to prevent Georgi from scoring the way he did? My answer at that time, which I still stand by, in principle: it doesn't matter. This was my journey, and part of it was getting lost in the wilderness and damaging my feet. This was my journey, coming back and learning to walk again, and somehow forcing my feet back into some semblance of functionality on the wrestling mat. This was my journey, to hit a car on my cycle, then dislocate my wrist days later, and then dislocate it seven times more during competition. And this was my journey, to upset the 2002 World Champion at the 2004 Olympic Trials, to make it here, to Athens. I can't honestly say what would've happened if I had had full use of my feet; that is, if part of the road that led me to this point were taken away, would I have gotten back to this place, this level, this opportunity to represent my country?

When I left the mat, the media was waiting for me. The previous day, a wrestler who had lost had cried relentlessly over the defeat. The media had a field day discussing how we should handle ourselves after a match. Maybe the press thought I'd be broken-hearted too.

"Hi, how're you all doing?" I asked the reporters and camera people. They had traveled and gone through the same security-clearance issues and travel hassles to get here as I had. I knew they were doing their job, but I still appreciated that they showed up to watch me wrestle, that they would help me write this final chapter.

"Aren't you disappointed?"

"How bad does this hurt?"

"What's it mean not to have a shot at the gold medal?"

I smiled. I couldn't help it. Of course I wanted to have a gold medal; who wouldn't? I explained to the reporters that I had made a mistake, and like the good wrestler that he is, my opponent had used that mistake to defeat me. I could've said something like, "Nine times out of ten, I would beat that guy," but in Sydney I had been that "one time" loss for Karelin. I didn't want to take away from Georgi's accomplishment. I told the media that I was disappointed I didn't wrestle my best match—because that's my goal, win or lose, to wrestle my best match—but that they should give Georgi credit. It was his time to shine.

As far as crying or pouting or claiming foul—no way, none of that. It just isn't in me. The journey to get to the semifinals had been filled with so many obstacles. I had nothing to complain about.

Now I was down to my last match.

To finish my career with an Olympic medal, I'd have to end it with a win. Not many wrestlers get to finish with a win in the medal round at the Olympic Games.

After losing in the semifinals, the question wasn't: "What would've happened if . . . ?" No, it was: "What's next?" I still had a chance to get an Olympic medal. My second Olympic medal. Instead of pouting or second-guessing myself about the match with Georgi, I needed to focus on what it would it take to win the bronze.

Georgi had earned his shot at the gold medal. He would lose 4–2 in a come-from-behind win by Russian Khassan Baroev in the gold medal match later that night. Baroev had been selected over Yuri Patrikeev for the 2004 Russian Olympic team. It sure seemed like a small world to me then.

I gathered my thoughts.

Emotions were running high. I looked at the flag again. I know I sometimes talk about the flag nonstop, and sometimes people tire of hearing me talk about what it means to me. But the truth is, that flag is a part of me, part of my soul, and its no small part of my motivation to do my best every time I represent my country, coaches, and teammates, the state of Wyoming and Star Valley. I thought about how much that flag had given me in terms of opportunities: growing up on a family farm, being in our church, getting an education, making a life out of athletics.

I started to cry.

"You are getting ready to wrestle for an Olympic medal," I scolded myself. "You can't lose focus as to what is important here. Look past the fact that this is your last match. You don't want to go out there and not represent your country proudly. If you don't wrestle to the best of your ability, you will not win a medal."

So I toughened up and put on my game face.

Before the bronze medal match, I talked to Coach Fraser. "I'm going to leave my shoes on the mat," I said.

He had this sort of clueless look on his face. Surely, I thought, he knows this is it for me.

"This is my last match," I said, "the last time I will wrestle is here. I will retire."

He kind of nodded at me. It was sinking in then, for him—for both of us. I knew Fraser was aware that this would be my last Olympics, but in the heat of competition, the last thing a coach is thinking about is that this is the end of the road for a wrestler he is coaching.

"Would it be okay to leave the flag on the shoes?" I asked.

"We don't want to disrespect the flag, don't let it touch the floor," Fraser said. Good point, I thought. The last thing I'd ever do is disrespect the flag.

Fraser kind of patted me on the back and walked away.

The Iranian I was to wrestle for the bronze, Sajad Barzi, had put together an impressive run at the Olympics. He was good, but no one had any idea he would be so successful at the Olympics, knocking off so many other talented wrestlers, including Deak-Bardos, the Hungarian who had won the silver medal at the World Championships.

Sajad is about 6-foot-7, so he has a leverage advantage against smaller wrestlers, especially someone like me who is 6-foot-1. He could throw any wrestler at the Games with that leverage advantage. I knew if he got a good lock on me, I could not physically stop him in the middle of a throw.

As we moved to the mat for the match, I thought about how big and strong Sajad was and what an unknown he had been, wondering how I would do against him. I wasn't nervous, but I had some fear that I wasn't ready for this match.

By the time the announcer introduced us, I just wanted to wrestle and take care of business.

As the match started, I was still surprised at Sajad's size. Iran has a good wrestling history and program, but not in Greco; freestyle wrestling is, however, one of their national sports. Ironically, Matt Ghaffari was from Iran and started in freestyle. So now, yet another circle was completing itself, for it was Matt who got me deep into this sport, taught me some lessons, and it was Matt whom I had beaten in 2000 to make the Olympic Team. Now I'd have to beat another proud Iranian wrestler to reach my final goal.

I sized up Sajad. "Whoa, is he big!" I thought to myself. "Okay, here we go. How are you going to beat him?"

My goal was to get him tired and then "turn" him from the *par terre* position to his back to get "exposure points," which are awarded when you have an opponent on his back and are near pinning him. By this time, it was our fifth match each in two days. Many of the other heavyweights from other countries don't push themselves like the U.S. coaches push us—we emphasize conditioning far more than many countries do for their heavyweights. We actually train beyond tired, pushing to exhaustion. I knew Sajad wouldn't be at my cardiovascular level.

So my goal was to not get scored on, get him making some small mistakes as he tired, and then find a weakness and score a point or two wherever possible. His arms were unbelievably long and strong, but I knew weakness would set in as he tired. And then I would get him off balance and use my experience and conditioning and position to score. I took him out of bounds once, scored a point early, and then scored another point from the clinch position. Sajad seemed to grow frustrated that what had worked for him against everyone else wasn't working on me. I could feel him slow down a little at times. I knew it could be fatigue, but a strong, young guy like that could've been playing possum, waiting for me to think I had the advantage and then get careless and overconfident, allowing him an opening. But it was only 2–0 at the end of the second and final period. And if three points aren't scored in a match, it automatically goes to overtime.

Even in overtime, the match wasn't decided yet, because he still could throw me, get three points, and win the match. We started in the clinch, and anything can happen from that position. From the film we had watched on Sajad, he had made a lot of his best throws from the clinch, grabbing his opponent. So I knew it was his best position. I had to keep working on him, tire him.

And I did.

I earned that last point—the last one I'd ever score as a wrestler—in the clinch, ironically the same move I had used to beat Alexander Karelin to win at the 2000 Olympics.

Beating Sajad wasn't my best match technically as a wrestler, but it was one of my best-thought-out, best-executed matches. I had an Olympic bronze medal, just two years after stepping on the wrestling mat with feet that were barely usable for pushing off.

In five years I had an Olympic gold, a World Championship gold, and an Olympic bronze. All of those years of being told I couldn't do it had ended with me beating back the doubters a final time, on the world's biggest stage. I looked at the flag, and after shaking hands and offering hugs, bent down to unlace my shoes a final time.

I looked up and saw my parents and friends, including pole vault star Stacey Draglia and her husband, who are good friends of mine, and U.S. multi-gold-medal swimmer Gary Hall, a rebel who I respect, a man who came to Star Valley to spend time with Dave Draney. All of the dots in my life connected at that point, and the picture this path painted brought tears to my eyes. It was all here. It was all ending. And that was all right.

To see those people who cared about me there supporting me meant a lot. I had no twinge of regret. I gave it everything I had, represented my country the best I could. The only sadness came from knowing that I would never wrestle again. I had done my best in practice, given 100 percent, so I couldn't have done anything more as an athlete. I was able to live my dream. Actually, since my goal had always been to make it to the Olympics, I had lived my dream twice and medaled both times.

Once again the American flag kept me going, reminding me of my coaches and teammates, my family in the stands, the troops overseas, the people back home in Star Valley. The shoes didn't want to come off that final time—or maybe I didn't want them to, or maybe both. It had always been about the journey, first and foremost. Now that journey was at an end, in a place no one thought I'd be, not in 2004, not after everything that had happened.

So I looked at the flag, took all the courage I could from it, and took off my wrestling shoes. As they sat in the center of the mat, under the lights, even the people who had been booing during the match burst into applause.

Of all the painful work I had done walking and learning to wrestle again, those last steps were the most difficult to take. A goal I had set in 1996 was coming to an end, this journey that had been extended to Athens because of what had happened in 1996 at the Olympic Trials weigh-ins. But I took pride in the fact that I had given 100 percent and gone out a winner—two goals that every wrestler, every athlete, has for their final competition, especially one on the world stage.

I had been blessed to represent my country in the final wrestling match of my career and to wear the red, white, and blue to the medal stand. It was all I could ever ask for.

And I paused to think about it: it truly was so very much more.

Twenty-One

NEVER STOP PUSHING, PERIOD

WHEN I TOOK my shoes off and left them in the center of the mat to signify that I was done competing in this great sport, everything I had put off thinking about hit me all at once.

I can't even say that the gold medal in Sydney meant more than the bronze in Athens, not after 9/11, not after how the world had changed and continues to evolve day after day. How did I perform? Did I do my best? Yes. Could I have done even better and won gold again? Yes. But after losing in the semifinals, I regrouped and was prepared to do my best again rather than wonder about what might have been, or wallow in what had transpired.

I learned from what had happened in the semifinals and didn't let it happen again in the bronze medal match, which was in no small part why I won the bronze.

Because I wrestled my best, I was able to say I performed the best I could in my final time out. Every competitor wants to say that.

At the Athens Olympics, I was wrestling for the American flag and all it stands for. Are we a perfect country? No. Do we always do the right thing? No, but then no other country can make such a claim either. What I was wrestling for were the ideals that made this country, built this other country, and shaped the world. Those ideals are still alive today in every city in America in some way, shape, or form.

Why does it seem like so many people around the world want to come to America to work in American business, to live in homes on American soil, to be able to say what they want, when they want, without fear that they will be arrested in the middle of the night and tortured because they are speaking their minds? Because in America, we believe in freedom, and liberty, and the pursuit of happiness. This country actually came into being largely because of people who had been denied these fundamental rights in the countries they left behind.

I looked at my wrestling shoes and thought about the troops in the far reaches of the world, coming under fire, fighting for their lives, defending America's policy and ideals, sacrificing their lives back home, their families, for a country they believed in so deeply that they were willing to die and be buried under Old Glory. There were men and women in Iraq and Afghanistan taking off their boots that night, or worse, having them removed for them after being the victim of some tragedy, like the hero I think of every time I see the American flag, Pat Tillman. That flag means so much, or should, to every American, regardless of who they vote for or what they believe is proper U.S. policy here and abroad.

Living in a free society is easy for those of us who awaken each day cloaked in freedom and liberty, but it's not so easy for those who have to defend it in combat boots. This moment was for all of those who made the sacrifice to put on those boots, wear that uniform with the American flag on a sleeve, and hold a weapon to defend their country, their own lives, their freedom. That saying about freedom not coming for free is true, but most of us can never grasp the sacrifice that it has taken through the years, and to this very day, and to points beyond. Freedom will always come at a cost, defended by those men and women in uniform.

After I got the American flag in my hands, I remembered what Coach Fraser had said, that I couldn't put it on my shoes because the flag would touch the floor, and that's disrespectful; in fact, once a flag touches the ground it is supposed to be burned. I would never subject the American flag to that, because what the flag represents had made it possible for this small-town Wyoming boy from a cow farm in Star Valley get to this moment, to this point in his life.

When I was told after the Olympics that I might be able to do some speaking and share my story with others, I didn't see that coming. I mean, this was my story, the hand I was dealt, so there was nothing that I thought was worth publicizing. Everyone has a story. But then I listened to people who would tell me that others could relate to my story of overcoming adversity and far exceeding the potential that people had seen in me at almost every step along the way. This was just the hand I was dealt, and these were just the situations I had to deal with along the way, but my story could help others.

Being a teacher, I feel comfortable standing up in front of a class of thirteen-year-olds; and if you can do that, you can step in front of thousands of people from a Fortune 500 company and talk about surviving adversity, knowing that around the corner is a huge success, but that we have to take the steps to get there and overcome the obstacles in that path. Working with a professional speaking teacher, Marilyn Townsend, we dissected my improbable path to success beyond what I had even imagined and structured a seven-part program that diagrams a logical, attainable route that can be used by anyone who is ready to accept life's challenges.

1. Go back to basics
2. Turn a negative into a positive
3. Enlist other people
4. Go out and train hard
5. Take care of business
6. Aim high when you are feeling low
7. Don't rest on your laurels

Having people like Tiger Woods and Tim Duncan come up and tell me how my win over Karelin inspired them meant a tremendous amount to me. To have people like Jay Leno, Oprah, and Rosie O'Donnell view my story as so inspiring that they'd choose to have me on their show and share it with their audiences truly humbles me. Hearing those people tell me what my journey means gives me a very warm feeling. When people tell me how much I inspire them, I don't know what to say besides "Thank you." I really do appreciate that.

I guess they are feeling what I am feeling, partly because I ask myself, "How would someone feel, after their whole life has been a series of battles and challenges, to in the end have the most improbable dreams come true?"

Everything that came to me initially after the win over Alexander Karelin was easy, because of all those early years where I struggled: to get the farmwork done, to push myself in special ed so that I could continue in mainstream classes and keep up with my classmates, to obtain a college degree when I was told it was out of my reach, and even, when I made it into Nebraska, that I didn't belong there.

The irony is that I hadn't changed through all those years. Sure, I had matured and learned lessons along the way, but I was still the farm boy from Wyoming who wanted to live every moment of every day and somehow reach the best of my ability.

My story is about an average person—below average in some ways, such as academically, but above average in other ways, such as work ethic—from a farm in rural western Wyoming. But each and every person has his or her own hardships and challenges that shape who they are. Some will face a challenge and not appreciate what the hardship can do for them in the future. But the true reward is to persevere and do your best—win or lose, succeed or fail. I'm a firm believer in losses or failures providing the best stepping-stones to the future, because you can learn from where you came up short and prevent that from happening in the future. Whereas, with a win or success, the tendency is to bask in the glory of the accomplishment and not learn where you could have done things even better.

We all are dealt many obstacles in life, which makes life tougher, makes our path to what we want to achieve that much more difficult. But instead of viewing these obstacles as something we have overcome, they often lead us to change course or, worse, back down. No matter the outcome, when you attack a challenge you will be a better person for the experience. The test can't always be measured in "pass" or "fail." Failure to realize one short-term goal shouldn't take away from the long-term goals. Failure means you must accept the challenge again with more resolve, more knowledge, and a better understanding of who you are and what it will take to come out on top the next time, and the times after that.

Wrestling has taught me that anything is possible if you are willing to put your mind, body, and soul into your efforts. You can literally exceed your own goals and dreams in sports. I thought one Olympics would be unreal, a medal amazing, and a gold medal almost inconceivable. I won the gold and went back and medaled again four years later. And though the World Championships don't get the attention that the Olympics do, they are, except in Olympic years, our Super Bowl, and my one gold medal in the Worlds is as meaningful as my two Olympic medals.

I am proud that I was not a kid who had everything handed to him. I believe that especially at a young age, hard work has to be part of the equation, whether it's working to earn money to buy a used car instead of receiving a new SUV for your sixteenth birthday, or working to pay your way through college so that you appreciate it more and realize it is your own investment, which will make you work harder in most cases. Nothing has been handed to me or my family, and it was only through the sacrifice of putting the farmwork above what we wanted to do that we succeeded together. So when I was faced with an undefeated Russian, I was prepared to beat him, because I had carried cows across slick and frozen pastures; I had stepped in holes and learned better balance, and built up my legs and chest; I had graduated from college when I was told I had no right being there; and because I had been able to treat my failures only as areas that could make me stronger. I was actually preparing for that Karelin match my entire life; I just didn't know it until I stepped off the medal stand in Sydney, Australia, with a gold medal around my neck and the American flag hanging high in front of me.

I think back on the many times when I had to overcome challenges that were unique to me or obstacles that were placed in my way. I recall having to return to Nebraska for both the teaching methods class the one semester and then having to leave my training camp in Arizona to student teach in Lincoln, only because I had a B that I thought should've been an A, which would have allowed me to student-teach in Arizona. If neither of those situations had popped up, I would've graduated a year and a half earlier (because I took the 1996 spring semester off to train for the Olympics). Yet I went back and did the methods class again. I did the student teaching where they said to do it, when they said, and had someone evaluating me who wanted to find every reason to fail me, to berate me, to make me feel like I didn't belong.

If I had given in or backed down at any point, I would not have been ready to make an Olympic team, much less two, and win Olympic medals. I had to work astoundingly hard to reach what many people would consider to be easy, basic goals, such as reading or even making a varsity team. We all are given obstacles in life, and we either learn to beat them, or they defeat us—it really is our choice. And if it defeats you, so what? Turn it into something you can build off of, and be stronger the next time, be better conditioned, mentally or physically, so that you don't tire. Learn how your opponent defeated you, and find a way to win by doing something different or doing something better the next time. When these chances to face these obstacles are presented, do not back down, do not run the other way. Use them to grow, to learn, to lay a foundation for future success. Remember that the harder the challenge, the higher the risk, the more will be the benefit, whether you have 100 percent success or just a fraction of that.

Because I kept getting up and dusting myself off every time I was knocked down, even the most formidable challenge I'd ever face as an athlete was simply just another opportunity to do my best, to show what I was made of, to demonstrate that I had prepared properly through practice and had gone the extra mile so that I wouldn't be tired late in the match when I needed my wind the most. To others, my path is illogical, improbable. But taken as the steps that they were, rungs on a ladder, it was a perfectly logical climb, moving forward when the climb was steeper, pausing and gripping tighter when the rungs were slippery, finding that reservoir deep within me for sustenance when I was tired and felt I could go on no longer. That I did continue on, that there was water when I went to the well all those times, is what got me to the top, allowed me first to achieve my potential, and then to go after dreams that should have been, for all practical purposes, far out of my reach.

I am here. You can get here too.

INDEX

A

accidents. See also injuries
  accident-prone at birth, 67
  car accident, 89
  in childhood, 68–72
  four-wheeler flips, 281–82
  motorcycle accident,
    292–93
  in teen years, 72–75
Afghanistan, war in, 136
after school chores, 13–15. See
  also farming
Afton, WY. See Star Valley,
  WY
Afton Elementary School
  (Afton, WY), 8–12
anger, dealing with, 12–13
aplastic anemia, 65–67
Armageddon (movie), 236
arrow in stomach, 70–71

Athens, Greece, 303–5. See
  also Olympic Games, 2004
  Athens
attention deficit disorder
  (ADD), 22–23
automobile accident, 89
Ayari, Omrane, 162

B

backbreaker move, 151–52
Bahrain, 298
bale wagon accident, 71–72
Banta Tournament (Finland),
  148
Barkley, Charles, 134
barn burns, 58–59
Baroev, Khassan, 312
Barzi, Sajad, 1, 3, 313–15
basketball, 285, 293
Baumgartner, Bruce, 111–12

bicycle accident, 71

body-lock move, 211, 214

Boozer, Carlos, 306

Bo's death and burial, 153–54

Bracken, Kevin, 142, 299

branding, Rulon's, 68

Bridger-Teton National Forest
(WY), 8, 219. *See also*
wilderness, lost in

Brown, Ron, 104

Bruce, Ed "Coach Bruce," 3

Buendorf, Larry, 206

burn on forearm, 74

Burton, Alice, 51–53

Byers, Dremiel, 149, 285–88,
294, 297, 299–300

C

Cancun, Mexico, 278–79

Cassidy, Butch, 47–48

Chadron, NE, 125–26

Chandler, Dan, 160, 173

charitable giving, 49–51, 59–60

chopping wood, 68

Christensen, Bob, 83, 84–85,
88

Church of Jesus Christ. *See*
Latter Day Saints Church

the clinch position, 180, 309,
315

Cornhuskers "Huskers,"
100–102

Couric, Katie, 195

Cuba, 114–15

D

Dawes Junior High School,
127–32

Deak-Bardos, Mihaly, 162,
203–4, 214–15

dislocated wrist, 293–96,
297–98, 310

Down Under Bowl (New
Zealand), 81

Draney, Dave, 136–37

Dream Team, 161, 305–6

Duncan, Tim, 305–6

E

Eastern Idaho Regional Medical Center, 255–57

Edmunds-Tucker Law, 44–45

education. *See also* University
of Nebraska; values for
living a good life

elementary school, 8–12,
200

importance of, 36–37, 77,
81–82

learning disability, 8–12,
22–23, 94, 95, 96, 107–8
Park Junior High School,
126–27
Ricks College, 81, 83–84,
88–90
Star Valley High School,
75–78
exercise. *See* physical fitness

F

failure, meaning of, 323
faith, 35, 60, 83, 88, 194, 243,
285. *See also* values for
living a good life
falling out of truck bed, 69–70
family. *See also entries beginning with "Gardner"*
farming as family effort,
27, 32, 39–40
overview of Rulon's family,
35–40
as role models, 134–35
Rulon's desire to be a
father, 34–35
thinking of family keeps
Rulon alive, 245–46
Farkas, Corey, 148, 160, 172,
286, 296–97
farming

barn burns, 58–59
cows and calves, 24, 25–26,
201
as family effort, 27, 32,
39–40
gravity-flow irrigation
system, 16–19, 79, 80
hard work for long hours,
13–19, 24–26, 79–80
hay, growing, bailing, and
feeding to cows, 26,
71–72, 74
odd jobs required to sup-
port, 35–36
"picking up strings," 19–20
purchase of land for, 54
self-esteem gained from, 26
in summertime, 16, 26
young children driving, 69
feet. *See* recovery from frostbite
Feldman, Bernie, 123–24
football, high school, 30–31,
75, 81
football, Univ. of Nebraska,
100–102
four-wheeler accident, 281–82
Fraser, Steve
advice on being No. 1,
149–50
announcing retirement to,
313

coaching at 2000 Olympic
    Games, 163–66
friendly bets with team
    members, 141–46,
    216–17
Greco-Roman wrestling
    career, 141
on Moreyko, 214
on Rulon/Karelin match,
    185–88
on Rulon/Patrikeev match,
    212–13
on Rulon's chances in
    Sydney, 185–88
on 2001 World Champi-
    onships win, 216
freestyle wrestling. *See*
    wrestling
freezing. *See* wilderness, lost
    in (winter, 2002)
frostbite. *See* recovery from
    frostbite

G

Gable, Dan, 173–74
Gardner, Alice Burton (great-
    grandmother), 51–53
Gardner, Alton (grandfather's
    brother), 51
Gardner, Archibald (great-

great-grandfather), 43–44,
    48–50
Gardner, Clarence (great-
    grandfather), 50–55
Gardner, Diane (sister), 38, 69,
    72
Gardner, Elworth (grandfather),
    51
Gardner, Evon (sister), 37
Gardner, Gary, 84
Gardner, Gay (father's first
    wife), 35
Gardner, Geraldine (sister), 37
Gardner, Marcella (sister),
    38–39, 69
Gardner, Mary Larsen (great-
    great-grandmother), 44, 49
Gardner, Randy, 261–62
Gardner, Reed (father)
    bleeding ulcer diagnosis, 58
    marriages of, 35
    raised by grandfather, 55
    on Ronald's illness, 67
    Rulon back-talks to, 78–79
    Rulon's respect for, 20,
        21–23, 35, 134
    as strict disciplinarian, 20,
        22–23
    working odd jobs with,
        35–36
Gardner, Reynold (brother)

college scholarship, 77

friendship with, 20–21, 39

"If it doesn't kill you...", 31

rivalry and rough play
with, 73, 74–75, 80–81

wrestling matches, 74, 76

Gardner, Rollin (brother), 37,
64, 260, 262–63, 278

Gardner, Ronald (brother)
aplastic anemia diagnosis
and treatment, 65–67

character and strength of,
63–65, 67

Rulon's vision of, 61–63,
68, 243

Gardner, Russell (brother), 38,
79–80, 281–82

Gardner, Virginia (mother)
nursing school, 35, 36–37

Rulon's respect for, 20,
21–23, 35, 134

school shopping, 27, 28

standing up to school
system, 10

supportive, positive out-
look of, 78

Ghaffari, Matt
beats Rulon at U.S. World
Team Trials, 147–48

career of, 111

dominates Rulon in 1995

Worlds, 118–19

friendship with and sup-
port from, 111, 112, 113

No. 1 ranking, 118

Rulon's win at 2000
Olympic Team Trials,
113–14, 151–52

Ghalstyan, Haykaz, 162

Giunta, Giuseppe, 162–63

goals, measurability of, 25

God, awareness of, 62, 243.
See also faith

golf course summer job, 105

Grand Prix events, 141–42,
203–4

Granite Awards (Univ. of
Nebraska), 99, 100

Grant, Herbert J., 54–55

GrapplersWorld.com, 170–71

gratitude, expressions of, 55,
138, 169, 201, 245, 254–55

gravel in Rulon's back, 69–70

Great Depression, 54–55

Greco-Roman wrestling. See
also Fraser, Steve; Ghaffari,
Matt; Karelin, Alexander;
specific events

game plan for last match,
313–15

importance of wrists, 294

international tournament

in Cuba, 114–15
introduction to, 104–5
re-ranking tournament,
   110–11
training for, 122–23
grind matches, 290

H

hands above head for eight-
   hour flight bet, 146
Hansen, Mike, 86–88
Hauck, Mike, 104–5
Heiner, Mark, 249, 255, 265,
   267–73
heroes and role models,
   134–38, 201, 277–78
Hicks, Dan, 142–45
high school sports, 30–31
homestead laws, 47
hospital visits. See also
   recovery from frostbite;
   wilderness rescue and
   thawing
   arrow in stomach, 70–71
   automobile accident, 89
   burn on forearm, 74
   gravel in back, 69–70
   knee cut on concrete,
      72–73

leg cut on barbed wire, 69
right shin cut with wire,
   73–74
hyperbaric chamber, 275,
   276–78
hypothermia, 139–41
hypothermia facts, 7, 139–41,
   218, 235, 254

I

Idaho Falls, ID, 255–57,
   275–80
injuries. See also accidents;
   recovery from frostbite
   broken arm, 146–47
   broken finger and rib,
      shoulder separation, 207
   broken rib, 148, 207
   dislocated wrist, 293–96,
      297–98, 310
   groin muscle ripped,
      150–51, 159
International Olympic Committee (IOC), 281

J

Jensen, Alan, 261–62
Jesus Christ, vision of, 62, 243
Johnson, Rick, 14

K

Karelin, Alexander
    career, 113, 174–75
    first match against, 147
    gold in 1996 Olympics, 124
    gold medal match against
        Rulon, 172–75, 178–84,
        324
    reputation, 167–68, 169,
        170–71
    at 2000 Olympic Games,
        162
Key West, Florida, 240
Kissinger, Henry, 167
knee cut on concrete, 72–73
KSL TV, Salt Lake City, UT,
    192

L

Laramie, WY, college meet,
    97–98
Larsen, Mary, 44, 49
Latter Day Saints Church
    basis of, 45
    Gardner, Archibald, 43–44,
        48–50
    Gardner, Clarence, 50–55
    history of, 43–45, 46–47
    manifesto forbidding
        polygamy, 45
    Ricks as part of, 88
    support from, 274
learning disability, 8–12,
    22–23, 94, 95, 96, 107–8
leg cut on barbed wire, 69
Leibovitz, Annie, 194–95
Leno, Jay, 193
Letterman, David, 193–94
LifeFlight, 158–59, 265–66,
    271–72
Lowney, Garrett, 160

M

Martori, Art, 112
Math 101, 95–96
McBride, Charlie, 102
media
    gold medal win blitz,
        189–90, 192, 193–95
    as Rulon recovers from
        freezing, 274–75
    Rulon's approach to,
        196–97
mental conditioning. *See also*
    physical fitness
    for 2001 Worlds, 204
    academic toll on, 97–98
    anger experiences, 12–13,
        152, 177–78

importance of, 76–77,
105–6

learning from mistakes, 30,
86, 156, 311, 322–23

for Olympic gold medal
match, 167–69, 171–75

positive self-talk, 30,
155–56, 244

self-evaluations, 131–32,
322–26

working hard for, 109

micromatches, 289–90

Milan, Hector, 146–47

military service, thoughts on,
135–36, 298

mistakes, learning from, 30,
86, 156, 311, 322–23

Moreyko, Sergei, 213–14,
308–9

Mormons and Mormonism.
See Latter Day Saints
Church

motorcycle accident, 292–93

Mourning, Alonzo, 161

N

name-calling by other children, 11–12, 200

National College Athletic

Association (NCAA) Finals,
98–99, 99–100

National Duals, 97, 99

National Junior College Athletic Association (NJCAA)
Tournament, 85–86, 90

Nebraska. *See* University of
Nebraska

Neumann, Tim, 91–94, 97–99

O

O'Donnell, Rosie, 194

off-balance move, 309

Olympic Games, 2000 Sydney
arriving in Canberra,
159–60

Closing Ceremonies as
flagbearer, 193

crowd chanting, "*U-S-
A...U-S-A*", 176–78, 182

draw and first bouts,
161–63

Fraser's analysis of
Rulon/Karelin match,
185–88

hypothermia affects
remembrance of, 42

media blitz after match,
189–90, 192, 193–95

mental conditioning for, 167–69, 171–75

Olympic champion, first 24 hours, 192–93

Opening Ceremonies, 160–61

Rulon/Karelin match for gold medal, 178–84, 324

Yevseychyc match, 163–66

Olympic Games, 2002 Salt Lake City, 41

Olympic Games, 2004 Athens Moreyko match, 308–9

pool of talent for, 308

Sajad Barzi match for bronze medal, 1, 3, 313–15

Tsurtsumia match, 309–10

weight classes cut for, 281

Olympic Training Center (Colorado Springs, CO), 150–51, 156–57, 283–86, 288–91

Olympic Trials (1996), 123–24

Olympic Trials (2000), 151–52

Olympic Trials (2004), 295–300

Oprah, 193

Osborne, Tom, 101

Osmond Elementary School (Afton, WY), 12

P

Pan American Games (2000), 151

Parella, John, 103–4

Parker, Robert Leroy "Butch Cassidy," 47–48

Park Junior High School (Lincoln, NE), 126–27

par terre position, 210, 314

Patrick, Dan, 192

Patrikeev, Yuri, 148, 155, 209–12, 301–2

patriotism

America makes everything possible, 319–20

defending Powell in Athens, 304–5

effect of 9/11, 205–6

representing America, 154, 177–78

for "Star Spangled Banner," 189, 193, 316–17

perseverance, value of, 43

Persian Gulf, 298

Petkovic, Momir, 291–92

Petrosyan, Anatoly, 291–92

Phoenix, AZ, Sunkist Kids training facility, 122–23

physical fitness. *See also*

mental conditioning
from carrying calves, 24,
25–26
conditioning program at
Ricks, 84
from farming, 17–18, 24–25
as feet recover from frostbite, 283–86
going the extra mile,
290–91
Olympic Training Center
sessions, 150–51,
156–57, 283–86, 288–91
shark bait wrestling game,
156–57
for 2001 Worlds, 204
working hard on, 109
pizza delivery and weight gain,
92–93
Pocatello, ID, 275–76
Podubbny Tournament
(Russia), 155
politics in sports, 165–66, 178
polygamy, 44, 45
positive self-talk, 30, 155–56,
244
Powell, Colin, 303
Poznan, Poland, 141–45
prayers for Rulon, 246, 264,
269, 279–80
Pre-Professional Skills Test

(PPST), 96, 107–8
public speaking, 203, 278–79,
320–21
Pytlasinski Grand Prix (1997,
Poznan, Poland), 141–42

R

reckless driving, 86–87
recovery from frostbite
basketball and, 285
driving to and from treatments, 275–77
four-wheeler accident
impedes, 281–82
hyperbaric chamber, 275,
276–78
at Olympic Training
Center, 283–86
physical therapy, 2, 279
professional treatment
during, 275–76, 279–80
surgeries, 278–79, 280
wrestling as motivation
for, 2, 4, 282–83
"Reflections of the 20th Century in Star Valley,
Wyoming" (Star Valley
Independent), 46
re-ranking tournament for
Greco-Roman, 110–11

retiring from wrestling, 1, 297, 307, 313, 316–17, 318

"reverse lift," 147

Rexburg, ID, 83

Ricks College (Rexburg, ID), 81, 83–84, 88–90

right shin cut with wire, 73–74

role models and heroes, 134–38, 201, 277–78

Rolex watch bet, 216–17

S

Samaranch, Juan Antonio, 167

scars and scrapes. See accidents; injuries

Schwab, Danny, 57, 219, 257–64, 265–67

Search and Rescue team, 259, 261–62, 263, 269, 271–72

Secret Service, U.S., 206

self-evaluations, 131–32, 322–26

self-motivation. See mental conditioning

September 11, 2001, terrorist attacks, 205–6

Shandera, Joe, 128–30, 131

shark bait wrestling game, 156–57

The Shining (movie), 246

Simpkins, Trent, 219, 258–59, 263–65

Skinner, Dusty, 259–62

snowmobiling. See also wilderness, lost in
abandoning the snowmobile, 229–30, 231
climbing mountains, 220–21
crossing ponds and Salt River, 222, 223, 225–26, 227, 229, 230
with friends, 219–20
getting wet and lost in river valley, 42–43, 221–29, 230

Soldadse, Georgiy, 209

spicy-hot chicken wings bet, 145–46

staff infection in leg, 123–24

Stai, Brendan, 101–2

Star Valley, WY
backlash from sudden fame, 198–200
community support, 59–60, 154
description of, 46, 51
flour mill and sawmill built in, 48–49
Great Depression in, 54–55
for mental centering, 106

pre-2000 Olympics visit to, 153–54

regional economy, 47

Rulon's personal feelings for, 197–98, 202

Tonight Show satellite link to, 198

welcome home parade, 195–96

working odd jobs with father, 35–36

Star Valley High School, 75–78

student teaching experience, 127–32

student teaching requisites, 125–27

Sunkist Kids wrestling club, 112, 122

Surofchek, Dave, 160

survival pack, 219

Swift Creek's Intermittent Spring, 50

swimming in the cow trough, 28

T

teachers' college, 107, 114, 121–22

teaching methods class, 116–18, 120, 121–22

Thue, Jeff, 89

Thurman, Timothy, 256–57, 276, 277, 280, 281–82

Tillman, Pat, 135–36

Tonight Show, 194, 198

track and field, in high school, 31, 75, 80

Tsurtsumia, Georgi, 309–10, 312

U

University of Nebraska (Lincoln, NE)

academic advisor, 93, 95–96, 108–10

attitudes toward non football-playing jocks, 120–21, 133

Coach Neumann, 91–94, 97–99

Math 101, 95–96

Rulon's final assessment of, 132–33

student teaching experience, 127–32

student teaching requisites, 125–27

teachers' college, 107, 114, 121–22

teaching methods class, 116–18, 120, 121–22

wrestling for, 97–100

U.S. National Championships, 118, 149, 150, 294

U.S. Olympic Sports Festival (1993, San Antonio), 104–5

USA Wrestling. *See also* Fraser, Steve; Greco-Roman wrestling

    camaraderie among team members, 142–45, 146

    Greco-Roman program, 104–5, 110–11, 113

    instead of football, 103

    party at Olympics, 192

    promoting wrestling for, 305

Utah State, 89

V

values for living a good life. *See also* mental conditioning; patriotism; physical fitness

    acceptance and 'What next?', 310–12

    accountability, 86–88

    befriending left out kids, 64, 132

    don't sell out for fame or fortune, 194

    faith, 35, 60, 83, 88, 194, 243, 285

    hard work, 13–19, 24–26, 32, 79–80, 134, 323–24

    keep your eye on ultimate goal, 131

    mental toughness and focus, 76–77, 201–2, 232–33, 312–13

    overcoming obstacles increases strength, 31–32, 169, 323, 325

    overview, 321–26

    seven-part program, 321

    Star Valley as source of, 197–98

    teamwork, 39–40, 84–85, 100, 300

    think through the process, 242–43

    turn negatives into positives, 78, 132–33, 185, 288, 318–19

W

Walton, Casey, 259–64

Walton, Lane, 239, 259–64

Weigert, Zack, 101

weight issues, 8–12, 92–93

wilderness, lost in (winter,

2002). *See also* snowmo-
biling

checking time, 236–37, 240

drinking from Salt River,
247–48

hearing friends at 1:30 am,
56–57, 238–40

hindsight, 34

hypothermia facts, 7,
139–41, 218, 235, 254

keeping "warm," 233–36,
242, 244

losing mental acuity, 244,
246, 250–51

plane shows up, 6–7, 8,
248–51

sunrise, 246, 248

sunset, 33–34

thoughts on accomplish-
ments and remaining
desires, 34–35

vision of Jesus, God, and
Ronald, 61–63, 243

walking out attempts,
229–30, 231–32, 242,
244

wilderness rescue and
thawing. *See also* recovery
from frostbite

crawling to rescue heli-
copter, 158–59

Eastern Idaho Regional
Medical Center, 255–57

gratitude for search party,
254–55

letter from Mark Heiner,
267–73

LifeFlight, 251–53, 265–66,
271–72

snowmobile rescue
attempts, 257–64

Star Valley's hospital,
253–54, 255

World Championships (1997),
146–47

World Championships (2001)

Deak match for gold,
214–15

early matches, 208–9

gold medal notoriety at,
207–8

Moreyko match, 213–14

Patrikeev match, 209–12

postponement due to 9/11,
206

World Championships (2002),
287

World Championships (2003),
288

World Team Trials (1995),
118–19

World Team Trials (1998), 147–48

World Team Trials (2003), 287

wrestling. *See also* Greco-Roman wrestling; injuries; USA Wrestling; *specific events*

    emotions don't mix with, 76, 85–86, 90

    in grade school, 28–29

    in middle school, 29–30

    as motivation for healing, 2, 4, 282–83

    Olympic matches, 42

    retiring from, 1, 297, 307, 313, 316–17, 318

    Reynold's skill at, 39, 76

    Rulon's love for, 103, 282–83

    as Rulon's Mormon mission, 88

    at University of Nebraska, 97–100, 118–19

wrestling shoes, significance of, 3, 4–5, 298–99

wrist, dislocated, 293–96, 297–98, 310

Wyoming, 15–16, 18, 46, 98. *See also* Star Valley, WY

Y

Yevseychyc, Juri, 163–66, 208–9